THE ORIGINS
OF THE TWELFTH
AMENDMENT

Recent Titles in
Contributions in Political Science

THE ORIGINS OF THE TWELFTH AMENDMENT

The Electoral College in the Early Republic, 1787–1804

TADAHISA KURODA

Contributions in Political Science, *Number 344*
Bernard K. Johnpoll, Series Editor

GREENWOOD PRESS
Westport, Connecticut • London

Library of Congress Cataloging-in-Publication Data

Kuroda, Tadahisa.
    The origins of the Twelfth Amendment : the electoral college in
the early republic, 1787–1804 / Tadahisa Kuroda.
        p.   cm.—(Contributions in political science, ISSN 0147–1066
; no. 344)
    Includes bibliographical references and index.
    ISBN 0–313–29151–9 (alk. paper)
    1. Electoral college—United States—History.   2. Presidents—
United States—Election—History.   3. United States—Politics and
government—1783–1809.   4. United States—Constitutional law—
Amendments—12th.   I. Title.   II. Series.
JK529.K87   1994
324.6′3′0973—dc20   93–44508

British Library Cataloguing in Publication Data is available.

Library of Congress Catalog Card Number: 93–44508
ISBN: 0–313–29151–9
ISSN: 0147–1066

First published in 1994

Greenwood Press, 88 Post Road West, Westport, CT 06881
An imprint of Greenwood Publishing Group, Inc.

Printed in the United States of America

∞™

The paper used in this book complies with the
Permanent Paper Standard issued by the National
Information Standards Organization (Z39.48–1984).

10 9 8 7 6 5 4 3 2 1

For Akiko,
Stephanie, and Timothy

Contents

Preface

It is a pleasure to acknowledge the support and assistance of mentors, colleagues, friends, and family members who have had a hand in this production. I have been fortune to have teachers like William Dusinberre, Robert R. Ramsey, Jr., Robert D. Cross, and Eric L. McKitrick; Flora B. Harper and Peter D. Pelham, Jr.; Joseph C. Palamountain and Edwin M. Moseley. I have benefitted enormously from the encouragement of colleagues and friends, including David H. Porter, Jr., David W. Marcell, Eric. J. Weller, and Phyllis A. Roth; Daniel Balmuth, William E. Brynteson, Joel Gordon, Richard B. Jensen, Allen F. Kifer, Patricia-Ann Lee, and Margaret J. Pearson of the Skidmore College History Department; Mary Ellen Fischer and Erwin L. Levine; Carolyn J. Anderson, Beverly Becker, David J. Burrows, Ralph A. Ciancio, Robert P. DeSieno, Giuseppe Faustini, Henry C. Galant, Warren Hockenos, Kenneth G. Johnson, Robert J. Jones, James M. Kiehl, Susan A. Kress, Mary C. Lynn, Donald J. McCormack, E. Darnell Rucker, Robert H. Van Meter, Paul H. L. Walter, Isabelle Williams, and Joanna S. Zangrando. I have drawn upon the inexhaustible good will of Martin I. Kaminsky and Derick C. January. Members of my family deserve thanks for their support throughout the years: Yasuko Yamada and her three remarkable daughters, Chica, Meiko, and Mizno; Teruhisa Kuroda and Reiko Kuroda Mrozik; Yataro and Yasu Ishikawa; Hisazo Nagatani and Otoshiro Kuroda; and, most of all, my wife, Akiko, and our children--Stephanie M. Kuroda and Timothy E. Kuroda.

This study is primarily the outgrowth of teaching courses in American history to undergraduate students at Skidmore College and coping with the host of questions and issues which the materials and the students raised. It is impossible to single out the many students who have unknowingly contributed to make this project, and I will simply thank them collectively.

I want also to recognize the moral support of participants in the 1988 "Classic Texts in Early American History" Institute at the University of

Connecticut, funded by the National Endowment for the Humanities and directed by Christopher C. Collier. Eric J. Weller, then Dean of Faculty, and the Trustees of Skidmore College provided an ad hoc research grant and a sabbatical leave during the spring of 1990, and a National Endowment for the Humanities' Travel to Collections Grant helped to complete the research in the summer of 1990. Librarians at Skidmore and at all the institutions I visited offered generous help, as did Wendell Tripp of the New York State Historical Association and Ene Sirvet of the John Jay Project at Columbia University. I also appreciate the cheerful assistance of Chrisana McGill, especially in helping to secure permissions from those libraries and archives, and of Daniel J. Berkery, who prepared numerous tables for the appendices.

THE ORIGINS
OF THE TWELFTH
AMENDMENT

Introduction

Americans elect the President of the United States through the complex medium of the electoral college. The Constitution allocates to each state electors equal in number to its representation in the two houses of Congress. In our own day, political parties prepare a list of electors loyal to their candidates, and the people usually vote for one set or another. In most cases, the candidate whose slate wins the majority or plurality of the popular vote in a state is assured of receiving all of its electoral votes. The electors gather in their home state, and each of them casts one vote for President and another for Vice President. The candidate who receives a majority of the electoral vote for President and the one who gets the majority for Vice President win these offices.[1]

This process makes more evident the federal nature of our republic. The framers of the Constitution had reconfigured the political landscape by distributing supreme powers in some areas to the central government and in others to state governments and by resting all on the sovereignty of the people. The structure and authority of the Congress reflected this balance; so did the invention of presidential electors. But in presidential elections, the full potential of the state as a corporate body, separate and unique in territory, interests, and inhabitants, remained unrealized until electors in each state voted as a unit.

The winner-take-all feature of the mature electoral college has weighty consequences. Under it, large states enjoy substantially more influence in the outcome than small states. They frequently provide the leading candidates, who in turn devise strategies to appeal to them. Urbanized and filled with diverse populations, these states affect the issues which will be highlighted in the campaigns. Like gubernatorial candidates, presidential hopefuls must pay attention to the particular combinations of people and interests which form a plurality or majority vote in the state, but unlike them the latter must be successful in many states, especially the larger ones.[2]

Many students of the electoral college believe that the modern electoral college bolsters the two-party system and serves to moderate the temper of national politics by teasing out candidates of the extreme left and right. These and other claims for the influence of the electoral college are accepted as correct by some and disputed by others; still others categorically reject them as deviations from the principles of direct, participatory democracy.[3]

This study examines the evolution of the electoral college in the early years of the republic and determines how and why it assumed its modern aspect, not at all self evident from the words in the Constitution. Indeed, a reading of Article II suggests that the electoral college could have developed into something very different. For example, nothing in the text requires electors to vote according to the wishes of the people or of the legislatures which appoint them; each elector could act independently. Meetings of electors could have become deliberative bodies to screen candidates and make a choice. Moreover, states could and did adopt a variety of methods for the selection of electors, including district elections. In practice, however, states moved toward a winner-take-all system.

In order to reconstruct the reasons for this development, it is necessary to engage in a careful examination of presidential electors at the state level during the formative years, the parallel evolution of party politics, and the relationship between them as evidenced in a series of presidential elections in the early republic. That relationship helped to build the federal institutions of the young republic in a manner that brought state and nation together after the upheaval of the Revolution. In the period from 1787 to 1804, new institutional arrangements for the governance of states and nation had to be worked out within the larger context of contending republican ideals, economic interests, personal ambitions, and public opinion. Not only did the Constitution grant to the central government control over tariff revenues and standing armies, but it also required the election of public officials and provided the federal administration with patronage. The creation of the presidency and the requirement for states to provide for the appointment of electors established one of the major points of intersection between the new national government and the states. Through the 1790s, national issues, especially those related to fiscal and foreign policy, took their place beside state issues as major concerns for politicians and voters. Thereafter state parties became vitally interested in advancing the cause of their national counterparts and, of course, national parties wanted strong state organizations, because winning local and state offices became a prerequisite for success in presidential contests. The development of national parties and their ability to operate within democratic parameters shaped the political traditions of the new nation. Republicans and Federalists came to see that in their pursuit of power and position, they had to work within limits sanctioned by the people. In the process, they defined the operations of the electoral college and legitimized them in the Twelfth Amendment. The most explicitly partisan amendment adopted up to that time (perhaps, to the present), and specifically designed to affect the impending presidential election, this Jeffersonian reform insured Republican success in the 1804 election. In spite of the critical role that it played in the shaping of the electoral college, the Twelfth Amendment has not enjoyed much attention. This account offers the first comprehensive, modern examination of the history of that amendment. It makes clear that although the institution of the electoral college may have been invented in Philadelphia in 1787, it assumed its modern form in the crucible of partisan politics in the early republic.[4]

I

A REPUBLICAN HAND:
NO KINGS, NO QUEENS

1
Origins of
the Electoral College

The fifty-five delegates who came to the Philadelphia Convention between May 25 and September 17, 1787 represented a political elite with years of experience in the affairs of their states and nation. All the delegates were white men, thirty-four of them lawyers. They were knowledgeable, astute, pragmatic, and bold individuals--anything but naive when it came to politics. They agreed in general on the need to bolster central authority by giving it the power to levy taxes and regulate trade. Many were also convinced that this stronger government must be kept safe for the people and the existing states, and hence sought to avoid an excessive concentration of power at the center by establishing a system of checks and balances, separation of powers, and a federal arrangement.

In spite of their considerable aggregate abilities and their shared goals, they divided sharply on specific proposals for the composition and powers of the legislative, executive, and judicial branches and on the lines to be drawn between central and state authorities. Ardent and reluctant nationalists, rival economic interests, free and slave societies, and large and small states clashed in debate. Differences over how to compose the Congress and how to count slaves for purposes of taxation and representation nearly exploded the Convention, and compromises were made with considerable difficulty. Other problems like the method for selecting the President, not quite so fundamental, tested the resolve of the delegates over all of the five steamy months in the City of Brotherly Love. These conflicts compelled accommodation and compromise, if an acceptable document was to be hammered out, and the resulting Constitution reflected the reconciliation of competing ideas.

In the letter submitting their work to the Confederation Congress, the delegates wrote,

That it will meet the full and entire approbation of every State is not perhaps to be expected. But each will doubtless consider that had her Interests been alone consulted the Consequences might have been particularly disagreeable or injurious to others. That it is liable to as few Exceptions as could reasonably have been expected we hope and believe.[1]

In short, the Constitution was not quite what any one group wholly wanted, but the best that could be devised under the circumstances.

What was true for the Constitution as a whole applied with particular appropriateness to the provisions relating to the election of the chief executive. As James Wilson, the Scottish educated Pennsylvania delegate and later Supreme Court justice, remarked, "the Convention were perplexed with no part of this plan so much as with the mode of choosing the President."[2] In a similar vein, the diminutive, scholarly Virginian, James Madison wrote to Thomas Jefferson in France and explained wearily: "On the question whether [the Executive] should consist of a single person, or a plurality of coordinate members, on the mode of appointment, on the duration in office, on the degree of power, on re-eligibility, tedious and reiterated discussions took place."[3]   A major reason for these difficulties over the executive derived from the delegates' mixed feelings about an executive. Many had fought a revolution to overthrow King George III and establish a republican government and society; they feared that executive authority harbored monarchical tendencies and did not want a new King George, even if a Virginian and not a Hanoverian. They had provided no separate and independent executive for the Articles of Confederation, the nation's first constitution. In the states, they gave the bulk of power to the legislatures which elected governors, who served for short terms, enjoyed no veto, and had circumscribed patronage powers. Only in New York, Massachusetts, and New Hampshire did voters make the choice, and, in the latter two, failure to form a majority behind a single candidate triggered a contingency election in the legislature.[4]

Throughout May and June the Philadelphia Convention considered the Virginia Plan and then the New Jersey Plan, both of which provided for an executive chosen by the legislature, the method the delegates preferred through July and August of 1787. But they could not escape certain liabilities associated with this familiar method. The executive might become dependent on legislators, incapable of initiative, and worried about pleasing them in order to gain re-election. The delegates sought to overcome this difficulty by linking legislative election to a long term of seven years with no opportunity for additional terms.

Still the delegates' anxieties persisted. For example, the decision to subject Presidents to impeachment by the Congress meant that they might not even serve a full seven years. Moreover, denial of re-eligibility meant that the nation could exhaust its pool of competent candidates. If it needed the services of a leader like George Washington for more than a single term, it would be blocked or it might ignore the prohibition and violate the Constitution. Ineligibility might also remove a motive for good behavior and lead Presidents, according to the brilliant and acerbic Gouverneur Morris, "to make hay while the sun shines."[5] Finally, a Congress, composed of persons known to powerful interests and foreign nations and gathered conveniently at the nation's capital, could be corrupted by promises of favor from foreign countries and political parties, and engage in horse-trading votes for President.[6]

Hence the delegates listened to other options. While the most nationalistic members from large states at various times favored direct election by the people (meaning adult white males and excluding women and blacks for the most part), most saw little merit in it because of its impracticality. The opponents identified many problems: (1) a census as a prelude to the first election could not be taken, (2) states had varying suffrage requirements, (3) registration and supervision of a national election would be expensive and time-consuming, and (4) a national election might produce disturbances, even riots, which would destabilize the republican experiment.[7]

Special objections came from the small states and from the South, which formed a loose coalition in favor of the legislative mode. The former feared that the popular vote would give an insuperable advantage to large states like Massachusetts, Pennsylvania, and Virginia, which would likely provide most of the successful presidential candidates. The latter rejected the popular vote because of the presence of slaves who could not vote. Virginia, for example, had a population of 748,000, and slaves accounted for 306,000 of that total--a sum greater than the populations of Connecticut, Rhode Island, New Hampshire, New Jersey, Delaware, South Carolina, or Georgia, and in the same range as New York or Maryland.[8]

Delegates questioned whether the people, living in a rural society with little in the way of modern transportation and communications, could agree on any single candidate. After all, only two Americans in 1787 had national reputations: heroic George Washington and the benign and tottering octogenarian Benjamin Franklin. Most Americans did not yet know John Adams, James Madison, and Thomas Jefferson well enough, let alone George Clinton, Patrick Henry, John Dickinson, John Jay, and Charles C. Pinckney.

Delegates realized that direct election, even if physically possible, meant disregarding geographical and political boundaries which identified Americans as citizens of states with distinctive problems and interests. Elbridge Gerry, for example, warned that such a proposal would "supersede altogether the state authorities," while John Dickinson announced that "he had no idea of abolishing the State Governments as some gentlemen seemed inclined to do."[9] The United States, already stretching from the Atlantic to the Mississippi and from Massachusetts to Georgia, would comprise one district. Could any state or group feel that its interests would be adequately protected? As discussion about the makeup of Congress moved delegates to conceive of the United States as a union both of people and states, the delegates could not support direct popular election which totally ignored the latter.

In their search for possible alternatives to legislative election, the Convention heard proposals for more than a dozen other modes for choosing the executive, some of them bizarre. Virginia's Dr. James McClurg recommended election by Congress for a term based on good behavior. James Wilson proposed that fifteen members of the Congress be chosen by lot to make the selection. North Carolina's Hugh Williamson thought that legislative election for three executives--one each for the northern, middle, and southern states-- would be the answer. Madison reverted to direct popular election with each voter casting ballots for three persons, two of whom would have to be from outside the voter's home state, as a way to encourage the formation of a majority. Massachusetts delegate Gerry proposed that the governors of the states should make the choice of President. Gouverneur Morris urged that each state nominate its best citizen, and the Congress or some other group choose from the list. It was fortunate that the convention delegates could proceed without daily public reports of their speeches. They were able to express their views freely, listen to each other's arguments, and to change their minds without fear of immediate public scrutiny of their work and without having to answer charges of vacillating on issues.[10]

In their discussions, the delegates began to listen to the idea of creating presidential electors. In early June, James Wilson suggested that states be divided into districts within each of which qualified voters would elect electors who would choose the chief executive. Alexander Hamilton's plan for a consti- tution, presented on June 18 as an alternative to both the Virginia and New Jersey plans, recommended that the executive be chosen by electors themselves elected by electors who were chosen by the voters as a way of finding a quali- fied person who would be truly national in outlook and free from state biases. On July 19, Oliver Ellsworth of Connecticut proposed that electors be appointed by state legislatures and apportioned so that states with less than 100,000 people would have one, those with between 100,000 and 300,000 two, and those with over 300,000 three electors. This formula had been earlier discussed as a possible one for the composition of the United States Senate. This allocation produced a total of twenty-five electors. Ellsworth's motion remained the only one using electors to gain a majority vote, albeit a temporary one, in the Convention prior to the formation of the Committee of Eleven in September.[11]

These early plans for electors stirred resistance. North Carolina delegate Hugh Williamson anticipated future critics by complaining that electors were too elaborate, expensive, and redundant, and that they placed an unnecessary additional barrier between the people and their rulers. Hamilton's conception of a neo-monarchy raised fears of creating an executive far removed from both the people and the states. Ellsworth alleviated worries that states would be bypassed and provided a formula for making some distinction between small and large states while confining the differences among them to a narrow range of one to three electors. Still the total of twenty-five meant that small states would be represented by just one person, thirteen would make a majority, and a few had the power to select the President.   James Madison also pointed out the rigidity of the allocations of electors to states in a nation where the population grew at a rapid pace and shifted markedly from region to region. Thus a state's population in both absolute and relative terms would always be changing, and its proper weight in presidential elections difficult to calculate.[12]

Moreover, Ellsworth's motion presumed or at least left open the possibility that electors from all the states would have to gather in one central place to vote.   This prospect raised worries over inconvenience and expense, which threatened lack of attendance and loss of influence in elections. The delegates knew the history of absenteeism in the Continental Congress, and the question of the location of the nation's capital remained a serious bone of contention in part because of the problems of communications and travel for distant members. Moreover, a single body of electors, while not open to the same amount of corruption as a standing body like the Congress, could still be influenced by cabals, foreign agents, and parties.[13]

All of these plans anticipated that electors would make the choice by coalescing around a particular candidate, but made no provision for ensuring selection or enhancing majority formation. The frequent assertion that voters in the states would prove partial to local candidates served as a warning; electors could show the same tendencies. The whole body of electors might have to sit a long time and ballot more than once in order to determine the victor. Such a process would invite deals among electors and subject them to temptations and influence.

The delegates hinted at differing expectations of the qualifications of presidential electors. Madison, Wilson, Morris, and Rufus King had spoken favorably of direct popular vote, and expressed faith in the growing general awareness among the citizenry about national figures. Their decision to support presidential electors derived from their opposition to legislative choice and their realization that they could not gain a majority for direct election. They expected electors to be respectable folk, but representative of ordinary citizens. Most of the other delegates who spoke on the issue felt that electors would have more information about candidates from the entire country than the average citizen, and that this breadth of view would improve the chances of a majority forming behind a single candidate. Hugh Williamson, on the other hand, thought that electors would be men decidedly of the second or third rank, and Caleb Strong predicted that men of real prominence would prefer service in the Senate or House.[14]

No delegate argued that electors would be disinterested persons exercising their own judgment without reference to prevailing opinion and interests in their states. Few in the Convention could have imagined the typical elector to be an unsophisticated, politically inexperienced, detached notable.   The political culture of eighteenth-century America dictated that men of standing in the community, those with the resources, education, family connections, and experience, devote themselves to political service. And though the ideology of

the American Revolution undermined the tradition of deference which strengthened public support for elite leadership, it had not yet brought reality in line
with ideals. The delegates themselves were living testimony to the persistence
of gentlemen in politics.   Rather than disinterested citizens, the framers
anticipated individuals who would in general express the views, interests, and
biases of their communities and states in the office of presidential elector. They
also worried about undue influence. Whether the plans of Wilson, Hamilton,
and Ellsworth sufficiently guarded against this danger remained an open
question. But the delegates surely understood that electors would be moved by
state loyalties.[15]

Not too surprisingly under the circumstances, the delegates lost their
momentary enthusiasm for electors and reverted to the legislative mode for a
single term without re-eligibility. Their considerations about how to choose the
President continued along several axes, one of which encompassed the competing interests between the large and small states. This division had surfaced most
dramatically in the rival Virginia and New Jersey plans over the composition of
the Congress. On July 16, Connecticut, New Jersey, Delaware, Maryland, and
North Carolina barely prevailed over Pennsylvania, Virginia, South Carolina,
and Georgia, with Massachusetts divided, and established equal representation
for all states in the Senate. While this action removed the most serious source
of disaffection for the small states, it did not end all of their concerns. While
the Virginia and New Jersey plans appeared similar on the surface in calling for
the legislature to choose the executive, they differed in their understanding of
the composition of that legislature, and the Connecticut Compromise left unset-
tled whether the legislative mode meant a concurrent vote of the two houses,
which favored small states, or a joint vote, which advantaged the large.[16]

Yet, the votes of state delegations on the many proposals and amendments
affecting the mode of selecting the executive did not always reveal clear lines
between the large and small states. If it is agreed that large referred at the time
to Massachusetts, Pennsylvania, and Virginia, and that small referred to the
others--some of which had vast territorial claims and the potential for population
growth, it was the exception rather than the rule that votes came down cleanly
in two blocs. For example, James Wilson's motion on June 2 to use electors to
choose the President lost by a 2-7-1 vote with only Pennsylvania and Maryland
voting aye. Massachusetts, Connecticut, Delaware, Virginia, and the three
southern states of North and South Carolina and Georgia voted no. New York
divided. On July 17 Gouverneur Morris's proposal to allow citizens to choose
lost by a 1-9 count with only Pennsylvania in favor. Two days later, a motion
by Oliver Ellsworth and Jacob Broome to try electors passed 6-3-1 with
Connecticut, New Jersey, Pennsylvania, Delaware, Maryland, and Virginia
forming the majority, the three lower southern states staying as a bloc, and
Massachusetts divided. When the convention decided to return to choice by the
national legislature on July 24, New Hampshire, Massachusetts, New Jersey,
Delaware, and the three lower southern states voted yes.[17]

Other considerations, including the intrinsic difficulty of the subject, compounded by progress made in shaping other sections of the proposed constitution which forced delegates in recursive fashion to examine prior decisions about the executive, and the experience of many states with the legislative mode influenced the votes of delegates. Even mundane considerations, such as absences by one or a few members of individual state delegations, could alter positions of state delegations. For example, the resignation of George Wythe in mid-June reduced Virginia's representation to six persons. George Mason, a pronounced critic of popular election of the executive, and Edmund Randolph, who had introduced the Virginia plan, favored the legislative mode, while Washington and Madison supported various alternatives. James McClurg and John Blair could determine the vote of the state. On July 19, Virginia agreed to the Ellsworth motion to use electors but opposed having them chosen by state legislatures, and on the July 24 it voted against a motion to revert back to the legislative mode. Yet two days later when the convention voted on a complementary motion made by Mason to restore the seven-year term and ineligibility, Virginia voted aye. On the final vote to accept the package of legislative mode, seven-year term, and ineligibility, Virginia divided, with Blair and Mason voting aye and Washington and Madison nay. Randolph and McClurg were absent.[18]

New Hampshire delegates John Langdon and Nicholas Gilman arrived in the Convention for the first time on July 23. Without hearing any of the previous debates on the subject which might have influenced them, they voted for the legislative mode on July 24; they could later reconsider after being brought up to speed by other delegates. New Jersey's delegation voted for the Ellsworth plan on July 19, but several days later supported the call for a return to the legislative mode. Perhaps it was behaving in a way consistent with a small state which hoped to have more influence in the latter. But it may be significant that in the interim William Livingston, who had been absent from July 3 to 19, rejoined the Convention, while William Paterson, who had been friendly to the use of electors and the allocation of 1-2-3 electors to states based on size, itself a significant departure from the principle of parity for all states, left Philadelphia on July 23, not to return until September. Delaware, like New Jersey, favored the Ellsworth plan and later supported reversion to the legislative mode. Its five delegates may have been simply willing to consider all options without making any commitments, but it is also possible that at least one member was absent on July 24 for the delegation divided on one vote. It is for certain also that John Dickinson returned on July 25, and he supported the legislative mode. In short, all delegations did not uniformly vote the way they were supposed to all the time from the vantage point of large and small states.[19]

The votes taken on August 24, however, showed clearly the division between large and small states. On this occasion, John Rutledge of South Carolina proposed a joint, rather than concurrent, ballot of the two houses of the legislature as an amendment to the legislative mode, seven-year term, and ineligibility. With its ostensible purpose of forcing the smaller Senate to vote together with the larger House in a single group, Rutledge's motion gave advantage to the more populous states over the lesser ones. Still it was true, as Madison pointed out, that the advantage stood at about 4-1 rather than 10-1, as strict adherence to population would have produced. John Langdon of New Hampshire conceded that experience in his state legislature showed the disadvantages of the concurrent vote. Seven states voted aye, while four registered nays. The former included Virginia, Massachusetts, and Pennsylvania, which had rarely voted together on prior measures dealing with the selection of the executive, the southern states of North and South Carolina, and New Hampshire and Delaware. The four dissenting states consisted of Connecticut, New Jersey, Maryland, and Georgia, all among the smaller entities in the union.[20]

New Jersey delegates Jonathan Dayton and David Brearley, who had spoken out against the joint ballot, then countered with a motion that each state in the joint session have one vote. Such an arrangement would avoid the disputes which arose from concurrence, but would retain the principle of equality of states. Delaware now joined the previous minority of four, but the majority of the three large states, the Carolinas, and New Hampshire defeated the Dayton-Brearley motion. It is important to note that on these crucial votes the three large states found allies among some of the smaller entities and that they held their ground on the joint ballot should the legislative mode survive in the final text. The amended language made the legislative mode less appealing to those delegates who had hoped that either a separate ballot or parity in voting would enhance the influence of their states. Whatever alternative might yet be proposed now appeared against the backdrop of an election by a joint ballot, which favored the large states and had other virtues as well over a concurrent vote. After these votes on August 24, the large states and their allies had little reason to support any mode which gave more weight to the smaller ones in the selection of the President. And the smaller states did not threaten to walk out of the convention the way they had when the composition of the Congress was at stake.[21]

On August 31 the Convention directed an ad hoc Committee of Eleven, chaired by David Brearley of New Jersey, and including a delegate from each of the eleven states in attendance, to resolve remaining uncertainties with presidential elections. Other members included Nicholas Gilman of New Hampshire, Rufus King of Massachusetts, Roger Sherman of Connecticut, John Dickinson of Delaware, Daniel Carroll of Maryland, Gouverneur Morris of Pennsylvania, James Madison of Virginia, Hugh Williamson of North Carolina, Pierce Butler of South Carolina, and Abraham Baldwin of Georgia. On September 4 this committee proposed a new method for electing the President which took account of the many points made in earlier debates. It created the office of presidential elector and assigned to states a number of electors equal to the total number of Representatives and Senators each had in Congress. Presidents were to serve for four years and be eligible for re-election. The Brearley committee simultaneously recommended that Presidents have substantial authority in foreign affairs and appoint ambassadors and judges with the advice and consent of the Senate. Gouverneur Morris provided an extensive rationale for the committee's plan. After the initial shock of such a proposal wore off, the Convention accepted this recommendation for a stronger, more independent, executive with minor modifications.[22]

The final text of what became Article II, section 1, of the Constitution, reinforced two major compromises the Convention had earlier accepted. The Connecticut Compromise between the Virginia and New Jersey plans had defined the legislature as representing both the people and the states, and now every state would have the same weight in presidential elections that it had in the Congress. Second, the Convention had agreed to the three-fifths clause to settle disputes between the free and slave states over taxation and representation in the House. The device of presidential electors implicitly agreed to that formulation and avoided re-opening touchy issues. The Constitution provided for a first Congress consisting of sixty-five members in the House and twenty-six in the Senate, if every state ratified, and hence for ninety-one electors. A majority of at least forty-six electoral votes decided who would be President, a more acceptable figure than the thirteen in the earlier plan recommended by Oliver Ellsworth.

Clearly, the delegates respected popular participation, for their plan made it possible to have popular election of electors, but they did not mandate this. And it would be a mistake to think of them simply as purely democratic. Wilson, Morris, and Madison spoke frequently in favor of direct popular vote, but their motives were complicated and included worries that other modes gave states too much influence. They were nationalists willing to accept democratic means to achieve their goal. Mason, Gerry, and Butler often criticized this mode as impractical, though expressing no objections to it in theory. In sum, the framers were not numerical majoritarians who only counted heads but complex majoritarians concerned with a heterogeneous people, composed of factions and organized into states. For example, reapportionment of the House and, accordingly, recalculation of the electoral votes assigned to the states occurred after the federal census every ten years, not with daily, weekly, monthly, or yearly changes in population, for the framers did not see any virtue in such close attention to numbers. Nor did they consider voter turnout as a factor in the election of officials or electors; whoever turned out determined the outcome. The device of presidential electors and their allocation to states fitted well with this sophisticated understanding. As Madison later explained,

In our complex system of polity, the public will, as a source of authority, may be the will of the people as composing one nation; or the will of the States in their distinct and independent capacities, or the federal will, as viewed, for example, through the Presidential electors, representing in a certain proportion, both the nation and the states.[23]

2

The Ratification Debate

When the Philadelphia Convention finally adjourned on September 17, it opened the doors to allow the Congress, state governments, and the public to view its work. Now, in ratifying conventions, broadsides, and newspapers, proponents and critics of the new frame of government argued the issues once again. The Federalists, who supported it, and the Antifederalists, who did not, helped flesh out the meaning of the presidential election plan. In the Pennsylvania ratifying convention, James Wilson stated, "The manner of appointing the President of the United States, I find, is not objected to; therefore I shall say little on that point."[1] Later, during the furious campaign to win ratification in New York, Alexander Hamilton began number 68 of *Publius* with the often quoted observation that "The mode of appointment of the Chief Magistrate of the United States is almost the only part of the system, of any consequence, which has escaped without severe censure, or which has received the slightest mark of approbation from its opponents."[2] To the extent that Wilson and Hamilton were speaking mainly to audiences in Pennsylvania and New York and making a judgment of the relative prominence which presidential electors gained in Antifederalist arguments, their words can be taken as generally correct.

It would be untrue, however, to conclude that Antifederalists were uniformly happy with Article II, section 1. Enough delegates in the ratifying conventions in Virginia and New York objected to the four-year term and re-eligibility that they secured a majority vote in favor of amendments to alter the Constitution. In Richmond George Mason complained that "the President is elected without rotation," while in Poughkeepsie Melancton Smith argued for a seven-year term without re-eligibility.[3] James Lincoln protested in the South Carolina convention that re-eligibility threatened America with a monarchy which would require another revolution to displace. Reports of convention proceedings in newspapers carried these criticisms to audiences in other states.

Antifederalists sometimes stretched the truth and argued inconsistently about presidential selection. Agrippa in letters to the *Massachusetts Gazette* showed that he knew some of the inner workings of the Philadelphia Convention. He identified a large group of delegates who wanted the single seven-year term and a rival group who preferred service during good behavior. Agrippa then linked the cause of those who favored re-eligibility with those who wanted good behavior tenure, and argued that their persistence in the final twelve days of the Convention led to the plan before the country. Not only did he make more of James McClurg's bizarre suggestion for life tenure--which may in fact have been a ploy to highlight the errors of those who argued for a lengthy term--than it deserved, but offered an alternative which seems equally bizarre: "The President shall be chosen annually and shall serve but one year, and shall be chosen successively from the different states, changing every year."[4] Benjamin Gale of Connecticut lamented that re-eligibility meant in effect a perpetual President and Senate; then he decried the powerlessness of the people, whose sole task was to have their legislature choose seven electors "to choose a *King President* for four years, and then to have another *squabble* again."[5]

Other critics struck more directly at the use of electors. The Columbian Patriot attacked the number of electors assigned to individual states, and complained that the ten allotted to Massachusetts was "nearly tantamount to the exclusion of the voice of the people in the choice of their first magistrate."[6] In number 14 of his essays, The Federal Farmer, though satisfied in general with the election scheme, considered an increase in the number of electors highly desirable and reassuring. In the *Gazette of the State of Georgia*, Georgian asked in disbelief, "What number of men choose a President for the important and almost unlimited trust in the United States?"[7] He answered incorrectly that there would be ninety-three for the first election after which he predicted a subsequent decline to seventy-six with Georgia's share decreasing from five to three. He feared that the few could be tempted by ambition and money, and wondered, "Who can set bounds to the depravity of human nature, if not restrained by wholesome constitutional laws."[8]

Benjamin Gale considered presidential electors a gimmick which gave the pretense that the people choose the President and Vice President. He envisioned his state legislature would encounter difficulties; the lower house would identify qualified persons, and the upper house would prefer others. The ensuing stalemate meant that the state would send fewer than its full complement of electors or none at all. The process "fettered and muzzled" popular will. James Monroe of Virginia denounced electors as unacceptable for they would magnify the influence of state governments rather than the people in the choice of President.[9]

Another Virginian, William Grayson, found Article II, section 1, filled with contradictory principles. While election in the first instance rested with electors, based on federal numbers, that in contingencies depended on states with an equal vote. As far as he was concerned, "It seemed rather founded on accident than any principle of government I ever heard of."[10] He could readily conceive of a plot whereby a group of northern states could steal the election from a popular candidate. If a northern candidate could get as few as two electoral votes, he could emerge as one of the top five whose names would be submitted to the House. In the House a majority of the delegations from New Hampshire, Rhode Island, Connecticut, New Jersey, Delaware, Georgia, and North Carolina, amounting to but fifteen Congressmen, could cast the votes of their seven states for their candidate. This result required the work of two electors out of the ninety-one and fifteen of the sixty-five members of the House. Grayson seemed unaffected by James Madison's rejoinder that his plan required the complicity of Georgia and North Carolina, two southern states.

Republicus objected that electors had to cast at least one of their votes for a person from another state. This was a constraint on the free exercise of judgment and would lead electors to vote for persons about whom they knew little. If electors failed to make the choice, then the House would come to the rescue, something which Republicus felt would not occur twice in the same century. Echoing Grayson, he asked, "Is it necessary, is it rational, that the sacred rights of mankind should thus dwindle down to Electors of electors, and those again electors of other electors?"[11]

The contingency provisions also drew the fire of Rawlins Lowndes in the South Carolina convention. He anticipated that electors would have no problems in the first election, for they would support George Washington. But what would happen thereafter? He saw the potential for a total stoppage of government. George Mason agreed with this analysis and upped the odds which he had given in Philadelphia so that there was only one chance in fifty that electors could make the choice. Then in a House election, the people would be excluded from participation. Aristocratis concurred. The House could and would choose a candidate who may have ranked as low as fifth in the electoral count, and thus Congress, not the people, will come to determine who would be President.[12]

A few critics took notice of the office of Vice President. Thomas McKean of Pennsylvania thought the position divided executive power with no apparent compensating gains and judged it a "useless officer."[13] The Federal Farmer did not go quite that far, but concluded that the office "is not very important, if not an unnecessary part of the system."[14] George Clinton, writing as Cato, believed the office to be not only unnecessary but dangerous: "for want of other employment" the Vice President is President of the Senate, "thereby blending the executive and legislative powers, besides always giving to some one state, from which he is to come, an unjust pre-eminence."[15]

Prone to suspect conspiracies, Antifederalists expressed alarm with Congress' power to set the time for choosing electors and for having them vote. Clinton worried that there was no date set for the end of the first term. In a worst case scenario, A Customer, writing to the Maine *Cumberland Gazette*, imagined this unhappy scenario:

Suppose they should think it for the public good, after the first election, to appoint the first Tuesday of September, in the year *two thousand*, for the purpose of choosing the second President; and by law empower the Chief Justice of the Supreme Judicial Court to act as President until that time.[16]

James Monroe saw a danger too. The Congress might set the date for choosing electors so far from the date for casting their votes that the electors could combine. The Federal Farmer agreed that a long interval invited corruption. A Georgian favored fixing unalterably forever the day for choosing electors and having them vote. Such would not have satisfied Joseph Taylor of North Carolina, who feared that the Congress "by their army, and the election being on the same day in all the states, might compel the electors to vote as they please."[17] Antifederalists did not always agree on solutions, but they expressed fears of monarchical, aristocratic, and elitist conspiracies which would deny to the people the choice of their President.[18]

The Federalists were not helpless in the face of these attacks and responded with arguments informed by the debates in the Philadelphia Convention. James Wilson, James Madison, Alexander Hamilton, and their allies, familiar with the pros and cons of lengthy terms, re-eligibility, legislative mode, popular vote, and electors, educated the national audience which would be decisive in determining whether or not the Constitution would be ratified.

They repeated over and over again that the mode of electing the President depended ultimately not on states or electors but the people. James Wilson claimed in the Pennsylvania Convention that all authority for the new government derived via representation from the people and that "the Democratic principle is carried into every part of the government."[19] He conceded that the Senate departed in limited respects from this foundation but that the House and the President rested upon it. "The choice of this officer," he argued, "is brought as nearly home to the people as is practicable; with the approbation of the state legislatures, the people may elect with only one remove."[20] Tench Coxe advanced a similar position, and contrasted the American President whose authority came from the people, served a short term, and returned to society with that of the British monarch.[21]

Writing to the *Connecticut Courant*, The Republican described the President as "an officer appointed by the people," acting through the medium of electors, while James Bowdoin told the Massachusetts Convention that the people authorized the President to act on their behalf.[22] Alexander Hamilton explained:

It was desirable that the sense of the people should operate in the choice of the person to whom so important a trust was to be confided. This end will be answered by committing the right of making it, not to any pre-established body, but to men chosen by the people for the special purpose, and at the particular conjuncture.[23]

Edmund Randolph, who had previously favored the legislative mode, now defended the scheme of electors vigorously and asserted that they "must be elected by the people at large,"[24] though nothing in the text required state legislatures to allow such. Federalist claims that the President was popularly based had clear advantages in the fight to win support for ratification but overstated the case made behind closed doors in Philadelphia.

Federalists denied that re-eligibility threatened republican principles. Edmund Randolph, for example, admitted that he had favored a single term at one time but had changed his mind after hearing extensive commentary by others. Re-eligibility would strengthen executive independence and make the President "more solicitous of promoting the interest of his constituents."[25] North Carolinian William Richardson Davie reported a similar conversion and pointed to the safeguards which the institution of presidential electors placed against corruption. Charles C. Pinckney and Benjamin Franklin emphasized that re-eligibility maximized the choices given to the people.[26]

Federalists presented an array of arguments to justify the resort to electors, mediating between the people and their President. Noah Webster reminded his audience that direct popular choice in ancient Rome paved the way for "excessive bribery and corruption," while Hamilton believed that electors would be much less likely "to convulse the community" and would be deliberate and judicious.[27] John Dickinson, writing as Fabius, explained that electors were more likely than the citizenry at large to have information about the candidates, and they were shielded from "undue influence." Madison showed that direct popular choice in a large, diverse society faced insuperable difficulties, while electors meant ease and convenience. The Republican considered the likelihood that electors could form majorities the chief advantage, and Wilson joined this Federalist chorus. A surprisingly harmonious note came from The Federal Farmer, perhaps the most widely read Antifederalist, who praised the use of electors and concluded, "I confess there appears to be a judicious combination of principles and precautions." The election of the President and Vice President "seems to be properly secured."[28]

Federalists frequently asserted that the use of electors freed the choice of President from corruption and cabal and thereby sought to alleviate anxieties on this point among Federalist and Antifederalist ranks alike. Webster rehearsed the constraints which the framers had written into the Constitution: the electors are "chosen by the several legislatures--under their inspection--separated at a vast distance--and holding no office under the United States. Such a mode of election almost precludes the possibility of corruption."[29] Fabius praised the provision that the Congress set the common dates for the selection of electors and for the electors to cast their votes. Independent and free from undue influence, "the electors may throw away their votes, mark, with public disappointment, some person improperly favored by them, or justly revering the duties of their office, dedicate their votes to the best interests of their country."[30]

Edmund Randolph and Richard Hobbs Spaight concurred that the setting of common dates precluded improper communications among electors from different states, and Judge James Iredell of North Carolina liked the idea that electors in one state might not even know who were electors in other states. The person who emerged the victor at the end of such a process would deserve the confidence and respect of the entire nation. Familiarity and opportunity for communication, to the contrary, would open the door to influence.[31]

Charles C. Pinckney educated his audience on the virtues of minimizing the role that foreign governments played in the election of the President. Particularly effective in confounding their plots were the provisions for electors meeting in their home states, rather than gathering at a central location. True, failure of the electors to form a majority threw the contest into the House, but only the top five candidates, previously chosen by electors, could be considered there. Wilson thought that these same protections also guarded against influence from "the lesser evils of party intrigue" and predicted that once the new government came into being even this source of influence would be counteracted.[32]

Wilson and Demosthenes Minor of Georgia also took the opportunity to appeal to those who were concerned that the Constitution left little room for the states: there could be no electors without the actions of state legislatures, and without electors there could be no president. Noah Webster stroked the small states. The dual vote meant that an elector from a large state might cast his second vote for a person from a small state; or that an elector from a small state could "shop around" for a candidate from all the states before casting his second vote.[33]

Federalists were not always consistent in explaining how much discretionary authority a state legislature had in deciding how to choose electors. Thus Edmund Randolph insisted that they must allow for popular election on a general slate, while Noah Webster indicated that they should appoint electors. In the North Carolina convention, an informative exchange occurred on this point. Samuel Johnston observed that some believed the people should choose electors, while others thought that the legislatures should do so. James Iredell replied that it could not be done properly by the legislatures, for their discretionary authority extended only to how the people chose. Archibald Maclaine disputed the Judge's reading, and William R. Davie, who had been a delegate in Philadelphia, replied that "it was left to the wisdom of the legislatures to direct their election in whatever manner they thought proper."[34] Wilson supported this interpretation in the Pennsylvania Convention, where he explained that electors could be chosen by the people if the legislature so determined and left open the possibility that it might decide otherwise. Some time later, Wilson elaborated. Electors

will, in all probability, be appointed in one of the two following modes --by the citizens--or by the legislature. If the former; the business will be managed in the same manner as the election of representatives in each state. If the latter; it will be managed by those to whom the different states have intrusted their legislative authority.[35]

He could not have known that practice would depart from these expectations.[36]

Clearly, Federalists rallied around the Constitution and they put aside differences which had separated them in the Convention. They answered their critics with sound argument, and they showed that the Antifederalists could not agree among themselves on what would be the right mode of election. However, they also created and left ambiguities which clouded future development of presidential electors. First, they insisted time and again that the people chose the President, while defending the use of electors who might or might not be chosen by them. They also allowed that resort to electors recognized the existence of states. But did they mean the states as administrative units or as corporate entities? Legislatures had the duty to provide for the selection of electors, but how would they exercise this authority, and would they converge on one mode? Once chosen, should electors vote proportionately to represent divisions among the people of the state or as a unified bloc and discount minorities?[37]

Article II, section 1 sought to maximize participation in presidential elections by rejecting the establishment of a single electoral college located at the nation's capital. Electors chosen for the specific purpose of electing a President, holding no federal office--not even postmaster--having no legislative business, congregating in their own states, having little time to consult electors in other states, being required to vote on the same day and for two persons for President, and being disbanded promptly afterwards, would be insulated from corruption. Federalists made much of these claims and spoke about how the Constitution shielded electors from improper influence; they could vote in whatever way they chose. And yet, they realized that they and their opponents had vital interests in advancing their candidates for President and Vice President. How could they achieve their goals and frustrate their rivals if the institution of presidential electors functioned according to the way Federalists described in 1788?

The framers of the Constitution in Philadelphia thought that electors would probably vote for one candidate from their home state or region, and hence not form a majority behind anyone, especially after George Washington, everyone's choice to be the first President. Although Abraham Baldwin of Georgia had expressed confidence that "the increasing intercourse among the people of the states would render important characters less and less unknown," and Wilson had argued that "continental characters will multiply as we more and more coalesce, so as to enable the electors in every part of the Union to know and judge them," most sought reassurance.[38] They underestimated how quickly the new government would create national figures and had resorted to a clumsy device whereby each elector cast two votes for President, one of which must be for a person from a state other than that of the elector, to improve the chances for majority formation. The dual vote also had additional appeal to small states. Although these features may have answered critics in 1788, they were laden with difficulties which would surface in 1789 and thereafter.[39]

As insurance, the Constitution established a dual contingency plan for election by the House of Representatives in the event of a tie between or among candidates with a majority vote or a nonselection by electors. The former was possible because one-fourth plus one of the two undifferentiated votes cast by electors made a majority and hence as many as three persons could conceivably have a majority and yet be equal. In the latter case, the names of the five candidates with the most electoral votes would be submitted for consideration. The generous inclusion of five, rather than a smaller figure like three, made it more likely that someone from a small state would be in the contest. In addition, each state had one vote in a House election. It would have been strange for the large states to have supported these contingency provisions unless they believed that their interests were sufficiently protected in the allocation of electors. The alternative they had in their hip pocket was appointment by a joint vote of the Congress as the Convention had approved in August. Precisely because they had every reason to try to determine the outcome through the electoral college, choice by the House was only a contingency. But a major challenge remained. Madison believed it essential "to render an eventual resort to any part of the Legislature improbable."[40] How were they to accomplish this desideratum in an expansive, sparsely populated, predominantly rural, republican society suspicious of factions, interests, and parties?[41]

Mainly because of the double vote for President, the delegates created the office of Vice President for the runner-up who did not need to muster a majority vote. Here the framers were too clever for their own good. As electors cast two votes for President, not one for President and one for Vice President, they could not know for sure which of the two persons they supported would become President and, of course, there was the possibility that neither would be successful. The process, rather than the intentions of individual electors, would discover who would hold the top office and in turn who would hold the second position. This provision, more than any other, invited the very kind of manipulation that the framers had intended to discourage by inventing presidential electors.

With most of the rest of the Constitution already written, the framers had difficulty finding duties to assign to the Vice President whose only role was to preside over the Senate, break tie votes, and receive the electoral votes from the various states. An afterthought, the office befuddled Vice Presidents, starting with John Adams who moaned, "My country has in its wisdom contrived for me the most insignificant office that ever the invention of man [designed] or his imagination conceived."[42] In 1789 when the first Congress debated how to address George Washington and considered "His Serene Highness" and "His Excellency" before settling on the more republican "Mr. President," one Representative had no trouble finding a suitable title for Adams's office: "His Superfluous Excellency."[43] In 1804 George Clinton of New York refused a possible eighth term as Governor on the grounds of age and poor health, but accepted the Vice Presidency because there was so little to do and so much time for recreation.

It is difficult to conclude that the framers in Philadelphia consciously sought to create an elitist, undemocratic institution in presidential electors, as some progressive historians have suggested. It is also improbable that they reacted solely to immediate issues in the Convention without reference to political experience or theory. The final provisions drew upon many different ideas, and almost every aspect can be traced to earlier arguments and counterarguments presented over a period of several months--some theoretical, political, personal, and mundane. Yet, the device of presidential electors at this stage was more effective in answering criticisms of every other method considered in the Convention and in the ratification debate than in providing a blueprint for the future. Much of what later defenders of the institution have found laudable and some of what later critics have considered deplorable derive from the creation of a particular electoral college by those who implemented the Constitution rather than the ambiguous invention of 1787.[44]

3

The First Presidential Election

The advocates of the Constitution, cosmopolitan as they were, had a greater chance of affecting the outcome of the first elections for President, Senate, and House than their opponents. James Madison had claimed that the great extent of the republic would filter out provincial elements in favor of more national, civic-minded, and virtuous ones. Antifederalists had agreed that persons attached to local interests would suffer as the geographic extent increased from a parish, county, and township to districts, states, and nation. Hence Federalists may not have fully appreciated the implications of presidential electors. A federal distribution of powers and a central government subdivided by separation of powers made it difficult for the new system to function without some agency to coordinate the actions of different branches and different governments. More particularly, the difficulties built into the process to manipulate the votes of electors made it necessary for those interested in winning presidential elections to assert themselves prior to the appointment of electors to get persons who could be relied upon to vote for the right candidates. It is a supreme irony that the framers made a Constitution which sought to minimize the influence of political parties but actually required parties to make it work. The first Washington administration brought forth the beginnings of the Federalist Party and the opposition of the nascent Republican Party. Thereafter presidential electors and political parties developed in tandem, simultaneously and a little awkwardly, moving like two persons in a three-legged race, to produce the outlines of the modern electoral college.[1]

Delaware began the parade of states to ratify the Constitution in December of 1787, and Pennsylvania, New Jersey, Georgia, Connecticut, Massachusetts, Maryland, South Carolina, and New Hampshire followed, making the requisite nine for adoption. The Philadelphia Convention had recommended that Congress determine the dates on which the states which had ratified should appoint electors and on which those electors should vote. The Convention had also asked the Congress to announce the time and place for the beginning of the new government and urged that thereafter Representatives and Senators should be chosen. But even after waiting for Virginia and New York to ratify in June and July, Congress stalemated over the location of the new government and failed to move. For the time being, Congress left the capital in New York City.[2]

It was not until September 13, 1788 that Congress adopted an election ordinance which provided that electors be appointed on the first Wednesday in January, that they assemble and vote on the first Wednesday in February, and that the Congress begin the new system on the first Wednesday in March by counting the votes for President. Apparently, Congress thought that the entire process could take place in the dead of winter without difficulties.[3]

Within New England, Rhode Island alone remained outside of the union under the Constitution. Connecticut moved promptly to make accommodations for the new system. In his speech opening the October session of the legislature, Governor Samuel Huntington asked the legislators to act with dispatch, and they promptly agreed to elect the five Representatives at large; the state completed these elections by the first week in January. The legislators also succeeded by mid-December to appoint their Senators.[4]

The Connecticut legislature decided with apparent confidence that its members should appoint presidential electors. Accepting the broad discretionary authority given to them, the members saw no need to pass a law formalizing the procedure but moved by simple resolution. They chose prominent state officials and supporters of the Constitution, and they instructed the electors to convene in Hartford on the first Wednesday in February to give their votes. They chose this method over popular election not because of time constraints for they authorized a potentially complex, two-tiered election for Representatives during the same period.[5]

On the appointed day, the seven men dutifully met at the courthouse and cast seven votes for George Washington, five for John Adams, and two for Governor Huntington. They took care to write out the words "seven," "five," and "two" to make any erasure or alteration noticeable. They also tried to eliminate challenges to their votes for lack of specificity by identifying George Washington as "late Commander in chief of the Armies of the United States of America," John Adams as "late Minister plenipotentiary of the United States of America at the Court of Great Britain," and Samuel Huntington as "Governor of the State of Connecticut." The electors signed their names and showed that the legislature had misspelled one of them, a potential disqualification for those favoring strict accounting. The official records indicate that they voted for "a President of the United States of America, & a Vice President,"[6] introducing an ambiguity as to whether they voted for two persons for President. Newspapers quickly reported the results and spread the news to other states.[7]

In New Hampshire Governor John Langdon issued a proclamation on October 10, 1788, calling the General Court to a special session to provide for electors by the January 7 deadline. Langdon came out in favor of legislative appointment, but John Sullivan, the former governor and Langdon's brother-in-law, argued for popular election. The two houses sought to resolve the disagreement by creating a joint committee to prepare acceptable legislation. On November 12, the General Court adopted a proposal for popular election of five electors at large, each of whom had to win an absolute majority of voters--not votes. In the contingency that one or more failed to win a sufficient vote, the General Court would make the choice from a list of the top ten candidates.[8]

On January 1, 1789 the General Court appointed a committee to canvass the returns. The committee calculated that 20,142 votes had been cast and assumed that each voter chose five candidates. Hence the number of voters came to 4,028, a majority of which was 2,015. No one received the necessary minimum. The committee then prepared a list of the top ten candidates. Then, a huge problem surfaced. The house apparently considered the appointment of electors a non-legislative act, differing from the passage of a bill, and suggested that the two houses meet in joint session to make the selections. The senate, however, favored appointments by concurrent votes. In the Philadelphia Convention, John Langdon had warned of just such difficulties with the concurrent vote. New Hampshire faced the prospect of a deadlock and abstention from the presidential election.[9]

On January 7 the senate sought to break the logjam by appointing five persons and sending the names to the house. But the house refused to follow. It suggested instead that ten names be placed in a box, from which the secretary and clerk of the house should pull out five at random, but the senate rejected this bizarre solution. Finally, with midnight approaching and each house jealous of its prerogatives, the House conceded. It agreed to vote on those nominated by the senate but insisted that its action should not set a precedent for future presidential elections. Immediately the house confirmed the senate's candidates, indicating that the differences were not over the particular persons to be chosen but over the joint or concurrent vote. The five electors met at Exeter on February 4. They acknowledged that they had the duty to vote for "two persons for President of the United States" and cast their undifferentiated votes for Washington and Adams.[10]

In neighboring Massachusetts, the General Court which had adjourned on June 20, 1788 to wait for instructions from the Congress, reconvened on October 29. By then, newspapers had introduced the public to some of the major issues confronting the legislature: should Representatives be chosen at large or in districts, should Senators be appointed by joint or concurrent ballot of the two houses, and should presidential electors be popularly elected or appointed by the legislature.[11]

For example, the *Massachusetts Centinel* published an extensive essay in which the author argued that the President represented the people of the United States, not the member states, and like the national government the President operated directly upon individuals. It seemed only proper, then, that the people have maximum influence on the choice of the chief executive, just as they had in the election of governor. Appointment of electors by the General Court, though constitutional, posed several disadvantages. The legislature stood as an intermediary between the people and the President, and it required voters to select their state legislators at least in part on the basis of which persons they might appoint. Moreover, the General Court mixed legislative business with the separate function of helping to elect the President. As a sitting body, the Court would become the target of corruption and intrigue. But A Citizen of Essex, writing to the *Salem Mercury*, disagreed. Article II, section 1, began with the words *Each State* and the word *State* did not mean the people. Instead it was a summary mode of expression, just like Massachusetts. This writer believed that the schedule prepared by the Congress worked against popular election in large, diversified states and implied legislative appointment.[12]

The Federalist-controlled General Court debated a committee report which recommended election of Representatives by districts and appointment of Senators by concurrent vote and presidential electors by joint ballot of the two houses. The membership divided on the relative merits of the proposals, but not along Federalist-Antifederalist lines.[13]

The principal arguments on behalf of legislative appointment of electors rested on the open-ended nature of Article II, section 1. Allowing the General Court to exercise its discretion would strengthen state authority, a sure protection for the rights of the people. It also guaranteed appointment, whereas the people might not be able to coalesce around the requisite number of candidates. Delays, runoffs, and the like would jeopardize participation. Advocates of popular choice, like William Heath, answered that the Constitution gave legislatures the power to decide only how the people would elect. Daniel Cony asked how legislators could justify preempting the people's right to vote and insulting them as well.[14]

A subcommittee of the house reported a scheme on November 10 that set the General Court on the path to resolution. It assigned one or two electors to each district which chose Representatives and gave voters the right to nominate. The General Court by joint ballot would choose one or two electors from the top three in each district. Further discussions led to a breakthrough, which gave Massachusetts a singular mode of choosing presidential electors. People in each district which chose a Representative would vote for one elector, and, if no one received a majority, the General Court would appoint from the top two candidates. In addition, the legislature would appoint two electors at large from those who received no popular votes. Lawmakers escaped the inconvenience of having unequal districts and of having different districts for Representatives and for electors. They had a system for appointing electors which imitated the methods used in selecting Representatives and Senators.[15]

The absence of any organized party effort to promote a ticket of electors combined with the district mode to produce fragmented returns. More than 220 persons received votes for the eight positions. Suffolk, for example, had 21 candidates, Essex 24, Middlesex 27, Hampshire-Berkshire 46, and Worcester

42. When the General Court realized what had happened in early January, the members moved to alter the law of November 20 with regard to the at-large electors, for it no longer made sense to select these two from those who had received no popular vote.[16]

On Wednesday, January 7, 1789, the General Court met in joint session to make the appointments. In the Middlesex, Hampshire-Berkshire, York-Cumberland-Lincoln, and Worcester districts, the legislature appointed the candidate who had the most votes. In Suffolk, Essex, Plymouth-Barnstable, and Bristol-Dukes-Nantucket districts, the legislature chose the candidate who finished second. The General Court then appointed two others. In exercising their authority, the legislators did not seem to be choosing Federalists over Antifederalists, for all the candidates who finished at the top of the district lists had served in state government and supported the Constitution, but in taking the second over the first they seemed to prefer those who had served longer in public life, especially in the General Court. Theodore Sedgwick, the Speaker of the House, had informed Alexander Hamilton back in November that in spite of the divided opinion in the state, the legislative mode would carry the day for Adams unanimously. Apparently, Sedgwick had less confidence if strict district elections became the mode, for it would have given minority opinion a chance to garner some electoral votes. But Henry Jackson and Christopher Gore quickly determined that the electors were firm and reliable Federalists.[17]

On Wednesday, February 4, the ten Massachusetts electors came to the senate chamber in Boston. In spite of ill health and lengthy travel for some, they began their work at eleven o'clock. They chose William Cushing chairperson and without further discussion proceeded to vote solidly for Washington and Adams. Clearly they had gathered to perform the sole duty of casting a predetermined vote; they had not come to discuss, deliberate, and negotiate. They recorded the vote on the reverse side of two copies of an official notice in the hand of John Avery, Jr., Secretary of the State, declaring the names of the persons chosen electors by the General Court, and sent them to the President of the Senate. Newspapers quickly reported the results and began to compare these with returns in other states.[18]

Among the southern states, North Carolina alone failed to ratify the Constitution prior to the first presidential election. The convention in neighboring South Carolina voted overwhelming to ratify, but political sentiment in the Palmetto state was divided along a line separating the Charleston and Tidewater region from the up-country. Throughout the 1770s and 1780s, state government advantaged the wealthy in the former while population favored the latter. The low country interests sought to maintain their superiority in the first federal elections and showed unease at the signs of factionalism within the Tidewater and the emergence of a politically active west.[19]

Governor Thomas Pinckney summoned the legislature to meet on October 7, 1788 to address the congressional resolution of September 13. After extensive debate, the legislators passed a law which provided for district elections of Congressmen and legislative appointment of both Senators and electors. It allowed "such persons as shall be returned Members thereof and shall attend on that day [January 7]" to select electors.[20] Indeed the house had a quorum and the senate did not on the first Wednesday in January. Those present appointed all Federalists, who gathered at the city exchange in Charleston. They had the convenience of a written form which required only the insertion of names and numbers. Whoever prepared the form had anticipated votes for only two persons. The electors gave 7 votes to George Washington, 6 to John Rutledge, and 1 to John Hancock. The presiding officer, Charles C. Pinckney, sent the various documents to Charles Thompson, Secretary of the Congress.[21]

Georgia cut it very close and could easily have missed participating in the first presidential election. This youngest member of the United States was also the least developed. Nathaniel Pendleton and George Walton, two of the men chosen by the legislature to represent the state in the Philadelphia Convention, had failed to attend. Now Governor George Handley issued a proclamation on October 17, 1788, calling the legislature to meet in Augusta on November 4 to make provisions for the appointment of electors. But after waiting several days, the legislators lacked a quorum, probably because many members were simultaneously chosen to serve in the state constitutional convention. They urged voters to make certain to choose persons at the state elections on December 2 who pledged to attend an early meeting of the legislature to provide for presidential electors. The *Georgia Gazette* expressed regret at the aborted session.[22]

The new legislature did not convene until January 6, leaving very little margin for error. Fortunately, the Georgia House of Assembly had a quorum and on the next day chose five men who were present. They gave George Washington 5 votes; John Milton 2, James Armstrong and Edward Telfair 1 each, all of Georgia; and Benjamin Lincoln of Massachusetts 1. The assembly asked the executive to have the records of the electors transmitted to New York City.[23]

Maryland experienced other kinds of difficulties in participating in the presidential election. Maryland's conservative constitution set a freehold requirement to vote for the lower house and the electorate chose electors who picked the upper house for five-year terms. There were nine senators from the western shore and five from the eastern. Viva voce remained the practice for voting. Maryland had ratified the Constitution by an overwhelming margin, which belied sharp, internal political divisions. The refusal of Federalists to recommend amendments to accompany ratification drove Antifederalists to a vigorous campaign in the first federal elections.[24]

Governor John Eager Howard informed the legislature on November 5, 1788 of the need to provide for Representatives, Senators, and electors. The legislators divided principally on whether elections for Representatives would be at-large, as Federalists favored, or in districts, as Antifederalists preferred.

They seemed less concerned about electors. They adopted an election law on December 22, which provided that eligible voters should give six votes viva voce for a Congressman from each of six districts on January 7, 1789, only about two weeks away. They should also vote at that time for eight presidential electors, five of whom would come from the western shore and three from the eastern. This allocation approximated the weights given these sections in the state senate. The electors were to meet on February 4 in Annapolis to perform their duties. Federalists expected that their statewide majority would produce victories for their candidates, especially in a campaign which had to be completed in such a short period.[25]

A Federalist legislative caucus met in Annapolis, prepared a ticket for Congressmen and presidential electors, and advertised it in the *Maryland Journal*. In some instances, individuals, like John Allen Thomas, made known their candidacy by a public announcement. The *Maryland Gazette* carried an item on December 30 which identified both Federalist and Antifederalist tickets for these offices. Interestingly, the Antifederalist slate had several names taken from their rivals. A few Federalists were surprised to find their names on opposition tickets without prior knowledge or approval and urged their followers to be on guard against such trickery. When Antifederalists criticized tickets for limiting the voters' freedom of choice, Federalists answered that their counterparts in states like Pennsylvania saw the wisdom of unity in a contest of such great importance.[26]

The campaign was short but vigorous and a good portion centered on presidential electors. William Tilghman expressed concern that Article II, section 1 of the Constitution required electors to cast two votes for President and not one for President and one for Vice President. He strongly favored Washington for the top post but saw how the undifferentiated vote by electors could be used by Antifederalists to jeopardize the Virginian's election or to embarrass him by giving him a hostile Vice President. Henry Hollingsworth also recognized the possibility of an accidental choice. He thought that Americans wanted Washington for President and most sought Adams for Vice President but feared that the latter could come out on top.[27]

Federalist literature stressed that ratification of the Constitution did not insure any final triumph over its opponents. Civis wrote in the *Maryland Journal* that Antifederalists could injure the new administration by causing mischief in the first election, and Tom Plain-Truth issued a broadside which warned that the new government was not yet free from danger. A Marylander wrote to the *Maryland Gazette* and informed readers of the candidacy of George Clinton of New York, "the most powerful and inveterate anti on the continent."[28] His selection as Vice President could set the course for his elevation to the chief magistracy and disaster for the new system of government. Hence Maryland should defeat all Antifederalist candidates for electors. By January 21, the executive council had the results, which showed a clean sweep for Federalist candidates for Congress and presidential electors.[29]

Governor Howard issued a proclamation, dated January 21, 1789, announcing the names of the eight men who had been chosen electors. Two failed to attend when the others met at Annapolis on February 4. Later, the *Virginia Gazette* reported that indisposition accounted for George Plater's absence and "some unavoidable accident" befell William Richardson. Maryland had made no provision for filling vacancies, and thereby the absentees deprived Maryland of one-fourth of its vote. Elector Robert Smith complained that inadequate communication frustrated concerted action with electors in other states at this crucial moment. Apparently, the electors decided to insure Washington's election and gave George Washington and Robert Hanson Harrison, the Chief Justice of the State of Maryland, 6 votes each.[30]

Virginia, like Maryland, experienced difficulties in having its full weight count in this presidential election. The battle over ratification had been intense, and Antifederalists, led by Richard Henry Lee and Patrick Henry, may have reflected the wishes of the majority in the state. When Virginia became the tenth state in the new union, George Washington became eligible to be the first President. Recognized everywhere as the largest of the large states, Virginia had ten Representatives and two Senators in the first Congress and hence twelve electoral votes.[31]

Virginia had a strong tradition of local governance, based on the county court system which the planter-slaveholder class dominated, and its state government operated by consensus. While political parties did not yet exist, the 1770s and 1780s made evident the sectional divisions between the coastal areas and the interior. These differences surfaced in the contest between Federalists and Antifederalists, the significance of which George Washington recognized: "To be shipwrecked in sight of the Port would be the severest of all possible aggravations to our misery."[32]

The legislature had a clear Antifederalist majority, evidenced by Patrick Henry's success in calling for a new constitutional convention in response to the Circular Letter of the New York Convention. Nonetheless, there was substantial agreement about the election laws. The House of Delegates chose to authorize voters to elect Representatives and electors on a district basis. In most instances, such a choice meant great difficulty in defining districts for both offices since there were always two more electors than Representatives, and all districts would have to be redrawn with each census. Virginia was fortunate in that it had twenty-four state senate districts, two of which were combined to create a presidential elector district. It then established ten new districts for the Congress. Antifederalists prepared lists of approved candidates, while Federalists like Edward Carrington put forward their own candidacies to provide clear alternatives for voters.[33]

On the appointed day, voters went to the polls, where sheriffs supervised the election. The sheriffs of all the counties which comprised the presidential electors' districts were supposed to meet to tabulate the results. Those in seven districts complied fully; in 3 only some attended at the time and place designated by law; in 1 only 9 of 17 sheriffs (none of the 7 from Kentucky) showed. In the other district, there was a total breakdown as some sheriffs kept their polls open longer than did others, and hence failed to meet within 7 days of closing the polls as required. On January 26, the governor and council certified the results, named eleven persons electors, including Antifederalists Patrick Henry, John Pride, and John Roane, and left one position vacant. On February 4, Warner Lewis failed to attend the meeting of electors at Richmond, and the Old Dominion lost one-sixth of its potential electoral strength due to a failed election and an absence.[34]

According to Theodorick Bland, the three Antifederalists intended to vote for George Washington, a fellow Virginian, but looked for an Antifederalist for the second office. Henry Lee agreed that this would be the Antifederalists' strategy, for they had no intention of disowning the war hero. Edward Carrington understood that Antifederalists elsewhere pushed for George Clinton of New York for Vice President and expected him to garner some votes in Virginia and South Carolina. St. John de Crevecoeur expected that Clinton as candidate for President sought support in Virginia and would get aid from western Pennsylvania. Electors were not going to vote blind; they intended to vote to advance the interests of the particular parties they represented. The electors met in Richmond on February 4, and cast 10 votes for Washington, 5 for Adams, 3 for George Clinton, and 1 each for John Hancock and John Jay. Martin Oster, present in the city at the time, shortly afterward sent an accurate vote tally to Comte de la Luzerne and reported that electors Edward Stevens, John Harvey, Daniel Stuart, William Fitzhugh, and Anthony Walker voted for Washington and Adams; James Wood for Washington and Hancock; Zachariah Johnston for Washington and Jay; and Henry, Pride, and Roane for Washington and Clinton.[35]

The middle states of Delaware, New Jersey, Pennsylvania, and New York exercised yet other options. In October, Delaware's Governor Thomas Collins urged prompt action by the legislature, and it quickly chose two Senators, Federalists George Read and Richard Bassett, by joint ballot. Shortly thereafter, the legislature adopted a bill for the popular election of the lone Representative and the three electors. The voter chose two persons for Representative, one of whom had to be a resident of a county other than that of the voter.[36]

In an interesting contrast, Delaware's voters cast only one vote for elector even though there were three positions to fill. The legislature set up a process which would enhance the chances of each of the state's counties having an elector. The voter submitted his choices for Representative and elector on a single piece of paper. The judges of elections in the counties made the local tallies and sent a copy of the results to the President (the Governor) and his Council. The President aggregated the returns and appointed the highest on the list for Representative and the three highest for electors. Jehu Davis, the Vice President of the state, issued a public proclamation to announce the winners. When the electors met in Dover on February 4, Gunning Bedford served as the moderator and recorded only that there were three votes for both Washington and Adams.[37]

Another small state, New Jersey, took a different course. With little public discussion, the legislature adopted an election law which provided for the popular election of four Representatives at large and the appointment of Senators by a joint vote of the two houses and of the six electors by the Governor and council of state. In essence, the legislature gave to the executive branch the power to choose electors. This mode provoked a later reaction, when petitioners from Middlesex County complained of the return of Tory principles. On Wednesday, January 7, 1789 Governor William Livingston and eleven councilors met and chose six electors. The Philadelphia *Federal Gazette* declared satisfaction with the Federalist credentials of the six men who met at Trenton in early February. David Brearley presided. They gave Washington 6 votes, John Jay of neighboring New York 5, and John Adams 1.[38]

Whereas Delaware and New Jersey represented Federalist strongholds, Pennsylvania did not. Partisan conflicts dated back to 1776 when the state constitution had been adopted. The Constitutionalists framed that document and supported the Articles of Confederation. Their Republican opponents had gained control of the unicameral assembly, sent delegates to the Philadelphia Convention, and had successfully maneuvered the state to ratify the federal Constitution. The Pennsylvania legislature began its regular session in September of 1788, when William Findley of Westmoreland, a leading Constitutionalist and Antifederalist, urged that elections for Congress be based on districts rather than an at-large general ticket in which the entire state comprised a single election district, an area so large that voters could not be acquainted with the candidates. William Lewis of Philadelphia countered that Congressmen represented the state, not districts, and James McLene of Franklin believed that the tightness of the schedule set by Congress demanded the simpler, at-large option. Like a number of other states, Pennsylvania did not establish a permanent law with general language applicable to all elections. Perhaps the state's experience with a unicameral system did not provide any warning of prospective legislative deadlocks in a bicameral system, especially when rival parties controlled each house.[39]

In the end, the legislature agreed to the general ticket for both Representatives and electors. William Findley suggested with regard to the latter that the ambiguity of Article II, section 1 be read in a light favorable to popular choice, and he encountered little dissent. Legislative selection meant that the assembly would have to stay in session all the way until January or reconvene solely to perform that task. Federalists must have found the general ticket appealing, for they felt confident of directing a large turnout of voters in Philadelphia and of carrying the entire slate of candidates for electors. But they knew that what advantaged them in the Keystone state might not work elsewhere. As Tench Coxe observed, "It will give a precedent to the other states, where the majority are unfavorable, such as New York etc., which may require the early attention of our friends in those places."[40] Clearly, they recognized the way in which majorities could be leveraged to a winner-take-all system.[41]

The assembly proposed January 7, the first Wednesday in January, for the election of electors. New Hampshire and Massachusetts, both of which permitted voters to participate in the process, scheduled elections at an early enough time so that the results could be known by January. Presumably Pennsylvania could have held its elections in December, tabulated the results, and announced them by January 7.[42]

The Constitutionalists and Republicans put emphasis on the contests for Congress in November. In the aftermath of an apparent Republican victory in these elections, the Constitutionalists largely conceded defeat in the presidential contest in January. Although they went through the motions of making a ticket, they were never really in the race. Those who were interested in the outcome probably favored George Washington in any case, though they may have preferred Henry or Clinton instead of Adams or Hancock with their second votes. The Republicans tried hard to associate their opponents with the Antifederalism of Henry and Clinton, but they were no more successful in stirring great interest. The sheriff of Fayette County reported that in his area no supervisors for the election attended and the people were indifferent to the occasion.[43]

Federalists worked diligently for the sure victory. The *Federal Gazette* and *Pennsylvania Packet* published their ticket and urged voters to be patriotic and support both the Constitution and George Washington. Early reports from Philadelphia indicated a one-sided result, when the Federalist candidates received between 1,525 and 1,545 votes while the highest total received by an Antifederalist came to 16. Indeed the Federalist majority in Philadelphia determined the course of the election. But serious problems jeopardized the Federalist triumph. Returns from the western counties had been very slow to come in for the congressional elections, and many had not reached the President and supreme executive council for several weeks beyond the deadline set by law. Anticipating a repetition of this experience, the council had sent out a messenger, James Dunwoodie, to the western areas to bring the returns for presidential electors so that they could be counted, and the successful candidates instructed to be in Reading on Wednesday, February 4. Unfortunately Dunwoodie provided no word until February 2. He may have been desultory in performing his duties and mixed some private business with the public mission, but his own account suggests that he faced near insuperable obstacles. He could not cross the Susquehanna River for four days, had trouble delivering his credentials to various local officials, and failed to reach Fort Pitt before January 19. He then went to Bedford, where he expected the returns from Huntington to be sent; alas, they never showed. He had to travel through a country where the snow had not been broken until he arrived. By the time he reached Green Castle in Franklin County, he had traveled nearly 830 or 840 miles. Even then he did not have all the votes.[44]

On Tuesday, February 3, just one day before electors in all the states were to vote, the President and supreme executive council issued a proclamation naming the electors, all Federalists.   James Wilson did not wait for the proclamation, but, assuming that he had been elected, set off from Philadelphia for Reading on Tuesday.   He realized that his absence, even if not his fault, would result in Pennsylvania losing an electoral vote, and his state, like the others, had made no provision for filling any vacancy.   In Reading, the electors chose Lawrence Keene to handle administrative details.   They reported that they were choosing a President and Vice President and cast 10 votes for Washington, 8 for Adams, and 2 for John Hancock.[45]

The September 13, 1788 resolution of the last Congress under the Articles of Confederation had stated that the first Congress under the Constitution inaugurate the government on the first Wednesday in March.   On March 4, New York City celebrated the occasion, but those members of the House and Senate who were present found their chambers still under construction and, more to the point, many of their colleagues tardy.   Charles Thomson was embarrassed for his country: "What must the world think of us?"[46]   It was not until April 6 that a quorum in each body permitted the official counting of the electoral votes.   At last, the Senate chose John Langdon of New Hampshire to be the presiding officer for the occasion and asked Oliver Ellsworth to notify the House of its ability to meet jointly and proceed with the election of the President.[47]

Meeting in the Senate chamber, the members of the two houses watched and listened as John Langdon counted the votes of the electors.   In spite of various irregularities, such as the inconsistent spelling of the names of electors on official commissions and the loss of votes in Pennsylvania, Congress made no effort to look behind the returns from the states.   The tally showed George Washington with 69 votes, a unanimous vote of the electors appointed.   John Adams had 34, John Jay 9, John Rutledge and Robert H. Harison 6, John Hancock 4, George Clinton 3, Samuel Huntington and John Milton 2, James Armstrong, Edward Telfair, and Benjamin Lincoln 1.   With the House concurring, the Senate asked Charles Thomson to notify George Washington and Sylvanus Bourn to inform John Adams that they were President and Vice President of the new republic.   At last, Americans had inaugurated their system of presidential electors.[48]

4

New York Abstains

No state offers a better example of how rival political interests and ideas affected the choice of presidential electors in 1789 than New York, a late, reluctant, and divided supporter of the Constitution. Though not considered to be one of the large states, it had a diversity characteristic of the larger entities. It had long been one of the most complex ethnic and religious societies and its internal divisions between upstate and downstate counties and between agricultural and commercial interests reached well back into the colonial past. The events of the Revolutionary War accentuated these differences. The state was the scene of intense and extended military activity; its population included loyalists numerous enough to inflame the fear and hatred of those who opposed British rule; and New York City was occupied by the British through most of the war. The war and attendant issues of taxation, confiscation of estates, and proscription of loyalists left a legacy of hostility, suspicion, and reaction which lived on after the war came to a close.[1]

George Clinton, first governor of New York under the constitution of 1777, was the dominant political figure of the period. He gained re-election in 1780, 1783, and again in 1786 when he ran unopposed. Clinton's supporters came from "semisubsistence areas in central or northern New York" and were on the whole satisfied with the political outcome of the state constitution and the Articles of Confederation which granted substantial autonomy to New York.[2] Their opponents were concentrated in "New York City, Albany, the other towns, and commercial farm areas, especially in the south."[3] Their nationalism and support for a stronger central government derived at least in part from their desire to place political power where they could have access.

The Constitution was created with little official input from New York. It was destined to be accepted by the American states, and New York's Antifederalists could not prevent it even in their own state, where they held a strong majority. Shocked and divided among themselves by the outcome in the ratifying convention in Poughkeepsie, the Antifederalists in the ensuing weeks and months tried to shore up their ranks by uniting behind a common plea for amendments. The reputation and political careers of men like Melancton Smith and Samuel Jones, who had voted for adoption in Poughkeepsie, depended on how reliable they appeared in this quest.[4]

Governor Clinton called for a special session of the legislature to deal with the September 13 resolutions of the Congress, but took his time about it, not even issuing his proclamation until mid October and then setting December 8 for the convening of the senators and assemblymen. His desultory leadership exposed him to political criticism for obstructionism and strengthened opinion among opponents that he, in particular, remained an inveterate foe of the new Constitution.[5]

When the legislature finally convened, Governor Clinton reported briefly on the need to prepare for the inauguration of the new national government and followed with a lengthier reminder of the need for amendments to the Constitution. Legislators might well have expected an unhappy session. Senate clerk Abraham B. Bancker noted that the Federalists had a majority in the senate and the Antifederalists a majority in the assembly: "consequently we must expect many of our acts to be negatived by each other in the course of Sessions, which, by the bye, is likely to be a very long one."[6]

The Federalists were determined to protect their interests in the upcoming presidential and congressional elections and to deny the Clintonian organization any advantage. They knew that the Antifederalists hoped to build an alliance with their friends in Virginia to advance the candidacy of George Clinton. They wanted George Washington for President and a trustworthy partner, like John Adams, for Vice President, and sought to make certain that no Antifederalist, especially Clinton, embarrassed Washington or the new government with a successful challenge for either position. They also sought clear majority control of the United States Senate and House, which would examine all proposals for amendments to the Constitution. Having just barely won the ratification battle in Poughkeepsie, they were not about to lower their guard and be surprised by the Clintonians.[7]

Federalist John Laurance introduced a bill on presidential electors in the senate on December 13, 1788, which stipulated that the house and senate separately appoint four of the eight electors assigned to New York. Meanwhile, the Antifederalists in the assembly proceeded on their own course. They took their cue from Article XXX of the state constitution of 1777, which provided that New York's representation in the national Congress be chosen by concurrent nominations and by a joint vote of the legislature should there be disagreement between the two houses. They proposed an omnibus bill that placed ultimate power to appoint Senators and electors in a joint session of the legislature.[8]

The senate considered the assembly omnibus bill on December 31, only a few days before presidential electors were to be chosen. It rejected the joint ballot for U.S. Senators in favor of concurrence by the separate houses. Philip

Schuyler secured a change in the provision for joint selection of electors: each house nominated eight and those named by both would be chosen. In case of disagreement, each house would appoint four from those nominated by the other.[9]

On January 1, 1789, the house received the senate amendments, and on the next day it rejected them all. With the two houses in disagreement on the basic issues, the assembly proposed a conference of the assembly and senate to be held on Monday, January 5, 1789 at 11 A.M., and appointed Samuel Jones, Matthew Adgate, and Gilbert Livingston, all Antifederalists, to manage its case. The senate agreed to the request and selected Federalists Philip Schuyler, James Duane, and Ezra L'Hommedieu to present its position.[10]

Newspapers later identified January 5 as a fateful day for New York. The conferees were able men, committed to their respective points of view, and spoke before large audiences. Antifederalists did not want to repeat their collapse in Poughkeepsie; the outnumbered Federalists were determined to overcome the odds once again. Whether New York would participate in the first election for President and whether it would enjoy an active representation in the Congress in its formative stages depended on the resolution of seemingly irreconcilable political positions.

Matthew Adgate, a lawyer-speculator who had voted at Poughkeepsie against adopting the Constitution, began the conference by insisting on good Antifederalist doctrine that the state constitution took precedence over the U.S. Constitution. Article XXX of the former prescribed the joint ballot as the legitimate method for choosing New York representatives to the Confederation Congress, and that mode should therefore now be followed in the selection of U.S. Senators and presidential electors. Conceding that popular election of electors was desirable, he believed that present circumstances made this option impractical, presumably because too little time remained to carry it out. Adopting the Clintonian line, he argued that the method which gave maximum voice to the popular will, as expressed in the lower house, should prevail. He might have added that in New York freemen elected assemblymen while one-hundred pound freeholders chose senators.[11]

Ezra L'Hommedieu, the Federalist state senator, replied for the upper house. He maintained that the new Constitution not only superseded the Articles of Confederation but also made certain portions of state constitutions obsolete. In bicameral legislatures, moreover, the two houses inherently held equal rights; each had the power to negate a proposal by the other. Any other procedure defeated the whole purpose of separation of powers and checks and balances.[12]

Gilbert Livingston saw no inconsistency between the requirements of the federal and state constitutions. The federal document left open the choice of separate or joint ballot; the state constitution filled the breach by ordering the joint method. Since it had been adopted in 1777 when no one could know the shape of the central government, the state constitution provided in general terms for the joint ballot and its prescription applied to any future central government.

Moreover, a concurrent vote created prospects for stalemate, which would undermine the idea of representation and the integrity of the central government. If this issue were not resolved, every succeeding legislature could suffer paralysis.[13]

General Philip Schuyler, the upstate landowner, father-in-law of Alexander Hamilton, and inveterate political rival of Clinton, then spoke for the Federalist senate majority. He asserted that the Constitution made moot the often cited Article XXX. The Constitution created two houses of Congress where previously there had been one. Representatives may not be appointed by the joint ballot of the legislature regardless of what the state constitution says. It is true that the Constitution gives the state legislatures power to set the time, place, and manner of choosing Representatives and Senators, but the state's discretion derives from the federal Constitution, not the state's constitution. While it is not explicit about Senators, the Constitution implies, he argued, that the state should take concurrent action, but he offered no explanation why this should be so. A joint vote will in no way insure a clear, decisive majority, and it may obscure the concurrence which separate votes guarantee. Like the previous Antifederalist speakers, Schuyler believed all too simply that the arguments over U.S. Senators applied with equal force to electors.[14]

Samuel Jones concluded the assembly presentation by returning to the supremacy of the New York constitution. In the absence of explicit language forbidding the use of a joint ballot, the state constitution's requirement remained binding. In legislative matters, the senate served as an independent body and its concurrence was required for a measure to become law. In appointive cases, the senate and house voted together in order to make certain that appointments would be made. Most of these arguments applied as well to electors, but with a single important difference. Jones believed that the national government exercised some control over New York when it came to representation in Congress, but Article II of the Constitution gave exclusive control over the choice of electors to the states. Here, even more clearly than in the case of Senators, the state constitutional provision prevailed.[15]

James Duane summarized the senate case. He began by suggesting that the senate's course of passing separate bills for Senators and electors was a more prudent one than the house's omnibus approach. He saw grounds for working out the differences over Representatives soon, but this accommodation would not resolve the disputes over other issues. He reminded the assembly that senators had taken the same oath to observe the state constitution as had members of the house and that they had acted in accordance with the operative provisions of that document. The house members apparently mistook their interpretation of the constitution for the constitution itself and insisted on a narrow reading of political history which blinded them to the changes instituted under the new central government.

Replying more directly to Jones, Duane remarked that the legislature can act only in its legislative capacity with each house having a veto on the other.

The only exception to this rule and practice has been the joint ballot for delegates to the old Congress, an obsolete procedure. The New York legislature had made all other appointments, such as the state treasurer and the commissioners for settling the boundary dispute with Massachusetts, by law with each house voting separately. It is of no significance to argue that the combined body of the two houses in the present case would favor the house bill over the senate alternatives, for the numerical majority in such a case had no standing. The senate, as well as the assembly, represents the people, and it does so by acting independently and preserving the principles of bicameralism. Duane then made an important distinction which previous speakers had not. The state constitution required the joint ballot for the old Congress, and, if it is admitted that the same must continue now, New York would have to use that mode in choosing Senators. But, Duane explained, by no stretch of the imagination can this New York constitutional requirement apply to the choice of presidential electors. Electors are not members of Congress, indeed are to be totally independent of it, and serve no legislative function.[16]

Having observed the entire proceedings, senate clerk Abraham B. Bancker sent a bleak report to his uncle. He thought the conferees for both sides had managed the debates well in the presence of a large, interested crowd but had changed few votes, if any. Indeed, immediately after the conference, the senators retired to their chambers. There they voted down a proposal to recede from their amendments to the omnibus bill. In the assembly Antifederalists voted to sustain that very bill. Henry Sewall, a Massachusetts farmer-merchant visiting New York city on business, wrote to Maine Federalist William Heath, "The Governor continues to countenance antifederal measures, under the zealous intent of obtaining a new Convention," and Tench Coxe observed that "the Scene of emotion at Albany is almost as great as that at Poughkeepsie was."[17] Bancker could hardly be faulted for predicting that there was no chance for the state to be represented in the Senate or to be counted in the presidential election. He concluded, "All this contest was ostensibly about the Mode, but the fact is, they contended about the Men, whether they should be federal or Anti-Federal."[18] One of the correspondents for the *New York Journal and Weekly Register* observed that "the fifth of January would likely form a melancholy epocha in the annals of New York."[19]

In the wake of the defeat of the assembly omnibus bill, the senate initiated its own bill to elect Representatives; the assembly soon followed suit. By the end of January slim majorities in each house passed a bill providing for district elections in which the electorate could vote for one Representative who had to be a resident of the state but not necessarily of the district. The council of revision expressed no objection and the bill became law on January 27. New York could at last proceed to elect Representatives to the United States Congress which would begin its first session in New York City on the first Wednesday in March of 1789.[20]

No such success greeted efforts to pass another bill on U.S. Senators.

Governor Clinton's nephew, DeWitt Clinton, expressed concern over the political consequences of the prolonged struggle; he believed that some New Yorkers feared that the Congress might leave Manhattan in view of the absence of New York Senators. He further believed that they would not blame the senate but the assembly and Governor. Yet the younger Clinton did not advocate compromise and concession! It was imperative, he believed, for adopting and nonadopting Antifederalists to rally together on behalf of the cause of amendments. On January 19, Samuel Jones introduced a new bill in the assembly calling for the joint ballot for electing U.S. Senators, and it passed that body. To no one's surprise, the Federalist majority in the senate held firm and blocked its passage.[21]

Alexander Hamilton sent to Jones an extensive letter in which he tried to remove any miscalculation on the part of the opposition; the Federalists were not bluffing. Hamilton also mentioned the existence of a compromise proposal which he had apparently already discussed with Jones. He believed that in this proposal the senate would bend on matters of principle more than the assembly would. The Federalists were willing to make concessions because compromise might gain for the people of the state the advantages to which they were entitled under the Constitution and have the new government inaugurated propitiously. He urged Jones to exercise a moderating influence in the assembly.[22]

A man of substantial property, legal expertise, and personal charm, Jones appealed to many moderates and, like Melancton Smith, had voted for ratification in Poughkeepsie, but now stood firm; having bent once, he seemed determined to maintain his political ties to Clinton, Antifederalism, and, most of all, constitutional amendments. On Friday, January 23, Jones reported a separate bill for joint appointment of presidential electors. Jones had some hope that electors could still be chosen and vote on the first Wednesday in February. Melancton Smith likewise advised Assemblyman John Smith of Mastic to continue to push for the appointment of electors. Until the Congress under the Constitution set the time for choosing electors, the states could take the schedule prepared by the outgoing Congress as advisory. Smith was probably correct in his reading. The appointment of electors in other states produced various irregularities which Congress chose not to examine. Governor Clinton's certification of appointment would probably have been sufficient. Yet Smith recognized that electors in all the states would have to vote on the scheduled day and that this deadline could not be ignored.[23]

On Tuesday, January 27 with the assembly meeting as a committee of the whole, Federalist Richard Harison expressed concern about the propriety of acting upon electors after the passage of the first Wednesday in January. Impressed, however, by the importance of the issue, he recommended that the two houses vote separately for them. If they could not agree on the same persons, then each house should choose by lot seven of its members, and those fourteen would make the appointments from the list of nominees. If the fourteen reflected the division of opinion in the legislature, they might choose equal or nearly equal numbers of Federalists and Antifederalists. But since there were more Antifederalists than Federalists in the assembly, perhaps thirty-five to twenty-four, and the Federalist margin in the senate was small, eleven to eight at the most, the odds favored the Antifederalists in the selection by lot. An Antifederalist advantage among the fourteen could have led to the appointment of a unified delegation to the electoral college. Then again, selection by lot offered no guarantees.[24]

Samuel Jones replied that the assembly bill was properly framed and should be sent to the senate. Jones showed that his own position had shifted since the conference, and he staked out a position of his own on presidential electors. Conceding that the legislature enjoyed substantial discretionary authority over the mode and that several methods were appropriate, he pointed out that the Antifederalist bill accorded with the most common method. Although Harison responded that the present deadlock required a temporary agreement for this election only and that the press of time dictated compromise with the senate, the assembly rejected his appeal.[25]

Richard Harison then tried again, recommending that the two houses stop debating the bill and move directly to appointment. Such an action would leave for calmer times a permanent law which Harison hoped would give the people the right to choose electors. Antifederalist Speaker of the Assembly John Lansing forthrightly and surprisingly challenged popular election and raised a new argument: "Sir, if the people are to determine who is to be the electors, the vote of the state will in most cases be lost, and the choice of president and vice president will either be left to chance or to cabal."[26] Lansing preferred legislative appointment by a joint session with a unified electoral vote for New York.

After further discussion, the house reverted to the original joint ballot and sent its bill to the senate on January 29 to no avail. James Duane successfully secured an amendment in which each house would nominate eight electors and appoint four from the list submitted by the other, which the assembly rejected. Samuel Jones argued that the senate amendment suffered a fatal flaw because in theory it left open the possibility that the state would not have a full complement of electors. What would happen, he asked, if the two houses agreed on the eight outstanding persons to be placed on their respective lists and also on the top four names on the lists? Then each house would wind up appointing four from the other's list, but they would be the same four persons. Given the long dispute in the legislature, it seemed hardly likely that the two houses would name the same eight candidates and that they would then choose the same four from the lists, and yet that is precisely what Jones and then Livingston argued. Indeed, even if they were right, it could be answered that four electors agreed upon by the two houses were better than none. On February 3, the house rejected the senate amendment to its bill and got from the senate an agreement to hold another conference. The house appointed Gilbert Livingston, Matthew Adgate, and Samuel Jones, and the senate chose Lewis Morris, Philip Schuyler, and James Duane to manage their respective positions.[27]

The conference of February 3, 1789 provided the last possible opportunity for New York to participate in the presidential election, for electors in all states were to cast their ballots on Wednesday, February 4. For all the urgency of the occasion, the conferees said little that had not been already been said. As if unmoved by the recent explanation provided by fellow Antifederalist Samuel Jones on January 27, Assemblyman Gilbert Livingston began by reverting back to the argument that the state constitution required the joint vote. Assemblyman Matthew Adgate also paid homage to Article XXX and echoed the party line.[28]

Philip Schuyler regretted that a second conference had to be called on essentially the same matters which had been examined in detail on January 5. The federal Constitution in Article II provided that electors should be chosen in a manner directed by the legislature, and that legislature did not consist of only the lower house. In practice the only way a bicameral legislature could function was through concurrence, whereby each house checked the other. Each in its own way represented the people, and no member of the legislature was free from the control of the voters.[29]

Samuel Jones concluded the assembly case. He made clear once again that his position on electors did not derive from the requirement of the state constitution. But he believed that a joint ballot was a reasonable mode which conflicted with neither the state nor federal document. The senate will have a minority vote, but such status did nothing to diminish the legislative parity of the upper house. It will, however, recognize that the senators are elected by one-hundred pound freeholders, not by the broad electorate which chooses assembly-men, and that they are subject to election every four years, not annually. The assemblymen "are therefore more recently from the people, and more likely to represent their feelings."[30] Finally, Senator James Duane scored some debating points, seconded Schuyler's arguments, and brought the conference to an end.

On the next day, when electors in the other states met to cast their votes, New York's legislature continued the partisan struggles of the preceding months with no way out of the impasse. There were futile last minute efforts by Feder-alists to appoint electors, but the Antifederalists continued to insist upon a total victory, all eight electors. Without any electors from New York, George Clin-ton lost any prospect of drawing a considerable electoral vote in the nation and of lending credibility to the Antifederalist cause for amendments.[31]

The Federalist senate submitted its final plan, which would allow each house to select four electors, a division which reflected as well as anything the relative strengths of the two parties in the state. Had it been accepted, this proportional plan would have assured Clinton of at least four electoral votes. Obstinate to the end, the Antifederalists rejected the senate measure.[32]

Thus February came and went, and the New York legislature failed to agree on a mode for choosing electors, and hence failed to appoint any. New York cast no votes for President and Vice President, but this abstention did not detract from the legitimacy of George Washington's election. During the debates in the Philadelphia Convention, James Madison and Hugh Williamson had proposed that the candidate with the most electoral votes be declared the winner, if this person had at least one-third of the total. When they failed to get support for electing by less than a majority, they argued that the majority be based on the number of electors who voted. The convention rejected this language in favor of John Dickinson's motion for a majority based on the number actually *appointed* by the states, a figure which could be less than the number allocated to the states.[33]

New York's abstention did not adversely affect the Federalists in the short run. Jeremiah Mason celebrated the occasion which made the election of a Federalist President more certain. Hamilton recognized that New York's participation would have sent an important message of national unity to the first administration, but it might have caused difficulties as well. The Constitution's directive that each elector cast two votes for President left uncertain which of the candidates voted for would ultimately have the greatest number of votes. Antifederalist electors could have held the balance of strength between the Virginian and the next strongest Federalist candidate and tipped the scales in favor of John Adams or someone else. Because George Clinton maintained a close friendship with George Washington throughout these trying times and because many Antifederalists had a high regard for the former Commander, there was less likelihood of such plotting over the presidency in actuality than Federalist partisans imagined.[34]

In addition, the presence of electors from New York might have made doubtful Federalist possession of the vice presidency. In their desire to guarantee Washington's election and to defuse any Antifederalist conspiracy, Federalist leaders had arranged for some of their electors to throw their second votes to someone other than Adams. Antifederalists from New York and Virginia could have provided the core of votes for another candidate, who might have finished second in the balloting. Melancton Smith hoped that an Antifederalist Vice President "would be the means of promoting amendments."[35] Even a strong finish in third place would have given notice that Antifederalism remained a powerful force. In any event, the Antifederalists in New York pursued a course of action which made any of these outcomes virtually impossible.[36]

The obstinacy of the Antifederalists, though understandable given their stunning setback in Poughkeepsie and the bitterness of their rivalry with the Federalists, offered no compensatory advantage for Clinton and his supporters. Not content with a proportional share of electors, they insisted to the end on all of them. By demanding total victory for themselves, Antifederalists could be portrayed as indifferent to the interests of New York and inimical to the new central government. At a time when that government was about to begin in New York City with the nationally revered Washington in the highest office, and when popular opinion in New York state seemed to be shifting favorably to the Constitution, Antifederalists showed poor political judgment. Horatio Gates went so far as to predict that "Antifederalism will die away by degrees, and wise men will wonder at their Opposition."[37]

In April of 1789 state elections for the legislature and for governor, in which the legislative stalemate over Senators and electors was an issue, loosened Antifederalist control of the New York government. The Federalists retained their majority in the senate and secured the majority in the assembly. Clinton defeated Robert Yates's challenge for the governorship, but only by the greatest exertions on the part of his supporters and then by the narrowest of margins. In a special session of the legislature in July, the Federalist assembly and senate initially proposed concurrent selection of U.S. Senators. The council of revision rejected the measure on the grounds that it allowed each house to appoint one Senator and neither house by itself composed the legislature. The two houses then accepted appointment by joint ballot. They chose Philip Schuyler for one seat and Rufus King for the other seat, as some Clintonians joined in support for the latter. New York belatedly sent its Senators to the Congress meeting in New York City.[38]

New York could do nothing about the presidential election, which was long past. When the state failed to vote on time for President, it lost for four years the opportunity to make its influence felt in the selection of the national executive. The effect of New York's abstention went beyond the potential political costs for Antifederalists. New York could remain a nonparticipant, for the Constitution permitted such abstention. But what was constitutionally permissible was not politically defensible. Any course of action that deprived the state of its proper influence in national government and which denied to President Washington and the new system of governance the support that they needed could not win public approbation for long. Federalist apologists could make political capital in the short run by blaming their opponents, but they faced Hamilton's warning to Samuel Jones:

> The vanity and malignity of some men may be gratified by embarassing [sic] the outset of the government; but this line of conduct would be a species of political suicide in every man who has in any shape given his assent to the system.[39]

The arduous debates in the winter of 1788-1789 showed that Federalists and Antifederalists understood that popular opinion played an important role in political life. Both sides maneuvered to win public support by identifying with what they perceived as winning political positions and resorted to constitutional arguments of the kind to which they had become accustomed after so many years of rivalry. Federalists emphasized the supremacy of the national Constitution, the principles of separation of powers and checks and balances, and the concept of concurrent vote. Just as naturally, the Antifederalists argued for the controlling influence of the state constitution, the supremacy of the lower house of the legislature, and democracy based on numerical majority.

While the old rhetoric and posturing continued, Federalists and Antifederalists were drawn increasingly to an agenda, schedule, and calendar shaped by the Constitution. From their respective positions, they had argued about the meaning of that Constitution and in the course of the debate explored various methods of selecting presidential electors within the broad discretion given states in Article II, section 1. The framers of the Constitution in Philadelphia had created not one electoral college, gathered at some central place in the nation, but separate electoral colleges, convened within each state. Given the difficulties of rapid communication and national coordination, this system made it problematic for all of those deeply interested in presidential elections to "fix" the outcome by trying to reach those appointed as electors. Alexander Hamilton attempted to manipulate the vote of electors in neighboring states, such as New Jersey and Connecticut, by advising them to throw away some potential votes for John Adams in order to ensure Washington's election as President. But such tinkering to deflect a vote here or there was a far different exercise from building majorities in state after state in favor of a particular candidate.

New York politicians were groping toward a system that would make certain their control over electors prior to appointment. In this regard, it is important to observe that neither Federalists nor Antifederalists in New York believed that presidential electors were to be persons distant from politics and party, exercising their independent judgment about who should be President and Vice President. To the contrary, their argument and their interests indicated their mutual understanding that electors were to be disciplined and loyal to those who appointed them; independence was not a virtue but a defect in electors.

Federalists and Antifederalists also expressed views both in favor of and in opposition to popular vote for electors and to joint or concurrent legislative appointment. Because they wrangled for so long, they learned what most other states had decided upon as appropriate modes for selecting electors. It became quickly apparent that district elections of the kind adopted in large states, such as Massachusetts and Virginia, had the potential of weakening their influence in relation to that of small states, like Connecticut and New Jersey, which favored unified delegations. They could hardly be indifferent to the advantages and disadvantages of proportional and unified electoral votes, information which would affect their future decisions about presidential electors.

In the end, they exercised their option of appointing no electors and shortly recognized the sober fact that appointment of electors was an obligation which could not be deferred for a week, a month, or a season. The schedule moved on relentlessly; latecomers could not claim their seats in the electoral college. All of these practical political considerations dictated how politics under the Constitution would be conducted in New York, and New York politicians determined that abstention from a presidential election was a precedent not worth repeating. Both Federalists and Antifederalists were being drawn into the realities of elections and appointments and the possible effects of the new Constitution on their political futures. Politics and the Constitution fit like hand and glove and began to give living shape to the political life of the state and nation.

II

LEARNING TO PLAY

5

New Rules for the Game in 1792

By 1792, the nation experienced significant changes which affected the evolution of presidential electors. First, the framers of the Constitution had set the total membership of the House of Representatives at sixty-five for the thirteen states and had allocated representation and electoral votes accordingly. They had also determined that after the first census, representation should be based on one for every 30,000 persons. Hence both the absolute number of Congressmen and presidential electors and the relative number assigned to each state changed for 1792 and the remainder of the decade.

Second, an act of Congress, adopted in early 1792, governed future presidential elections. Having had so many important items of business on the table and receiving the census returns so recently, the first federal Congress hardly had time to give sustained attention to election laws. Finally, on March 1, 1792, the second Congress acted. The new law allocated electors among the states and required all states to appoint electors within thirty-four days of the first Wednesday in December, when the electors were to cast their votes for President. This schedule obviated the problems with inclement weather which could impede elections held later in the winter. At a maximum, electors served thirty-four days from the time they were appointed to the time they cast their votes, hardly a sufficient period for those keenly interested in the outcome to plan and coordinate how electors were going to vote throughout the nation-- unless of course the electors were already pledged to particular candidates. The Congress also stipulated that governors should certify the list of electors. When the electors met to give their votes, they should gather in each state at a place determined by the legislature, submit their ballots, and record their votes on separate lists, one copy of which was to be sent by special messenger and a second by post to the President of the Senate, the sitting Vice President, by the first Wednesday in January. A third copy was to be delivered for safe keeping to the judge of the federal district in which the electors met. The lawmakers assumed that they should not go behind the appointment of electors and their votes and should rely on state authorities to validate the process. The law directed the Congress and the Senate to be in session on the second Wednesday in February to witness the opening and counting of the electoral votes.[1]

Third, states had to make adjustments to both the reallocation of electoral votes and to the law. New to the exercise, several had the advantage of studying how other members of the union had chosen presidential electors in 1789; they were not, of course, obligated to follow precedents.

Among New England states, Connecticut and Massachusetts made a smooth transition to the census and the new election law. In the former, legislative appointment of electors meant that no new district lines had to be drawn; the legislators would simply appoint nine persons rather than seven. In the latter, the combined method of electing one elector in each congressional district and appointing two more in the General Court meant that once new congressional districts were defined the state could proceed to the selection of electors. New Hampshire, by contrast, changed to a very cumbersome mode of general election. Those qualified to vote for state senators voted for six persons to be elector, and any person who received a majority of the votes cast won. In the event of vacancies due to a failure to secure a majority vote, the Governor made a list of the names of the top candidates containing twice the number of vacancies and submitted it to the voters. If the second round failed to fill the positions, then the secretary of the state drew names of the potential electors out of a box.[2]

Rhode Island, which had joined the union in 1790, waited until October of 1792 to prepare for the appointment of electors. The legislature resolved to appoint four electors by joint ballot. The electors were to meet on the first Wednesday in December at the state house in Bristol to cast their votes. Underscoring the experimental nature of this procedure, the lawmakers agreed that this method set no precedent and left open the possibility that a future assembly might give the people the right to elect.[3]

In 1791 Vermont became the fourteenth state in the union. Its legislature passed an act which allowed for the appointment of presidential electors by the joint ballot of the governor, council, and the house of representatives in a Grand Committee. This body by majority vote appointed as many persons as there were electors assigned to the state. On November 1, 1792, the legislature resolved that the Grand Committee should meet on the following day, and invited the governor and council to join them, at which time they appointed four men. Several days later, the legislature determined that the electors should meet at Windsor to vote on the first Wednesday in December.[4]

Among the southern states, Georgia and South Carolina retained legislative appointment, Maryland continued with election at large, and Virginia stayed with election in districts, which the new state of Kentucky adopted. North Carolina, which ratified the Constitution in 1790, adopted a law in the 1792 session directing that the state be divided into four districts, each of which included several counties. The members of the General Assembly from each district were to convene on Monday, December 26, and choose three residents for electors. There had to be at least one elector in each of the Superior Court districts of the state and a total of twelve for the entire state. Everyone, other than a member of the legislature, who filled the office received compensation, and anyone who failed to perform the assigned duty faced a fine.[5]

In the middle states, New Jersey continued legislative appointment while Pennsylvania opted again for election at large. Delaware joined the small states of Connecticut, Georgia, and New Jersey and shifted to the legislative mode. The legislators' rationale for abandoning popular election pointed to the new federal election law which meant "great Inconvenience and Expence to the good people of this State, to be convened within the short Period limited by the Law of the United States and at an inclement Season of the year, for the purpose of appointing Electors."[6] Their justification for adopting the legislative mode simply declared that the Constitution permitted it.

New York went through a clumsy adjustment, which once again served as a useful case study of factors which operated on legislative discussions of the subject. The interaction of the federal census, a congressional election law, and the emergence of political parties all played a part. In anticipation of the presidential election, New York political leaders moved promptly to set up procedures for choosing electors. The legislators, like those in Delaware, quickly came to the conclusion that thirty-four days provided too short a time to conduct popular elections. It is not at all evident, however, that elections could not be conducted within the time prescribed, for Massachusetts, Pennsylvania, and Virginia, states as large as New York, and New Hampshire, Maryland, and Kentucky decided in favor of popular selection.

In all likelihood, the legislators responded to other factors. First, since New York held annual legislative and triennial gubernatorial elections in April and biennial congressional elections in December, popular elections for electors in the fall imposed additional costs and inconvenience. Second, debate over how to conduct such elections, whether by districts, at large, or some other means, could lead to delay, and they did not want to repeat the 1789 embarrassment of failing to cast electoral votes. Third, the assemblymen and senators believed they could represent their constituencies faithfully and were fully entitled to appoint electors under the provisions of Article II of the federal Constitution. Rhode Island, Connecticut, Vermont, New Jersey, Delaware, North and South Carolina, and Georgia legislatures took a similar position. Nonetheless, New York legislators thought it prudent to justify their decision explicitly on the shortness of time for an election, not on their constitutional prerogatives.[7]

On March 29, 1792 Samuel Jones, a leading Antifederalist actor in the deadlock of 1789 but now shifting toward Federalism, introduced a bill on electors in the state senate. He explained that under the Constitution the legislature could simply appoint persons for this office without passing any law; adopt a resolution which did not require executive approval and set forth procedures for making appointments; or adopt a law, which required the assent of the executive. In selecting the last option, the New York legislature brought the Governor into the process. In addition, any proposed state law required review by the council of revision, consisting of the governor and judges of the high court, which could veto any legislative action. Yet, their intrusion into the process posed no constitutional problem, for the legislature had decided to proceed in this fashion.[8]

In early April, the state senate worked up a measure, secured the concurrence of the house, and forwarded it to the governor and council of revision. The New York law of April 12, 1792 stipulated that the senate and assembly would appoint electors in the same manner as they had done for the Confederation Congress, that is, by joint ballot. The act required the legislature to convene on the first Tuesday in November to choose electors in the ratio of 4:3:3:3 for the southern, middle, western, and eastern districts. This ratio assumed that New York would have thirteen electors or some multiple of thirteen at a time when Congress was considering reapportionment in accord with the 1790 census. Behind this ratio stood the supposition that presidential electors should be broadly representative of the different regions of the state. Those appointed were to gather at the courthouse in Poughkeepsie, Dutchess County, to cast their ballots for President on the first Wednesday in December. Adoption of a law covering presidential elections marked a significant step forward for New York. Clearly, New York had learned from its earlier experience in 1788-1789; it at least had rules on the books, which would operate in 1792 unless new majorities in both houses changed the law and the governor and council of revision agreed. What had been a highly controversial and partisan issue in the 1788-1789 election appeared uneventful in 1792.[9]

The legislature elected in April convened in the fall in New York City, when the members had to refocus their attention on the state's presidential electors' law. They received a message from Governor Clinton pointing to a problem with the ratio of electors set by state law, for the Congress had reapportioned representation in the House and gave New York ten Representatives and consequently twelve electors. Samuel Jones introduced a motion to repeal that portion of the April law which set the 4-3-3-3 ratio, and the measure hurried through both houses by November 8. The absence of a quorum in the council of revision briefly delayed final approval.[10]

This episode had important implications for the future of presidential electors. Reapportionment after each decennial census meant that the state could expect to have a different number of Congressmen and electors every decade. Periodically legislatures would have to draw up new congressional districts, and that occasion could be expected to prompt highly partisan debate and argument. The difficulties of drawing acceptable district lines for Representatives would be compounded in states which decided to have district elections for presidential electors. Not only would these have to be redrawn every decade, but the lines could not be identical with congressional districts because the number of electors assigned to a state always exceeded the number of Representatives by two.

Massachusetts overcame this difficulty by inventing an ingenuous mechanism, and Virginia in 1788 encountered a situation where it had exactly twice as many state senatorial districts as presidential electors and could combine them appropriately. The convenient choices were narrowing to legislative appointment or at-large election of electors, and there were as yet few advocates for the latter.[11]

In addition to the census, the federal election law, and the changes in state practices for choosing electors, an even more momentous factor affecting the 1792 presidential election was the emergence of national political parties. The ratification of the Constitution no longer served as the only overriding issue in defining partisan lines. The Washington administration began to make a record, especially on matters of patronage and fiscal policy, which shifted attention to new issues and political figures, and these new weights altered balances throughout the nation. Federalists exploited Washington's popularity, and most Americans initially rallied behind him and his new administration. The nascent Republican opposition, which drew from the ranks of both Antifederalists and former Federalists, sought to send a message to the administration that it did not have a free hand to do as it pleased. The initiatives of Alexander Hamilton and the reaction of James Madison and Thomas Jefferson created divisions which took root and developed into national political parties. The differences had a distinctly sectional flavor; the administration had its most enthusiastic supporters in the Northeast and its most persistent critics in the southern states.[12]

However, it is well to remember that party organizations were immature. There were as yet no party caucuses or conventions, and hence no institutional means for making authoritative nominations for President. But unlike the election in 1789, the one for 1792 had an incumbent administration, and incumbency served to identify George Washington and John Adams as the candidates of the Federalists. Given the general respect for Washington, the opposition moved with caution and uncertainty.

There was no real question that George Washington was the right person for the presidency, and no candidate appeared to challenge him. His silence about his plans to serve a second term persuaded most of his ardent supporters that he would serve, if elected. Yet, the constitutional provision that electors cast two votes for President kept open the question for whom they would give their second vote. Because it was unthinkable that Washington would be anything but President, the election turned out to be a contest for Vice President. Nothing in the language of Article II of the Constitution compelled this reading, but political reality led to it. No less an authority than James Madison spoke of the upcoming contest as "the election of a vice P[resident]."[13] Of course there was an incumbent Vice President in John Adams, and he enjoyed enthusiastic support in New England and general support elsewhere. For those opposed to Hamilton and the Federalists, however, the election of an alternative would convey better than anything else their growing restiveness with national policy. There remained the potential for a Virginia-New York alliance behind the Republicans.

Virginians and New Yorkers had mixed while New York City served as the nation's capital from 1789 to 1791, and in mid-1791 Thomas Jefferson and James Madison made a swing through the Northeast in the course of which they visited New York and may have met Robert R. Livingston, Aaron Burr, and Clinton. The evident political importance of George Clinton and his identification with the Bill of Rights in 1791 also necessitated an accommodation with him. Finally, New York in 1792 carried the weight of 12 electoral votes out of the total of 132, a toehold outside of the South which might lead to additional votes in neighboring states in the Northeast.[14]

Although Thomas Jefferson himself might have been a worthy candidate, he was reluctant at this time to challenge Washington even indirectly and he may also have not been ready to face off against John Adams with whom he was personally on good terms. But it is worth remembering that he could have run, and it is at least hypothetically possible that Washington and Jefferson could have polled the most votes. The provision in Article II, often misinterpreted, states that "the Electors shall vote by Ballot for two persons, *of whom one at least shall not be an Inhabitant of the same State with themselves*." Electors in any state, except Virginia, could have cast their votes for the two Virginians. In reality, of course, there were serious political obstacles to the success of two candidates from the same state. Not only would they have the disadvantage of losing votes in their home state, but they would have to overcome the resentment of other states and regions to such an exclusive pairing.

By 1792 Virginia Republicans considered George Clinton a real possibility for Vice President. Their commitment briefly wavered when a controversy broke in the summer over a disputed gubernatorial election in New York in which Clinton claimed victory over John Jay in spite of obvious irregularities in the canvassing of votes. Several significant New York Republicans, Melancton Smith and Marinus Willett, suggested Burr as a better choice. John Nicholson saw some merit in this idea since circumstances in New York made Clinton's nomination problematic. Robert Livingston also believed that Clinton could not vacate the office which his supporters had gained for him at substantial expenditure of political capital.[15]

Clinton behaved with circumspection, neither actively seeking the nomination for the office of Vice President, which he probably wanted, nor completely closing the door to any offers. In October of 1792 the Governor broke a tie in his council of appointment to raise Aaron Burr from the United States Senate to the state Supreme Court, a move some saw as payoff for Burr's support of Clinton in the gubernatorial election dispute but which may have been a way to remove Burr from the vice presidential race. Clinton was alarmed by Burr's ambition. Meanwhile, John Beckley had traveled from Philadelphia on behalf of Republicans in Pennsylvania to meet with Melancton Smith in New York "to conclude *finally & definitively*" the choice of George Clinton for Vice President and to put aside any thoughts of Burr.[16] Beckley reported the agreement to James Monroe and James Madison and both were pleased. Monroe thought

Burr too inexperienced and preferred a man of "more advanc'd life and longer standing in publick trust" and one "who in consequence of such service had given unequivocal proofs of what his principles really were."[17] Monroe seemed to be describing Clinton, whom he admired! Madison conceded that Clinton had been damaged in his pursuit of national office, though not enough to make him abandon the Governor for someone of such relative youth and modest achievements as Burr. He concluded that the choice came down to Adams or Clinton for the second office. The sudden emergence of Burr, however, caught the attention not only of Clinton and Madison but also of Alexander Hamilton, who preferred Clinton--a man of integrity--to this opportunist whom he was eager to deny.[18]

Although adherents of the candidates had no formal mechanism for making nominations, the weight of incumbency and informal calculations among active politicians made the picture sufficiently clear for those interested in the election. Oliver Wolcott of Connecticut saw the opposition strategy by late November:

> The plan really is to elect George Clinton, and where a direct interest cannot be made in his favor, it is intended to diminish the votes for Mr. Adams. I think it is likely, unless some attention is given to the subject, that votes will be solicited for such men as Mr. Hancock, &c, &c. Not that they expect that any other effect will be produced than a plurality in favor of the real candidate.[19]

Federalists did what they could to shore up support for Adams.

Because the de facto nomination of the incumbents by the Federalists and the decision by leading opponents to concentrate on Clinton as an alternative to Adams, presidential electors coalesced more tightly in 1792 than in 1789. In Connecticut, Massachusetts, New Hampshire, and Rhode Island the electors cast all their votes for Washington and Adams. Vermont's electors met in Windsor, and, with Samuel Hitchcock absent due to illness, gave three votes to Washington and Adams.[20]

In the South, Maryland was afflicted as in 1789 by absences. Eight electors met in Baltimore without William Smith and Samuel Hughes of the western shore to vote for Washington and Adams. Virginia, North Carolina, and Georgia gave all of their votes for Washington and George Clinton. South Carolina electors gave 8 votes to Washington, 7 to Adams, and 1 to Aaron Burr. Kentucky gave its 4 votes to two Virginians, Washington and Thomas Jefferson.[21]

Among the middle states, New York did not go through any pretense that their electors were free to vote for whomever they wished. John Quincy Adams told his father that in the New York legislature "their Governor has a bare majority, determined to support upon all occasions his party and his politics." He expected "nothing but the voice of faction from New York," and hence no support for John Adams's candidacy.[22] John Beckley, clerk of the House of Representatives and unofficial national party organizer for the Republicans, saw the resolution of the disputed gubernatorial election as decisive in insuring New York's 12 electoral votes for a Republican candidate in the presidential race. Indeed, Greenleaf's *New York Journal* described the electors as "twelve of the staunchest friends of true republicanism."[23] Observers as varied as Abraham Bancker, Melancton Smith, and Alexander Hamilton agreed that legislative appointment had produced a solid Clintonian college of electors.[24] Governor Clinton certified the appointment of the electors, and they met as directed at the courthouse in Poughkeepsie on December 5, 1792. They made a sparse record of their actions and reported very correctly that they had voted by ballot for two persons, one of whom was properly from a state other than New York. The electors cast 12 votes for George Washington and 12 votes for George Clinton, without making any distinction between votes for President and Vice President.[25]

Elsewhere in the middle region, New Jersey and Delaware cast their votes for Washington and Adams. Pennsylvania's fifteen electors met in Harrisburg, where Thomas McKean reported that they gave 15 votes for Washington, 14 for Adams, and 1 for Clinton.[26]

The electors from all the states reported their results to the presiding officer of the U.S. Senate by the first Wednesday in January in compliance with federal law. Interested persons made do with reports in the newspapers about the electoral count. In many cases, these reports in the early weeks of December contained conjectures and inaccuracies, but by January they came very close to the mark.[27]

In February of 1793, the two houses of Congress made preparations for the official count of the electoral votes. The House chose William Smith and John Laurance to serve as tellers, and the Senate appointed Rufus King to perform that duty for it. On February 13, Representatives and Senators gathered in the Senate chambers where the President of the Senate and incumbent Vice President of the United States, John Adams, "opened, read, and delivered" the certificates of the electors from fifteen states to the tellers, who tabulated the results.[28]

The official count indicated that five candidates received at least one vote: Washington, Adams, Clinton, Jefferson, and Burr. But electors in thirteen states voted for only two, while those in Pennsylvania and South Carolina voted for three men. In no instance, did electors scatter their votes! They voted for Washington for President and someone else for Vice President. Rhode Island's electors made that explicit, though nothing in the Constitution prescribed such a distinction. Furthermore, the results indicated that New England stood solidly behind Washington and Adams, while the southern states preferred Washington and Clinton. The middle states, in particular Pennsylvania and New York, divided, and their votes determined the outcome of the national contest. Their status as holders of the balance of power critically affected presidential elections for the rest of the decade; here "were more discernible signs of party development than in most states."[29]

The electoral votes indicated that Republicans were not about to challenge

George Washington directly. The President received 132 electoral votes, a unanimous vote of the electors. John Adams won 77, George Clinton 50, and others 5. The Clintonian electors used their votes in such a way that they were in fact casting 1 vote for Washington for President and 1 vote for George Clinton for Vice President even though their formal report to the President of the Senate made no such distinction. Their work cut into the majority for Adams, who was sorely aggrieved at his total. Indeed, if Pennsylvania's Republicans had been able to carry their slate for electors, the totals would have given Clinton second place.[30]

John Quincy Adams tried to console his father.

Great pains it seems were taken to unite the opposition in favor of Governor Clinton, and canvassing letters were received by the electors in Rhode Island and Connecticut from New York, and even from Virginia. But in both the former States the electors and the people, instead of being influenced by those letters, resented very much such an insidious attack upon the liberty of their suffrages, and their unanimous votes may convince the abettors of anarchy and confusion that at this time they have 'overleapt themselves and fallen on the other side.'[31]

The results depended on the appointment of electors already committed to particular candidates and parties.

6

An Election without Washington

The second Washington administration brought intensified partisan political fighting. Juxtaposed on the alignments over fiscal policy, federal power, and patronage were philosophical and practical differences over the appropriate American response to the increasingly radical direction of the French Revolution and the outbreak of a European war. Monarchical or republican principles, loyalty to the former mother country or to our French ally, the security of American trade with England or the lucrative trade with the French West Indies, the prerogatives of the executive branch or the Congress and of the Senate or the House, and the effects of all of these matters on Hamilton's fiscal system divided Americans. The Washington administration tried to steer through this politically treacherous field with a policy of neutrality. In 1793 and 1794 several dozen democratic societies formed across the nation and publicized meetings and resolutions often critical of the national administration. In 1794 and 1795 occurred the furious debate over the Jay Treaty, which produced the sharpest and clearest division up to that time between Federalists and Republicans. Congress became the center of political debate and also of national party organization.[1]

The charged political atmosphere meant that the presidential election in 1796 would have been heatedly contested regardless of the candidates. But what made this presidential election novel was the prospective absence of George Washington from the lists. No longer invulnerable to criticism, Washington remained the great national figure. In early May the President wrote that "nothing short of events--or such imperious circumstances (which I hope and trust will not happen)" could prevent him from making a public announcement of his intention to retire from office.[2] Soon thereafter, he began communications with Alexander Hamilton about a valedictory address to the people. He disclosed that it was his wish "to withhold the promulgation of my intention until the period, when it shall become indispensably necessary for the information of the Electors, previous to the Election (which, this year, will be delayed until the 7th. of December)."[3] Robert Goodloe Harper observed,

> While it was understood that General Washington would consent to be reelected, no man however popular, had the least Chance of becoming an Elector if he was understood to be opposed to the old man.[4]

When Washington indicated that he had second thoughts about delaying his public announcement because it subjected him to continued abuse from the opposition in the press and elsewhere, Hamilton disagreed. He favored delaying a public renunciation of a third term until "the last moment":

> The proper period now for your declaration seems to be *Two months* before the time for the Meeting of the Electors. This will be sufficient. The parties will in the mean time electioneer conditionally, that is to say, *if you decline*--for a serious opposition to you will I think hardly be *risked*.[5]

In the absence of any formal nominating process or mechanism, Federalist leaders fastened upon John Adams of Massachusetts, the incumbent Vice President, and Thomas Pinckney of South Carolina, negotiator of the popular Pinckney Treaty, as their candidates. John Jay's supporters backed off after the Jay Treaty uproar. Alexander Hamilton and Rufus King preferred Patrick Henry as the second Federalist but settled on the South Carolinian to be paired with Adams. In late July, William Smith of Charleston described the nominating process, such as it was, as informal and tentative.[6]

On the other side, John Beckley had suspected for more than a year that Washington would not seek a third term, and communicated with opposition leaders on the prospect of Jefferson as the Republican candidate. Republican leaders, particularly in Congress, made known their preference for the Virginian. They attempted something more in choosing a running mate. A Republican congressional caucus met in Philadelphia in May but could not agree on Aaron Burr, Robert R. Livingston, Pierce Butler, or John Langdon and on the desirability of having a New Yorker on the ticket, but Beckley wrote Madison that a Jefferson-Burr ticket would be accepted everywhere. Later, seeing that the Federalists teamed a New Englander with a Southerner, the Republicans looked to the middle states and New England for a candidate to join Jefferson. Although many found Burr a promising choice, Republicans, including New Yorkers who knew him well, did not enthusiastically embrace him. George Clinton understood that he himself was not a strong candidate, but had no great wish to advance the fortunes of a man who could displace him as leader of New York Republicanism and be the beneficiary of an alliance with Jeffersonian Virginia. Robert R. Livingston, who might draw some Federalist votes in New York and New Jersey, did not want to risk an open pursuit of the office but made himself available. The knowledge that New York's annual state elections in April assured Federalists control of the legislature which appointed electors must have weakened Burr's standing. Yet, Republicans understood the need to play to the political power of the middle states and perhaps to moderate New Englanders as well, and Burr had family connections throughout the region. Republicans read the political mood well.[7]

Difficulties with prompt and reliable communications, the incompleteness of national party organizations, and the dual vote of the electors meant that opportunities abounded for confusion and error about candidates, strategies, and outcomes. Most well-positioned politicos knew that the contest for President was between Adams and Jefferson, but partisans faced problems trying to get their candidate elected President. The two votes for President made it difficult for anyone to try to manipulate the outcome with certainty. But there were those willing to try.[8]

The active John Beckley noted that Burr had been campaigning for six weeks throughout New England and calculated that "his efforts are more directed to himself than any body else."[9] He urged James Madison to consider diverting half of Virginia's electoral votes to someone other than Burr, such as George Clinton, to make sure that Burr would not finish ahead of Jefferson. In short, he was willing to drop one of the two leading Republican candidates in the hope of getting the other for President or Vice President, a strategy of expediency necessitated by the double vote of electors, which could damage Republican loyalties in New York.

Alexander Hamilton, driven chiefly by the desire to prevent Jefferson's elevation to the presidency, entered on a strategy that strained party unity. Unlike Beckley who pressed forward one of the two Republican candidacies, Hamilton encouraged New Englanders and southern Federalists to support Adams and Pinckney equally in hopes of elevating both above Jefferson. He favored this double entry, even though some southern Republicans might vote for Jefferson and Pinckney and thereby give the South Carolinian the presidency over Adams. Hamilton felt that Adams' probable anger at relegation to the second office again was balanced by the need to offset the dire threat to the nation posed by Jefferson's candidacy. Hamilton walked a tightrope on this occasion, for he realized that Adams's supporters might withhold electoral support from Pinckney to make Adams's superiority clear.[10]

Jonathan Dayton, the New Jersey Federalist Congressman, concurred in the critical importance of excluding Jefferson. He anticipated Adams's losing in Pennsylvania and the states south of Delaware and predicted to his friend in Massachusetts, Theodore Sedgwick, that the real choice came down to Jefferson, Burr, and Pinckney. John Laurance believed the outcome rested in the key middle states, especially on the choice of electors in Pennsylvania, where Federalists could not be confident, and in New York, where they were assured of loyal appointees. He then added, "I should not be disappointed if Mr. T. Pinckney should be President."[11]

Among Adams loyalists in New England, however, the talk about fully supporting Pinckney touched sensitivities and elicited resentment. Electors in some states had been all too ready to throw votes away from Adams in 1789 and 1792. The Vice President's friends began to pursue a strategy of having Federalist electors cast one vote for Adams and the second for anyone other than Pinckney. No one was more active in this effort than Oliver Wolcott, Jr., a personal friend of Hamilton but also a committed New Englander and Gallophobe. Theodore Sedgwick tried to counteract such a course which would inflict a wound on southern Federalism. He urged Federalists everywhere to live up to their obligations to support both men. Should Pinckney finish ahead of Adams, Sedgwick attributed it to "a constitutional mischief, and we must console ourselves with the purity and federalism of our chief Magistrate. But on the other hand, the mischiefs of a breach of faith are innumerable and will, probably, be endless in their efforts."[12]

New Englanders, suspecting Hamilton's motives and fearing the outcome, found themselves in a dilemma. George Cabot believed Massachusetts electors would "be governed by the best intelligence which can be had on the day of voting."[13] Stephen Higginson observed that a majority of the state's electors considered throwing away their second votes to make sure that the South Carolinian did not precede Adams. It is significant to note that Higginson saw dangers of Republican electors, realizing that they could not get Jefferson for President, casting enough votes for Pinckney to elevate that Southerner to the top office and to deprive Adams of his rightful place. That is, Republicans, though a minority, would choose between the two candidates of the majority party. The dual vote for each elector left open such a possibility. By 1804 Republicans feared that the Federalists would determine which of the Republican candidates would become President and moved decisively to prevent such undue influence. In 1796, however, Republicans had hardly given up on Jefferson. Northern Republicans supported Jefferson and Burr, and Southerners, particularly Virginians, intended to back Jefferson solidly and to scatter their second votes among other Republicans.[14]

In the Federalist stronghold of New England, Adams did well, in part at the expense of Thomas Pinckney. Adams supporters had little leeway since they truly wanted the New Englander to become President and the double vote threatened this goal. In Adams's home state, Governor Samuel Adams certified that the state had chosen sixteen electors through its combined election--appointment method. In accordance with a resolution of the General Court, they met at the statehouse in Boston and voted by ballot on December 7, giving Adams 16, Pinckney 13, Samuel Johnson of North Carolina 2, and Oliver Ellsworth of Connecticut 1 vote. Neighboring New Hampshire chose electors through a complex system of first round and second round elections in which candidates had to win a majority of the vote. The legislature filled vacancies by a convention in which the two houses met jointly. The electors met at Concord and gave Adams and Oliver Ellsworth all of their votes.[15]

Connecticut Governor Oliver Wolcott certified that on November 4, the legislature appointed electors who met at Hartford on the first Wednesday in December to cast votes. They filled out a form already prepared for them, which indicated how they were appointed, for what purpose, and how they proceeded in accordance with the appointment and the law, and filled in the blank spaces. Loyal to Adams, they gave the Vice President 9, John Jay 5, and Thomas Pinckney 4 votes.[16]

Rhode Island and Vermont, like Connecticut, stayed with appointment of electors by a joint ballot of the legislature. Gathering at the statehouse in Bristol, the Rhode Island electors noted that they voted by ballot for two persons, Adams and Oliver Ellsworth, "one of whom for President, and the other for Vice President of the United States," contrary to the instructions of the Constitution.[17] Vermont electors convened in the Rutland courthouse and, unlike the other New England states, voted loyally for the Federalist ticket.[18]

The Republicans, as expected, did well in their southern base. Maryland shifted from at-large to district elections of ten electors for 1796, and district elections approximated proportional representation in the state's electoral college. There were clearcut examples of candidates for elector who declared for whom they would vote. Acting as president of the electors, John Roberts submitted a curious report: Adams received 7, Jefferson 4, Pinckney 4, Burr 3, and John Henry 2 votes.[19]

Virginia stayed with its district election system. As in Maryland, voters had opportunities to know for whom the electoral candidates would vote should they be elected. Governor James Wood certified the list of twenty-one electors. The electors met and gave Jefferson overwhelming if not quite unanimous support: he received 20 votes, Samuel Adams 15, Clinton 3, Washington, Pinckney, Burr, and John Adams 1 vote each. Anticipating a potential question to arise, they reported, "And we further certify that each elector voted for one person who is not an inhabitant of the state of Virginia."[20] Meanwhile, North Carolina shifted from legislative appointment to district elections. Governor Samuel Ashe reported the election of twelve men who cast 11 votes for Jefferson and 6 for Burr. James "Iredelle" received 3 votes, while Washington, Thomas Pinckney, Charles C. Pinckney, and John Adams got 1 each.[21]

South Carolina retained the legislative mode. Governor Arnoldus Vander-Horst attested that on December 6 the legislature chose eight men. They gave their votes equally to Thomas Pinckney, a native son and Federalist, and to Thomas Jefferson.[22]

Georgia, like North Carolina, moved to district elections in 1796 and only "the votes of such counties as have made returns" counted. The electors gathered at the statehouse in Louisville and gave Jefferson and Clinton 4 votes each. Kentucky once again relied on district elections. The electors met at Brent's Tavern in Lexington, and, after choosing Caleb Wallace to be president of the meeting, they voted on ballots and deposited them in a box; an elector then drew each one at a time, numbered it, and recorded the votes, all for

Jefferson and Burr.[23]

Tennessee participated in its first presidential election. Its admission into the union by the narrowest of margins took place when Vice President Adams was absent from the chair of the Senate. Although Tennessee would have only three electors, "all parties considered it as a point of consequence at this moment; that the votes for President will be nearly equal, & of course viewing every vote of importance."[24] Tennessee's voters went to the polls in the fall, and their electors went solidly for Jefferson and Burr.[25]

The middle states often decided the outcome of presidential elections in the early republic. In Federalist Delaware, Governor Gunning Bedford certified that the two houses met on November 10, 1796 and chose the electors. They met at Dover on December 7, "sat down to a *federal* dinner, and after a few rosy libations were quaffed, they unanimously agreed" to support Adams and Pinckney.[26] "A truly *federal* mode this of deciding for the people on the weighty concerns of the State," lamented the Republican *Delaware Gazette*.[27] Federalist New Jersey continued legislative appointment, and produced electors equally loyal to the same duo. Pennsylvania retained election on a general ticket. The voters chose men who gave Jefferson 14 votes and Burr 13. Thomas Pinckney received 2 votes and John Adams 1.[28]

Participation in this presidential election went smoothly for New York for the first time. In March of 1796 the legislature adopted a law, which reaffirmed the power of the legislature by joint ballot to appoint electors. Unlike the 1792 measure, this law did not make any apology or offer any rationalization for this decision. The act applied to all future presidential elections, not just the impending contest, and marked a significant step forward. It was still possible for disagreements between a senate controlled by one party and the house controlled by the other to occur as they had in the 1788-1789 election, but no one could ignore the fact that a positive law determined the mode. Either house and either party could initiate steps to change the law, but they had to obey the existing law until they had gone through the proper procedures. New York would not be caught in stalemate as it had in the first presidential election and as Pennsylvania, for example, would in 1800.[29]

It is important to point out that voters in New York, not knowing for sure who would be candidates in the upcoming presidential contest, proceeded on schedule to elect assemblymen and senators in April. These elections were of the first importance and needed to be well managed, for the party which won would be in a position to choose presidential electors later in the year. But the ordinary citizen in New York had little direct influence on presidential politics. In the dark about the candidates, New Yorkers chose state legislators on the basis of local and national issues current in April. Washington's Farewell Address did not appear in newspapers across the country until September of 1796.[30]

On November 7, the newly elected assembly chose between two slates, giving the Federalists an overwhelming victory over Republican candidates, many of whom polled fewer than 5 votes. A Republican newspaper reported with feigned wonder, "After their respective nominations, by an *appel nominal* from each individual member, were gone through with, the two houses met in the great Court room, compared their lists, and were found *perfectly* to agree."[31]

Although Greenleaf's Republican paper published a number of articles designed to promote the Republican cause and reprinted from the *Aurora* a piece which defined the function of a presidential elector as acting the way the people would act if they could vote directly for President, New Yorkers in the know realized that such last minute appeals would have little effect. Federalist Robert Troup was pleased with the appointments and satisfied that the electors would act in accord with party policy: "We have none but good and true men, who will vote unanimously for Adams and Pinckney."[32] DeWitt Clinton saw these Federalist electors as inflexible: "I believe ours cannot be moved."[33] Former Governor George Clinton had even more to say about the electors, and he was not complimentary:

> The Electors in this State are all picked Men of the opposite Party many of them not of the most dignified Character and therefore the most obstinate Tools of Faction--Some of our sanguine Friends suppose that two or three may vote partially for the republican Ticket owing to the Influence of personal Attachment. I confess I am not myself of this Opinion and I am confident that at least Mr. Adams will have an unanimous Vote.[34]

Such characterizations of the electors by those opposed to their political principles began to create an unflattering image. Federalists offered similar descriptions after future elections. Critics accused electors of being puppets, who did not act for themselves but in accord with those responsible for selecting them. Yet, when they belonged to the political majority in the state, they wanted electors who were loyal to the core and could not be swayed; they wanted faithful, not independent and maverick, electors.[35]

On the first Wednesday in December, the twelve Federalist electors of New York gathered in the town of Hudson, where they cast 12 votes for both Adams and Pinckney. Their behavior appeared absolutely proper. They were then "attended by several gentlemen from this city and Claverack, partook of an elegant entertainment, prepared for the occasion by Mr. Gordon; and drank several patriotic toasts."[36] While Abraham Ten Broeck, Abraham Van Vechten, St. John Honeywood, Charles NewKirk, and Peter Smith traveled together back to Albany and others made their way home, Colonel John M'Kinistrey, a Columbia County assemblyman, carried a certificate of the votes to Philadelphia. Thereafter, word of their votes spread rapidly. Elector Lewis Morris shared information with his son, while Thomas L. Witbeck, a Burrite, learned that "the Electors of this State have been uniform" and was disappointed that Burr had not picked up a few second votes.[37]

As interested and strategically active a person as Alexander Hamilton was not absolutely positive of the national outcome as late as mid-December. He hoped that Adams and Pinckney had swept but suspected that Jefferson took the second spot. Benjamin Goodhue correctly saw that Jefferson could not become President but joined Hamilton in anxious worry that the Virginian would be Vice President. Meanwhile, Aaron Burr thought that Jefferson was ahead in a close race and had a chance. Lewis Morris, one of the presidential electors, did not know the national results at the end of December.[38]

Although the official counting of the votes awaited the meeting of the Congress on the first Wednesday in February, the newspapers reported many of the electoral votes accurately well before that time. When Congress met in the chambers of the House of Representatives for the official counting of the electoral vote, the Vice President opened and delivered the certificates of the electors from sixteen states to the tellers. The tellers tallied the votes, and provided Adams with a list giving the state by state votes for various candidates. At that point, Adams made an announcement, which must have been awkward for him.

I now declare that JOHN ADAMS is elected President of the United States for four years to commence with the 4th day of March next; and that THOMAS JEFFERSON is elected Vice-President of the United States for four years, to commence with the 4th day of March next; And may the Sovereign of the Universe, the ordainer of civil government on earth for the preservation of liberty, justice and peace among men, enable both to discharge the duties of these offices comformably to the Constitution of the United States, with conscientious diligence, punctuality and perseverance.[39]

Thirteen men received votes. Yet, the "scattering" of votes was not quite as extensive as might first appear. Electors in three New England states voted for only two men, and those in Connecticut and Massachusetts voted purposefully, giving the vote of every elector for Adams, giving more of the second vote for Pinckney than for anyone else, and throwing away the remainder to protect Adams's claim to the presidency and relegating Pinckney to the vice presidency at best. Electors in three middle states voted solely for two men. In Pennsylvania the overwhelming majority of electors voted for two men. In the southern states, electors in two states voted for only two candidates. Maryland, which allowed for district elections of electors, had a split delegation in its electoral college. Virginia and North Carolina electors overwhelmingly went for Jefferson and dispersed their second votes to assure his claims over that of Burr. The electors for the western state of Kentucky cast their votes for two candidates. Thus on a state by state basis, the electors did not act in a confused or random fashion. In nine states, all the electors cast their votes for two men of the same party. In the others, electors threw away an occasional second vote to secure the superior claim of one candidate on the party ticket over the other, or represented divisions among the voters produced by the district method of choosing electors.[40]

In Pennsylvania, it appears that one elector cast a vote for Thomas Jefferson for President and for Thomas Pinckney rather than for Aaron Burr for Vice President, and in Maryland, it is likely that one elector, Mr. Slater, voted for both Adams and Jefferson. South Carolina electors, of course, gave all their votes to Jefferson and Pinckney. These anomalies served as reminders that partisan lines between Federalists and Republicans had not yet been drawn indelibly in every state and in every individual, and even among prominent political figures there continued to be some switching across party lines throughout the decade. Nonetheless, the growing importance of partisanship was evident.

The national outcome, itself the net result of decisions in the separate states, surprised many: Federalist John Adams had been chosen President and Republican Thomas Jefferson Vice President. Federalists were not totally dismayed. For example, Robert Goodloe Harper of South Carolina was pleased that Jefferson lost the chief magistracy, and he defended the various mechanisms within each state which had allowed Federalists to marshall a majority for Adams:

Had the electors been chosen by districts in Pennsylvania, instead of a general ticket throughout the state, it is certain that instead of one vote there, Mr. Adams would have had at least 6, probably 7. By the same mode of election in New-York, Delaware and Massachusetts, it is believed that he would have lost one in each of those states. It is highly presumable that he would have gained one in South Carolina; perhaps two. So that had the sense of the people been taken in the fairest possible manner [by district elections], we may conclude that the result would have been still more favourable to Mr. Adams by 5 or 6 votes.[41]

Harper, a close political ally of Alexander Hamilton, reminded his constituents in South Carolina that electors did not vote for one person as President and another for Vice President but for two candidates for President. This constitutional provision had led to some delicate political calculations. After learning the results, Robert Troup explained to Rufus King the maneuvering in both parties which produced this unlikely result.[42]

Hamilton observed that some on both sides tried to make the best of the awkward outcome:

Our Jacobins say they are well pleased and that the *Lion* & the *Lamb* are to lie down together. Mr. Adams['s] *personal* friends talk a little in the same way. Mr. *Jefferson* is not half so ill a man as we have been accustomed to think him. There is to be a united and vigorous administration. Sceptics like me quietly look forward to the event-- willing to hope but not prepared to believe.[43]

Theodore Sedgwick shared with Hamilton disappointment that Federalist electors had not voted equally for the party's candidates. He believed the most important object for all Federalist electors should have been the exclusion of Jefferson from either executive office.[44]

The results had the effect of sowing the seeds of division between Jefferson and Burr and between Hamilton and Adams. Virginia's electors made a point of not voting for Burr and seemed to make no effort to reward a New Yorker, whose state was solidly committed to the Federalists. The Adams Federalists did not forget what they considered a close call. Stephen Higginson informed Hamilton that Adams loyalists believed that there had been a conspiracy by an inner clique, and "at the head of this Junto, as they call it, they place you & Mr. Jay."[45] Similarly, Elkanah Watson, the upstate New York Federalist and well-known proponent of canal construction, wrote to his friend John Adams to congratulate him on assuming the presidency. But his note reflected on the motives of the Hamiltonians in the state who "are both mortified & disappointed, on the grounds of the known independence of your mind."[46] Adams replied in a temperate fashion, saying only that

> If they have been "disappointed" it has been in the Election of the V.P. not in mine: and that by no means on the ground of "the known independence of my mind." I assure you I think differently of those gentlemen, if I guess who they are that you mean.[47]

The results also raised questions about the institution of presidential electors. Robert Goodloe Harper thought that the Adams and Jefferson victories rested less with the actions of Federalist electors and more with the constitutional requirement that electors cast two undifferentiated votes for President. Indeed, Federalists shortly began to submit proposals to amend the Constitution to compel electors to differentiate their votes for President and Vice President so that in future contests they could be assured of winning both offices and shutting out the Republicans entirely.[48]

7

Preparations for 1800

The Federalist and Republican parties had their origins and early development in the Washington administrations, but they matured further in the tumultuous single term of John Adams. With the shield of Washington removed, partisans had a field day as the republic was battered back and forth by the political turbulence set in motion by the French Revolution. The undeclared naval war with France from 1798 to 1800, the political repercussions of the XYZ Affair, and a host of controversial Federalist initiatives, like the Alien and Sedition Acts, military preparedness measures, and stamp and other taxes, and the equally controversial Republican responses, such as the Virginia and Kentucky Resolutions and defiant editorial attacks against the administration, created and maintained a warlike atmosphere. It took no great intelligence to see that the next presidential election would be bitterly and intensely contested and that the rival political parties would on that occasion further define the institution of presidential electors in partisan terms.[1]

Several major currents concerning presidential electors flowed together in 1800. One of these was the scrambling in state after state to revise the mode for choosing electors so that one party or the other would gain an edge. Virginia, Massachusetts, and New York, all among the largest states in the union, engaged in such action. Second, the course of the campaign made the constitutional provision for presidential electors a major issue. Third, in the United States Senate, Federalists initiated a measure to allow the Congress to review the returns from electors and to accept or reject those votes. Republicans saw in this action a step toward congressional election of the President and away from popular participation.

Republican Charles Pinckney of South Carolina, so certain that the impending presidential election would be close, warned his party to be attentive to every single electoral vote. Putting aside his support for direct popular government, he urged James Madison to press for legislative appointment instead of district elections for electors in Virginia. Madison and his allies knew that in the 1799 congressional elections Federalists had shown sufficient strength to carry five districts. Virginia's Republicans used their control of the legislature to prepare a new law on electors in January of 1800. Madison served on the committee to draft the measure which stipulated popular election by a general ticket. Opponents protested in vain that Virginia had operated with district elections in the past, people had not petitioned for this change, and proponents allowed no time to consult constituents. On January 17, the reform passed the house of delegates by a 78-73 vote and a few days later the senate concurred. By this change, Republicans leveraged majority control into a winner-take-all system, and denied to Federalists even a few electors in the home state of Thomas Jefferson. A Virginia Federalist predicted that the law would "exclude *one-third* at least of the citizens of Virginia from a vote for the President of the United States."[2] Republicans did not deny the validity of the complaint but pointed to existing Federalist advantages of winner-take-all systems in a number of northern states. In *A Vindication of the General Ticket Law*, Republicans rationalized that the general ticket gave the state a unified vote. Partisan motives prompted the measure.[3]

Of course, Adams's faithful supporters in Massachusetts felt the need to respond to Virginia. Massachusetts now sought to deny even one or two Republicans from winning spots as electors in the state's unique and complex mode of choosing electors. After a spirited and acrimonious debate, the two houses of the General Court gave themselves the power by a joint ballot to appoint sixteen persons and prepared the way for Adams to get all the votes of his state on a winner-take-all basis. Later, in November, the legislature took the further precautionary step of providing that those appointed meet one day prior to the day they were to vote and empowered those present to fill any vacancies. The Bay State was not going to fail to deliver every one of its sixteen votes. Republican critics accused the Federalists of depriving the people of their rightful place in the election of the President by this usurpation.[4]

A Republican critique in the *New England Chronicle* saw the act as a vote of no confidence in Adams's ability to carry his own home state. The *Albany Register* asserted that the legislature had deprived the people of their "invaluable and inalienable right of chusing [*sic*] their electors."[5] In so doing, the aristocratic faction in Massachusetts resorted to the same arguments heard in debates over this subject in New York and in neighboring New Jersey. Republicans opposed the change on the grounds that the people had freely exercised the right of suffrage since the adoption of the Constitution and had never consented to surrender it. The *Albany Register* concluded that the aristocrats feared the surge in republicanism even in Massachusetts and worried that they might lose as much as half of the electoral votes to Jefferson. Federalists, however, pointed to Virginia as the instigator of partisan manipulation in the Bay State, New Hampshire, and elsewhere.[6]

New York considered and rejected a proposal to change from legislative appointment to election in districts, but the debate over this issue demonstrated how much political philosophy as well as partisan advantage motivated the opposing sides. The Republican initiatives for reform staked a clear claim to political democracy. On February 9, 1799 John Swartwout of New York City, an associate of Aaron Burr, suggested two reforms which could be implemented within the state. First, he was troubled by the existence of four large senatorial districts in which state senators were elected. This system made it "impossible for the people to have sufficient knowledge of the characters, who are from time to time held up as candidates for seats in the Senate of this State."[7] Second, he reminded assemblymen that the preamble to the law on presidential electors in 1792 implied that legislative appointment of electors was a temporary expedient and that popular election was the preferred mode.[8]

The inseparable blending of national and local issues showed in the figure of Jedidiah Peck, assemblyman from Otsego. A former Federalist, Peck had run afoul of the Sedition Act, and Federalists had secured from United States District Judge John Sloss Hobart a warrant for Peck's arrest. Taken into custody in September, Peck had to await his trial until April of 1800, during which time he served in the Assembly and became a prominent advocate for democratic reforms. It was Peck who picked up Swartwout's banner and suggested that the legislature confine itself to determining how the people should choose electors rather than making the appointments itself. Outside the legislature some Republicans attempted to build up a petition campaign in support of the reform. Republicans once again demonstrated their growing proficiency for mobilizing public opinion and building local organizations, while Federalists counted on the wisdom of their positions to win support.[9]

On March 12, 1799 in the Committee of the Whole, Peck claimed that legislative appointment was unconstitutional and inexpedient. Under the current law, a majority of one in the legislature gave the entire electoral vote to one candidate. Assuming that they all appointed their electors, a majority of one in the five largest legislatures of the nation would select the president. This was "too great a weight to hang on so small a pivot," he continued, and allowing popular choice in district elections would broaden the base and "prevent parties from throwing so great a weight in the scales by so small a purchase."[10] Assuming the posture of the party outside of power, he and his fellow Republicans wanted to break the features of the existing system which permitted winner-take-all advantages to the Federalists.

Adam Comstock of Saratoga came to the aid of Peck and gave voice to key Republican principles. The right of suffrage, he believed, served as the very foundation of representative government and all power in a republic derived from the people. Claiming that "the least deviation from this principle is a step toward tyranny," he reviewed the language of Article II, section 1 of the Constitution.[11] The word *state* cannot mean the legislature, for, if it did, the sentence would make no sense. The word *state* must mean the people who comprise the state. If there is some doubt and ambiguity, a republic should interpret the language in favor of the people.

John V. Henry, an Albany Federalist, challenged Comstock's reading of the Constitution. The word *state* did not mean the people but the body politic, the people in their corporate character, and included the legislature as well as the people. When the Constitution gave the power to the people to elect Representatives, it did so explicitly. If the Constitution meant to give the power solely to the legislatures, it would have done so expressly. Then the legislatures would have to act as law-making body with concurrent votes of the upper and lower houses. The actual language provided more flexibility and permitted, for example, joint ballot by the legislature. Henry recognized that the legislature could exercise the option to give the selection to the voters, but it did not have to do so. So far Henry's reply provided a reasonable answer to Peck and Comstock.

The Federalist then made a terrible gaffe, according to Republican press accounts. He noted that the bill to provide for district election of electors actually limited the right of voters to choose whomever they wanted. He ran on:

> Whenever the people choose electors, it is not done with that purity which it might be done by their representatives. The people have not that information that their representatives have; their representatives have more expanded minds. Popular elections are bad, because the electors get misinformed by wicked and designing men--witness, the false impressions, made on the minds of the electors about the Sedition Law--they are no better informed, that the common law, under which they were before, is much more severe, and that the Sedition Law is an amelioration of the common law.[12]

It hardly mattered that Henry had a sound interpretation of the Sedition Act. In one moment, he assumed an elitist, anti-democratic posture and embraced the Sedition Act, linking both with the Federalist Party in New York.[13]

The Republican Comstock leapt at the chance to pin unpopular tags on the tail of the Federalist by sarcastically referring to Henry as such a good friend of the Sedition Law: "Wherever we find this doctrine prevail, the people considered as nothing more than the mere *Swinish Multitude*, they have been enslaved."[14] He had no difficulty himself in identifying with the democratic faith that the people were as competent to choose electors as to choose legislators. Carried to its natural limits, Henry's argument meant the legislature should take over all the voting rights of the people. Daniel Bull of Saratoga kept the Federalists on the hook by asking how far Henry was willing to go in his elitist scheme?

Josiah Masters of Rensselaer rose to support Henry but in the process dug a deeper hole for the Federalists. He noted that the people at large were not demanding the vote for electors; only a few petitions had been received. The legislature did not take away popular representation when it appointed electors, and it performed this task better than the people: "The people are not so capable of choosing as the legislature. What do they know about the general government, or about foreign affairs. Nothing."[15] New York and other states had used the legislative mode in previous presidential elections without any question being raised about the legitimacy of this practice. He saw no need to change now.

Striking at the elitism of Masters and Henry, Peck tied them to aristocracy, Britain, and the Sedition Law. "We ought, agreeable to this reasoning," he said, "to have the privilege of choosing Billy Pitt, or any other European, because some of us should think that men of more wisdom might be got there than here."[16] He personally favored direct election in districts, the method used to elect Representatives and legislators. The smaller the district, the closer the officials are to the people. His was a straight Jeffersonian argument. Edward Savage of Montgomery agreed with his Republican colleagues and pointedly recalled that many opponents of the district election proposal now had favored it in the past. Indeed, the old Federalists in the 1788-1789 election had tweaked the Clintonians for refusing to allow for popular vote. On the other hand, the Federalists knew that the Clintonians had argued back then for the legislative mode.

William B. Woolsey of New York City correctly observed that the Constitution granted the legislatures a discretionary authority. Hence the question came down to expediency. He wondered, "Why shall we make the experiment now proposed at the hazard of loosing [sic] all our electors."[17] Here was a significant issue. A district election could result in the twelve New York electors' canceling themselves out; a legislative appointment which encouraged a unified delegation to the electoral college lent great weight to the state. Had Woolsey developed his position and had that been a principal defense for continuing the past practice, Federalists would have held the high ground, or at least higher ground than they assumed in this debate.

The committee of the whole then proceeded to a vote on the bill for district elections of electors and rejected the measure by a 47-54 tally. The Federalist majority in the New York legislature had confidently asserted the rights of the legislature through joint ballot to appoint electors, believing that they would thereby secure for the Federalist presidential candidates the entire vote of the state. In so doing, they assumed that this leverage would work to their advantage as it had done in 1796. They were quite willing to ignore the positions which some had taken in the 1788-1789 debate for the rights of minority representation in the electoral college. They also forgot the political dangers they courted in putting themselves against a rising tide of popular sentiment, and they aligned themselves in the public mind with authoritarian rule, aristocracy, the Sedition Act, and Britain. They gave the Republicans in New York ample ammunition to reverse their recent defeats in the assembly and at the ballot boxes. Should Republicans win a majority of the joint session of the legislature in the

April elections, they could take all of New York's electoral votes.[18]

Partisan maneuvering was apparent in the nation's capital as well as in the state legislatures. The Federalists had widened control of Congress in the aftermath of the XYZ affair and the Alien and Sedition acts. In the Senate, they prepared for the upcoming presidential elections by taking up a bill to deal with disputed returns. A central figure in this effort was James Ross of Pennsylvania. A Princeton graduate and an able lawyer with a distinguished bearing, Ross gained election to the Senate in 1794 as an arch-Federalist. In 1799 he lost a bitter gubernatorial contest to Republican Thomas McKean but retained his seat in Washington. Republicans controlled the lower house of the state legislature, and Federalists retained a margin in the upper house. Pennsylvania had adopted laws governing the selection of electors for each previous presidential election but had no general law on the books. The prospect of a legislative stalemate over a law to choose electors in 1800 gave rise to talk that the Republican Governor might have to proceed and appoint on his own authority by proclamation. The possibility of the Keystone state's throwing its entire weight to the Republicans probably served as the immediate reason for Ross's interest in creating a mechanism for screening electoral votes from the states.[19]

On January 23, 1800, the Senate agreed to create a committee to determine what measures, if any, should be taken to assure the legitimacy of the presidential election and made Ross chairperson of the committee, which included John Laurence, Samuel Dexter, Charles Pinckney, and Samuel Livermore. Later Wilson Cary Nicholas became the sixth member. By January 28 the Ross committee reported a bill, and over the next several weeks the Senate worked to perfect it while concurrently it dealt with the highly controversial proceedings against William Duane and the *Aurora* for violations of the Sedition Act and contempt of the Senate. By mid March, the Senate had an engrossed bill.[20]

The bill created a grand committee of thirteen persons, six chosen by ballot from the House of Representatives, six more similarly chosen from the Senate, and a chairperson elected by ballot by the House from three Senators nominated by the Senate. The grand committee was to meet on the day before the counting of the electors' votes at a joint meeting of the Congress and to examine and decide disputed returns.

The bill stipulated that each house choose by ballot two of its members to serve as tellers, who were to receive the certificates from the electors after the President of the Senate had opened and read them. The tellers were to record various pieces of information, including relevant dates, names, places, numbers of votes, and content of certificates from governors in the states. The President of the Senate then administered an oath to members of the grand committee and handed over to its chairperson all the certificates of the electors and other accompanying documents as well as "all the petitions, exceptions and memorials against the votes of the Electors, or the persons for whom they have voted, together with the testimony accompanying the same."[21]

The grand committee was to meet every day except Sunday, behind closed doors, and to determine issues by majority vote. Vacancies for members and chairperson were to be filled in the same manner as the original appointments. The committee could subpoena witnesses, make use of federal marshals, and take written testimony; those who told falsehoods could be prosecuted.

> The grand committee had extensive authority to enquire, examine, decide and report, upon the constitutional qualifications of the persons voted for as President and Vice-President of the United States; upon the constitutional qualifications of the Electors appointed by the different states, and whether their appointment was authorized by the state legislature or not, *or made according to the mode prescribed by the Legislature*; upon all petitions and exceptions against corrupt, illegal conduct of the Electors, or force, menaces or improper means used to influence their votes; or against the truth of their returns, or the time, place or manner of giving their votes: *Provided always*, That no petition, or exception, shall be granted *or* allowed by the Grand Committee, which *shall have for its object, to draw into question the number of votes, on which any elector in any of the States shall have been declared appointed.*[22]

The grand committee was to report on or before March 1, and indicate the number of legal votes for each candidate and the number of illegal votes which had been rejected and the reasons for rejection. The bill provided that "the report of a majority of the said Committee shall be a final and conclusive determination of the admissibility, or inadmissibility, of the votes."[23]

Critics sought various changes, usually without success. For example, they sought selection of the grand committee by lot rather than ballot and thereby give some opportunity for the minority in each house to have a greater weight than numbers alone would entitle it. They also favored having the grand committee operate in the House rather than Senate chambers and in the open. They tried to minimize the discretionary authority of the committee by giving it power to ask only if the appointment of electors in any state had been authorized by the state legislature or not. On these issues, Senators Ross, Uriah Tracy of Connecticut, and Jonathan Dayton of New Jersey, and other dyed-in-the-wool Federalists voted together in opposition.

On March 25, Republican Senator Wilson Cary Nicholas submitted an amendment which was in effect a substitute motion, which struck out the first ten of what had been fourteen sections in the Ross bill. Nicholas conceded that legitimate questions might arise about the returns of the electors: (1) whether an Elector has been appointed in a mode authorized by the Legislature of his state or not; (2) whether the time at which he was chosen, and the day on which he gave his vote were those determined by Congress; (3) whether he was not at the time, a Senator or Representative of the United States, or held an office of trust or profit under the United States; (4) whether at least one of the persons for whom he has voted is an inhabitant of a state other than his own; (5) whether the Electors voted by ballot, and signed, certified and transmitted to the President of the Senate, a list of all the persons voted for, and the number of votes for each; (6) whether the persons voted for are natural born citizens, or were citizens of the United States, at the time of the adoption of the Constitution, were thirty-five years old, and had been fourteen years resident within the United States. Yet it would be difficult in many cases to determine for whom an unqualified elector voted, since returns frequently listed only the candidates and the aggregated numbers of votes. In that case, should all the votes of the state be cast aside? Who should have this discretionary authority?[24]

Nicholas believed the Constitution required that the returns from the electors should be opened and counted before a joint session of the Congress, where the states had the same weight they had in the electoral vote, and that no legislative device, operating in secret, could be substituted for this procedure. Federalists stretched credulity in asserting that the necessary and proper clause of the Constitution entitled Congress to create a grand committee. They demonstrated an unseemly distrust of the people and their electors.

Hence he proposed that on the occasion of the counting of the electoral vote, the names of the states should be written on a piece of paper and placed in a box, from which one would be drawn at a time. The President of the Senate would then read the certificate of the electors and any petitions about the returns from each state in turn. If there was no exception, then the vote was counted. If there was an objection, the members present should decide the issue without debate by a simple yes or no vote. This motion failed 11-18. On March 28, the Senate passed a refined Ross bill 16-12 and sent it to the House. The partisan alignment was evident, and several Republican Congressmen issued circular letters to their constituents warning of the grave threat to their liberties posed by the grand committee.[25]

The House, which had a numerical majority of Federalists but contained a strong Republican minority, received the Senate bill on March 31, and worked through it in April, when it sent the measure to a committee of seven consisting of chairperson John Marshall of Virginia, Samuel Sewall of Massachusetts, Chauncey Goodrich of Massachusetts, Robert Goodloe Harper of South Carolina, John Nicholas of Virginia, John Dennis of Maryland, and James A. Bayard of Delaware. Although Marshall expressed some sympathy for a congressional check against abuses in the state returns, he saw the proposed bill replete with constitutional and logical difficulties. On April 25, Marshall reported a bill which moderated the Senate bill by trying to preserve the role the Constitution assigned to the House to choose a President in the event the electors failed to do so.[26]

By this point, the bill gave the House an equal role with the Senate in the process. The grand committee had become a joint committee and consisted of eight persons, four each chosen by ballot from each house of Congress; the Senate did not have any more representation than the House. Each house filled vacancies in its delegation. The President of the Senate was to deliver all petitions and related testimony, other than the packets containing the certificates of the votes of the electors, to the joint committee, and the Speaker of the House was to turn over any information he might have received to the same group. The joint committee required a minimum of three persons from each house to take any action and made a report to the House and Senate in which it calendared all the contested votes, the appropriate documents, and the law, resolution, or act of the state legislature governing the choice of electors, "but without giving any opinion thereon."[27]

In the meantime, each house chose by ballot two of its members to serve as tellers to count the electoral vote returns. The tellers recorded the votes and the names of the candidates for whom the votes were cast, the dates of the certificates, the names of the electors, the time of their election, the time and place of their meeting, and the substance of the communications from the governors certifying the appointment of electors. They drew out of a box the names of the states one by one, and the President of the Senate before a joint session of the Congress read the certificate of the electors and all other materials, including any from the joint committee. If no one objected, the vote of the state was counted. If at least one Representative and Senator supported the petition against counting the returns, the two houses separated and without any debate took a vote based on ayes and nays. If they did not agree to refuse the vote, the return was counted. The Representatives put the burden to win concurrence on those who wanted to reject the returns.

Opponents tried to amend this proposal in several ways. They sought to strike out the section providing for a joint committee. They favored having any question about receiving the electoral returns from a state settled immediately by a majority vote of the session of the House and Senate. But they were not successful, and the House adopted its bill 52-37 on May 1, and sent it to the Senate.[28]

The ultra-Federalists in the Senate acted swiftly to shape the House measure more to their liking. On May 8, 1800, they adopted several amendments, of which one was crucial: when the two houses met separately to vote on whether to accept or refuse the contested electoral return from a state, they must agree to accept those returns if they are to be counted. In essence, the Senate put the burden to win concurrence in the two houses of Congress on those who wanted to accept the returns. The insistence on this provision doomed the movement to create a committee, joint or grand.[29]

The House refused to accept the Senate amendments, and the Senate refused to withdraw them. On May 13, the House considered a resolution, which would have given to it primary responsibility for dealing with contests over presidential elections, namely, "that all questions respecting the Election of President & Vice President of the United States ought to be decided by the House of Representatives but that the Votes should be taken by States the Representation from each State having one Vote."[30] But with the session ending the next day, the House postponed further action. Partisan political motives operated everywhere, it seemed, but so did institutional differences between the House and Senate. Thus division within the Federalist majority in the two houses ended a serious effort to tinker with the returns of presidential electors. The threat of congressional intrusion also encouraged Republicans to seek a decision from presidential electors rather than to rely on the House.

8

The Election of 1800

The presidential election took place over a period of months from the spring of 1800 until the first Wednesday in December when the electors met in their states to vote. In most instances, the contest for President hinged on state elections for legislators who appointed electors; in five cases it depended on popular election. The sectional political bases for the parties remained an important feature in 1800. Once again Federalists counted on New England and Republicans relied on the southern states. Thomas Jefferson calculated, "Keep out Pennsylva[nia], Jersey & N[ew] York, & the rest of the states are about equally divided."[1] The division between the Federalist upper and Republican lower house of Pennsylvania's legislature, moreover, made it possible that the Keystone state would sit out the presidential election as New York had done in 1789. "If Pennsylva[nia] does not vote," Jefferson added, "then New York determines the election."[2] William Bingham in Philadelphia agreed that the state elections in New York in April would probably determine who would succeed in the presidential contest.

Jefferson knew from communications with Chancellor Robert Livingston and Aaron Burr that the key to getting majority control of the joint session of the New York legislature which would appoint presidential electors lay with the city of New York, which had twelve assembly seats and could make a swing of twenty-four in a joint session. It was simple arithmetic. If the Republicans lost New York, they faced long odds, "because it would then require a republican vote both from New Jersey and Pennsylvania to preponderate against New York, on which we could not count with any confidence."[3]

No issue was more important in New York's legislative election than the method of selecting presidential electors. Federalists assumed the political liability of an aristocratic party opposed to democratic reforms, for which the Republican press took them to task. The *American Citizen* publicized Federalist charges that the people lacked sufficient knowledge and discernment. An Independent Elector submitted a plea to voters to repudiate such Federalist claims. The author saw democracy advancing in other states, where the people voted for presidential electors. The *American Citizen* chose early April as the right time to begin coverage of the Ross bill, which drew all kinds of constitutional and political fire. The *Republican Watch Tower* editorialized that power derived from the people and noted that one party consistently favored recognizing more power for constituted authorities at the expense of the people. Here, it claimed, was the true difference between the Federalists and Republicans.[4]

From Albany, Gerald W. Bancker noted that the two parties campaigned spiritedly because leaders in both understood that the victors "shall bear the sway, and possess the iron rod of power, not only in the State but in the United States."[5] Robert Troup agreed that this was an election "to choose a legislature to appoint electors."[6] The presidential election in the fall had become clearly linked to legislative elections in the spring.[7]

In a brilliant tactical move, Aaron Burr organized the 1800 Republican campaign for the legislative elections in New York City. He secured the agreement of some of the best-known members of the party, including George Clinton, Horatio Gates, Brockholst Livingston, and Jacob Broome to run for the assembly, several of whom were not eager to do so. Burr may have taken a page from the book of Virginia's Republicans, who planned to run a similar star-studded slate for presidential electors in hopes of winning all of the state's electoral votes for Jefferson. In neither case did the makers of these tickets intend that the successful candidates exercise independent judgment; instead, the tickets were designed to bring success at the polls and support for the Republican team of Jefferson and Burr. Burr's slate included Clintonians, Livingstonians, and, of course, Burrites. He and his allies in ward committees prepared lists of prospective voters and turned them out on election day. Having the venerable George Clinton's name at the head of the ticket had, James Nicholson remarked, "a most powerful Effect."[8]

The Federalists got off the mark slowly. In New York city, they had trouble putting together a senate slate for the southern district. When they finally agreed, they could not find quality candidates for the Assembly and Congress, who were willing to spend extended time away from family and business in either the state or new national capital. Peter Jay tried a direct attack against the Republican assembly ticket by writing a piece for the *Daily Advertiser*. He chided the Republicans for bringing out their old war horses, but those veterans had clout. And the Republican ticket secured a majority of twenty-eight seats in the lower house. Victorious as well in three of four senatorial districts, Republicans reduced the Federalist majority in the upper house to seven. They crowned their triumph by taking six of the ten congressional seats. These successes pointed toward a dependable Republican majority in any joint session of the legislature that would meet in the fall to appoint electors. They also established the Republican Party as the majority party in the state and left the Federalists with almost no safe constituency.[9]

Disappointed and frustrated, driven by his passion to defeat the Republican presidential candidates, and alarmed at the ascendancy of Burr in state politics, Alexander Hamilton requested that Governor John Jay make a preemptive strike and have the current Federalist legislature provide for district election of electors instead of having the newly elected Republican legislature name the slate in the fall. He must have recognized how abrupt a shift in position he was recommending for the Federalist Party, for he admitted,

> in observing this, I shall not be supposed to mean that any thing ought to be done which integrity will forbid--but merely that the scruples of delicacy and propriety, as relative to a common course of things, ought to yield to the extraordinary nature of the crisis. They ought not to hinder the taking of a *legal* and *constitutional* step, to prevent an *Atheist* in religion and a *Fanatic* in politics from getting possession of the helm of the State.[10]

Hamilton anticipated support from all Federalists and condemnation from all Republicans, and he justified the action on the grounds of "public safety." Coincidentally, on May 7, Philip Schuyler made a similar suggestion to Jay. The temperate and responsible Jay rejected the idea, which, if attempted, might have provoked a furious popular outcry against the Federalists and undermined the people's faith in the elective process.[11]

Some might conclude that Hamilton was willing to resort to "guile, sophistry, and fraud" to prevent Jefferson's election, but what Hamilton proposed was not unconstitutional under either the federal or state constitutions.[12] Hamilton doubted that legislative elections in the city of New York captured directly the sentiments of the people toward the presidential candidates, while he supported direct popular choice of electors. Moreover, others in both parties sought partisan advantage by changing the mode for selecting electors in many states in 1800.

But such a defense ultimately fails to take Hamilton and Schuyler off the hook. First, suppose that Jay had agreed to their suggestion and called for a special session of the legislature. Would his rationale for a proclamation have provoked open resistance from Republican legislators and an outcry from the voting public against the Federalists? Second, assume that the legislators agreed to convene and met in Albany in the late spring or early summer. Consider all the things that could go wrong. This legislature, elected in April of 1799, had nominal but unreliable Federalist majorities. The assembly had voted in opposition to nativist constitutional amendments initiated by the New England states and divided closely on redrawing state senate districts and choosing presidential electors in districts. Could this assembly be counted on now to support a Federalist scheme to deny New York's electoral vote to Jefferson and Burr?[13]

The difficulties multiply with each question. Since New York had a permanent law on presidential electors, adopted in 1796 by a Federalist legislature,

Governor Jay, and the council of revision, the special session in 1800 would have to draft and pass through both houses a bill on which they agreed and then gain the consent of the council of revision. Unlike 1789 when failure to agree left New York with no electors and no electoral votes, the situation in 1800 favored Republican electors should the special session fail to find common ground. The legislature would have to devise quickly a new law for district elections, which would mean in all likelihood the creation of twelve districts, two more than the existing congressional districts and hence be composed of differing geographic areas and populations. Even if elections for electors proceeded in timely fashion and voters chose some combination of Federalist and Republican figures, Hamilton and Schuyler would not be out of the woods. Existing federal law required such elections to take place within thirty-four days of the first Wednesday in December and not before then. By that time, Governor Jay would face pressures from the Republican legislature, duly elected in April, to call the usual late fall session in order to take countermeasures. If he failed to do so, Republicans might very well have convened themselves. In fact, Republicans planned to do just that.

Most important of all, the Hamilton and Schuyler proposal might have had serious repercussions in other states, such as Pennsylvania, Maryland, and North Carolina, where Republicans could have taken drastic steps to counter the New York gambit. Perhaps Governor McKean in Pennsylvania would have proceeded to appoint electors by proclamation rather than await the breaking of the deadlock in his legislature which threatened the state's ability to vote. These hypothetical scenarios could be extended further, but perhaps they have served their purpose. What Hamilton and Schuyler recommended amounted to a change of the rules of the game after a full, free debate in the 1799-1800 legislature over the mode of choosing electors in which the Federalists insisted on legislative appointment. Then having suffered defeat in a free election, in which voters now more than ever understood that in selecting their legislators they were also voicing their presidential preferences, the Federalists sought to take what they had not won.

Hamilton's and Schuyler's suggestion was in that respect very shortsighted. Not only did it have a host of practical obstacles to overcome, but it also had the aura of men and a party identified with arbitrary and hence anti-democratic measures, for whom the ends justified the means. It sought to take with power from the top what Republicans had won by patient organizational efforts and cultivation of public opinion. Fortunately, Jay's character and "old school Federalism" nipped the idea in the bud.[14] The Governor recognized Hamilton's plan as desperate; it had no real chance of success and could undermine the young republic which depended on free elections. Defeated in 1800, the Federalists could fight again on another day (they could not have known that they would never recapture the White House or the governor's mansion on their own). Hamilton had to find another way out.

In early May, Republican Matthew L. Davis reported to Albert Gallatin that

New York City had carried the state elections and hence secured electors for the national Republican ticket; he suggested that political logic pointed to a New Yorker to be Jefferson's running mate. In this calculation, Davis had plenty of company. This consideration made George Clinton, who had a good record of winning electoral votes from Virginia, Robert R. Livingston, and Aaron Burr the prime candidates. On May 11 a Republican Congressional caucus, the party's first effective nominating caucus, named Burr to join Jefferson on the ticket.[15]

Federalists remained highly interested in Burr, whose energetic campaign had done so much to secure Republican victory but whose ambitions kept political doors open to them. Fisher Ames informed Rufus King that Burr was on the market to the highest bidder and concluded, "thus you see no affair can be more involved in doubt or more dependent on intrigue, caprice or accident."[16] Federalists knew that Burr made a journey to New England to survey Republican prospects. His foray into Connecticut and Rhode Island gave him rosy notions that both states might support the Jeffersonian ticket and that at worst the former would be so equally divided as to cast no votes. Some conjectured that Burr courted votes primarily for himself rather than the ticket, and these suspicions ripened later in 1800 and early 1801. Robert Troup had never seen Burr so confident as he was since the April elections. Indeed, he seemed to be on top in New York--and near the top in the nation.[17]

Federalist Speaker of the U.S. House of Representatives Theodore Sedgwick attended a Federalist congressional caucus on May 3, where the participants agreed to the strategy of supporting their candidates, John Adams and Charles C. Pinckney, equally and faithfully. But Samuel Dexter of Massachusetts worried over the possible consequence of a Pinckney victory: the denigration of the incumbent President would alienate his supporters and destroy any prospects for future cooperation between New England Federalists and their counterparts south of Delaware. Seeing these dangers, President Adams acted swiftly and decisively by asking for the resignation of two of Hamilton's confidantes in the cabinet, Secretary of War James McHenry on May 5 and of Secretary of State Timothy Pickering on May 10. There was little reason for Adams to respect the views of New York Federalists after the Republicans triumphed in the state elections and Hamiltonians assumed a hostile posture toward Adams's re-election. He had to be more attentive to the needs of southern Federalists who could help him win electoral votes. His selection of Samuel Dexter to replace McHenry and of John Marshall of Virginia to succeed Pickering represented urgent countermeasures.[18]

Nonetheless, Alexander Hamilton wrote to Speaker Sedgwick of Massachusetts, recommending uniform Federalist support for Charles Cotesworth Pinckney and John Adams as the last opportunity for blocking Jefferson. Echoing this line, Timothy Pickering of Massachusetts advised Rufus King that Republican electors in New York would probably decide the election, but Federalists still had an outside chance. If New England states should vote equally for John

Adams and Charles C. Pinckney and if South Carolina and a portion of North Carolina electors cast one vote for Pinckney and the other for someone other than Adams, then the South Carolinian might emerge with a surprise victory. After all, South Carolina had voted for Jefferson and Thomas Pinckney in 1796 and North Carolina's practice of choosing electors in districts allowed for the exercise of influence. By the same token, Adams supporters did not have to be reminded of this threat from within. Some critics suspected that Adams even preferred the election of Jefferson over Pinckney.[19]

Republicans kept close tabs of Federalist strategy. Jefferson noticed the "hocus-pocus maneuvers" of running General Pinckney to carry South Carolina and influence North Carolina. He also predicted that New Englanders loyal to Adams would not be duped by the plot to make the South Carolinian President.[20]

The summer and fall of 1800 featured contests in numerous states for control of the legislatures which would appoint electors and in others elections for electors. For example, New Jersey had a continuous record in support of Federalism, but Republicans had made gains in the later 1790s. The state's practice of legislative appointment of electors meant in practice that the Federalists with a numerical majority won all the electors, denying Republicans any portion of the state's vote for President. In the legislative elections of 1800, Republicans waged a vigorous campaign in which they denounced Federalist policy at the national level and demanded the direct popular election of the President. They hoped to win a legislative majority capable of implementing democratic reform for choosing electors, or at least making appointments of loyal Republicans. Party newspapers in neighboring states publicized the efforts of New Jersey cohorts, like Joseph Bloomfield, who identified the Federalist Party with the "undemocratic legislative mode. In spite of these efforts, Republicans failed. Federalist David Ogden reported with relief: "It is wonderful when we consider that the whole state has for a long time past been overrun by emissaries from the democratic hordes of New York & Pennsylvania."[21] Federalists took thirty-eight seats to twelve for their rivals. Surely, Federalists would appoint electors committed to Adams and Pinckney.[22]

South Carolina, another state which relied on legislative appointment of electors, held its legislative elections in October. Given that Federalists had made a determined pitch to the Palmetto state by putting Charles C. Pinckney on the ticket with Adams and that Republican leader Charles Pinckney made a concerted effort to place the state in Jefferson's column, the contests took on great importance. The two sides locked in a fierce tussle in which no stone was left unturned. According to the Republican Pinckney, in Charleston,

> it is said several Hundred more Voted than paid taxes. *The Lame, Crippled, diseased and blind were either led, lifted, or brought in Carriages to the Poll.* The sacred right of Ballot was struck at, for at a late hour, when too late to counteract it, in order to know how men, who were supposed to be under the influence of Banks and federal

officers and English Merchants, Voted, and that they might be watched to know whether they Voted as they were directed, the Novel and Unwarrantable measure was used of Voting with tickets printed *on Green and blue and red and yellow paper* with Men stationed to watch the Votes.[23]

Although Federalists carried Charleston and the bulk of its delegation to the legislature, Republicans had their hopes because of successes elsewhere and because a number of the successful candidates seemed susceptible to persuasion.[24]

Maryland had used district elections in the past, but Federalists advocated changing to legislative appointment. Both sides understood that the mode affected differently the fortunes of their parties in the impending election. Four candidates for the assembly claimed, "We deem it a sacred duty to pursue every *proper and constitutional* measure to elect John Adams president of the United States."[25] Another supporter of the Adams candidacy pressed for legislative appointment "for the present Election only, in order to counteract the artifices of the Anti-Federalists in Virginia and other States."[26]

Candidates for the legislature, Congress, and electors addressed public meetings and militia musters. They also resorted to the press. The *Maryland Gazette* published the announcements of Jeremiah T. Chase and Gabriel Duvall, rivals for elector for the district of Anne-Arundel County and the city of Baltimore. Duvall declared that if chosen, he "will vote for that able and distinguished patriot and statesman, THOMAS JEFFERSON, ESQUIRE,--THE FRIEND OF THE PEOPLE."[27] Chase, to the contrary, indicated that "he is decidedly in favor of John Adams, the friend of liberty and the constitution, as president."[28] No one could mistake that they were committed to particular candidates.

From late winter, Pennsylvania dominated the headlines, and rightly so. The Keystone state had problems deciding exactly what to do. The state had chosen to adopt a law prior to each presidential election specific to it. Given the heightened partisan competition in the later 1790s, outgoing Governor Thomas Mifflin had advised the legislature on December 7, 1799 that it must act with dispatch to provide for the presidential election either by continuing with the general ticket system or adopting a suitable alternative. The state senate had a majority of Federalists, while the house had a majority of Republicans. The former considered a measure to create district elections, which would assure the Federalists a share of the state's electoral vote, and the latter preferred the general ticket, which would allow Republicans an excellent chance of getting all fifteen electoral votes for Jefferson and Burr. The house observed that the general ticket system was convenient and had worked well in the past. Both sides initiated petition campaigns in support of their positions.[29]

The Federalist majority in the senate went out of its way to challenge Thomas McKean, who had defeated James Ross and taken office on December

17.   On January 13, 1800 Federalists drafted an address sharply critical of McKean's use of insulting epithets in the gubernatorial race and of his removal policy upon taking office, and on January 27 they approved sending the rebuke to him. McKean replied with equal venom, standing by his earlier claims that among the supporters of his opponent were enemies of the Revolution and foreign emissaries and asserting executive prerogatives and the principle of rotation in office.   Not surprisingly, partisanship stood in the way of an accommodation, and the two houses of the legislature could not agree on a new election law.[30]

Representatives of the two houses tried to work out a common position in conference, but without success. The house members claimed that the state was divided into two parties and that the people preferred Republicans. Republican spokesmen believed that statewide elections, like that those for governor and for electors on a general ticket, resulted in persons of superior qualifications coming out on top. Republicans therefore contradicted positions they had taken three years before when they occupied the minority status which now fell to the Federalists. They contended that legislatures, moreover, could never draw district lines totally satisfactorily, and the possibility of abuse and perversions made the district mode permanently unacceptable. Finally, the district plan resulted in the state's losing its influence in national elections:

If one set of districts, for example, choose eight electors of any certain principles, and the other set of districts choose seven electors of any other certain set of principles; it will follow, that as the seven will destroy an equal number out of the eight, there will be left to this deeply-interested State, but one effective electoral vote; while the least State in the Union by adopting the opposite method, will secure to itself three effectual votes.[31]

But senators did not accept this plain reading and expressed doubt about exactly where the majority of the voters stood. They believed that the people consisted of a majority and a minority, and both portions had a right to be heard. The minority benefitted from district elections, and both could take heart from having elections held in local units where the voters knew the candidates. Federalists, like Republicans, found it convenient to adopt the rhetoric of their opponents and found themselves driven by partisan considerations to defend their plans for an election law. The stalemate meant that Pennsylvania had no provision for appointing electors when the legislature ended its session on March 17, 1800 with no plans for reconvening before the next regular session in December, by which time electors in all the states were supposed to have voted.[32]

Virginians like John Nicholas and John Dawson, loyal to Jefferson and Burr, must have taken a good deal of consolation from the April election results in New York. But they expressed great anxiety about the status of the contest in Pennsylvania and New Jersey. Newspapers in other states carried frequent reports of the deadlock in Pennsylvania which was so reminiscent of the one which had kept New York from participating in the first presidential election.[33]

After the October legislative elections produced decisive Republican victories, Governor McKean called for the legislature to reconvene in November. On November 7 it received McKean's message, in which he indicated his strong preference for popular election of electors but conceded that at this late date there was no way to do so and meet the schedule set by federal law. McKean thought it essential that Pennsylvania participate in the presidential election and thus avoid the disgrace and stigma of abstention. He urged consideration of legislative appointment, a method used by some of the other states. The house, fortified by new members elected in October, received petitions from constituents who urged joint ballot as the expedient method for appointing electors. Its bill, providing for this mode, passed easily on November 10, 1800.[34]

The Federalists in the senate, bolstered by Philadelphians who had gathered at Dunwoody's tavern and created a committee to keep their partisans in the legislature firm, predictably refused to accept a procedure in which the two-person Federalist majority in the upper house would be swamped by the sizeable Republican advantage in the lower house. By a narrow but fixed 13-11 vote on November 13, the senate recommended that it appoint seven and the house choose eight electors; the house promptly refused to concur by 20-56. The two houses then appointed members to a conference. The house delegation suggested the joint ballot with each branch given some unspecified portion of the total number to be chosen. The senate delegation countered with objections to the former but left the door open on allocation of electors. The house conferees then decided to discuss allocation as the only alternative to deadlock. They accepted for the time being precedents set in other states and weighed the most recent reports on the course of the national election. The rival *Gazette of the United States* and the *Aurora* kept the emotional fires ablaze with attacks and counterattacks.[35]

By the concluding phases of the election, Federalists worked under serious national handicaps. New Yorker Robert Troup provided an able assessment. The party had no rallying point. Death had overtaken George Washington, the father of his country, and the party had no one equal to Jefferson, author of the Declaration of Independence, and Madison, Father of the Constitution. Party loyalists in the states had to carry the burden of unpopular measures of the national government without Washington to shield them. John Adams's decisions and Hamilton's responses inflicted irreparable harm on party unity. The public soon witnessed the extent of Federalist disarray, when a private letter from Hamilton fell into Republican hands and came out in pamphlet form on October 22. This event brought out into the open the simmering dispute between the Adams Federalists and the Hamiltonians on the eve of the presidential election. Adams's purging his cabinet of McHenry and Pickering and pardoning Fries and other "insurgents" provided the final straws. The break, which extended to both substantive national policy and personal differences, some of which went back to alleged Hamiltonian maneuvering in the 1796 election, offered Republicans an emotional lift. They must have been stunned and pleased by this turn of events.[36]

Federal law required the appointment of electors within thirty-four days of the first Wednesday in December, which fell on December 3. Accordingly, Federalists and Republicans had a final opportunity to influence the outcome. In every state, partisans took great care to make certain that they did not lose by carelessness what they had fought so hard to win during the spring, summer, and fall campaigns, and they had good reasons to be wary. Mistrust of each other's good intentions, the malleability of the electoral system, and the consequences at stake contributed to the anxiety and excitement. One by one the states showed the hands they would play.

New Jersey Governor Richard Howell certified that the council and assembly met at the statehouse to appoint electors on October 30. The Federalist slate overwhelmed the Republican ticket. When they met at Trenton, they gave all of their votes to Adams and Pinckney.[37]

Connecticut acted with similar dispatch to meet the thirty-four day requirement. Although a clearly Federalist state, Connecticut leveraged its weight in party and national affairs by electing Representatives at large and appointing its electors by a concurrent vote of the legislature. Republicans protested against these practices. Republican Abraham Bishop, for example, had caused a considerable stir back in September. Invited to deliver a Phi Beta Kappa address on the eve of the Yale commencement in September, Bishop chose to make a highly partisan speech. When he made the text of his intended remarks known, the society decided to cancel the affair. Bishop then delivered an address under the auspices of the White Haven Society, which raised questions about those who claimed that a national debt was a blessing, not a curse; that an army cherishes rather than destroys freedom; and that the friends of government are guardian angels, not Satan's legions. Critical of those who opposed popular election of electors, he singled out the elite which will appoint electors and then tell them how to vote. But the Federalists remained adamant and had their way. Connecticut's legislature by concurrent vote on October 31 chose electors, all sound Federalists, who met on December 3, in Hartford, and voted as expected. They filled out a form earlier prepared and gave uniform votes for the Federalist ticket.[38]

Delaware had no standing law governing the choice of electors. Federalist Governor Richard Bassett had called for an early session of the state legislature to remedy this deficiency. When the house and senate sought to consider a bill for legislative appointment, Caesar Rodney urged postponement. At this late date he argued for popular choice as Delaware had enjoyed in 1788. He recommended the alternative of a popular election for electors on November 20 of 1800 and every fourth year thereafter. Rodney received support from the New Castle delegation and solid opposition from Kent and Sussex representatives; his motion lost. On November 5, the legislature passed the original bill and promptly made the appointments by joint ballot. The electors gave their votes to Adams and Pinckney.[39]

In New York, wary Republicans anticipated a conspiracy in which either Federalist legislators would refuse to attend the meeting of the legislature and thereby prevent a quorum or Governor John Jay would refuse to convene the legislature and thereby prevent the appointment of Republican electors. One observer found Republican Tunis Wortman's office preparing circular letters to Republican members of the legislature to convene themselves since the Governor would probably not issue the usual proclamation for that purpose. The *American Citizen* came to the conclusion that Federalists, realizing they could not defeat Jefferson, derived "a malignant pleasure in exciting doubt."[40]

But on November 4, 1800 the legislature met at the call of the Governor. He urged the members to behave with prudence to advance the success of the national government and urged moderation of partisan passions. The house then proceeded to nominate candidates for presidential electors. Meanwhile, the senate put forward a totally different list. In the joint vote, the house list carried by a party vote.[41]

The New York electors met at the home of Stephen Holmes in Hudson, which attracted an audience of interested persons. Their certificate to the President of the Senate stated that they had voted by ballot "for two persons, one of whom was not, an inhabitant of the State of New York."[42] They reported 12 votes for Jefferson and 12 for Burr. The care with which they acted suggested that they did everything possible to make sure there would be no question about the validity of these votes.

Later, James Cheetham hinted that elector Anthony Lispenard may have wanted a secret vote so that he could support Burr and that DeWitt Clinton had foiled this plan by getting all the electors to show each other their ballots. But it should be noted that Cheetham was a close ally of Clinton in his battle against Burr for control of the Republican Party in New York, and his motives are not beyond challenge. Moreover, because the votes were recorded in the certificate sent to the President of the Senate, all the New York electors would have known if any one had departed from party discipline long before the votes were opened at the nation's capital.[43]

After voting, the electors headed back to their homes. One of them, Jeremiah Van Rensselaer, crossed the frozen Hudson River on route to Albany and fell on the ice, injuring his back and dislocating a shoulder. Had this mishap occurred on his trip to Hudson and he had failed to reach his destination, his electoral vote would have been lost, for New York had no law providing for vacancies in the office of elector.[44]

Vermont's Federalist Governor Isaac Tichenor wanted to impress on his legislature on October 10 the importance of choosing electors dedicated to the cause of "order and good government," who would support the positions of Washington and Adams.[45] On October 21, James Wetherell of Rutland County introduced a bill to divide the state into districts for the purpose of appointing electors, and on October 25 Udney Hay moved to create a committee to prepare for the popular election of electors. These efforts to deny a solid bloc of electors for Adams gave Republicans some hope. But the assembly majority, heeding the Governor's advice, rejected them. Later, Tichenor certified that a grand committee, consisting of the governor, council, and house of representatives, met on November 8 and appointed electors. They met at Salmon Duttons in Cavendish in the county of Windsor and voted for the Federalist ticket.

Maryland held its district elections for electors on November 10, about a month after the state legislative elections. The new legislature made no attempt to alter the mode for appointing electors as some feared. The electors met at Annapolis and gave 5 votes for Adams, Jefferson, Pinckney, and Burr, listed on their returns in that order, hinting that the electors knew that the first two were contesting for the presidency and the latter two for the vice presidency.[46]

Massachusetts, which had fought vigorously over shifting from popular election to the legislative mode earlier in the year, now moved with precision. By joint ballot on November 13, 1800, the General Court chose electors, many of whom had served in the same capacity in 1796. They gave a solid vote to Adams and Pinckney.[47]

Georgia's legislature had adopted a resolution for the popular election of four electors at the same time as the state election for legislators on the first Monday in October, but the measure had received a veto from Governor James Jackson who recognized that the state elections did not occur within thirty-four days of the first Wednesday in December. Jackson told the legislature on November 5 that he favored the popular election of electors but indicated that to hold an election so soon after the state elections made this option inconvenient and expensive. After declaring that it was permissible under the state constitution for sitting legislators to serve as electors, the legislature met in joint session on November 18 and chose electors. Between November 28 and December 1, the two houses provided that the Governor could fill any vacancy that might occur among the electors. On December 3, the electors filled out a form which had two columns, one for Jefferson and one for Burr. The electors' names appeared in each column.[48]

Governor Arthur Fenner of Rhode Island reported that electors were chosen on November 19 in accordance with the state law, providing for popular election at large by plurality vote on the third Wednesday in November in every fourth year since the previous election. Although there were last minute efforts to finetune the law in the General Assembly, the election occurred on schedule. In Providence, *The United States Chronicle* and *The Providence Gazette* printed the slates of Federalist and Republican candidates for electors; *The Newport Mercury* did the same for that city. Federalists, like A Freeman, claimed that their ticket consisted of "great Landholders, and firm Friends of the Government," committed to the re-election of John Adams, while Republicans, like A Number of Citizens, countered that theirs included patriots "warmly attached to her Liberties and real Interests."[49] The charge that Christopher G. Champlin and Ray Greene, father and uncle of two of the Federalist candidates for electors, participated in a meeting in Philadelphia designed to elect Charles C. Pinckney President over Adams, created a stir. But in spite of this distraction and Aaron Burr's appearance on behalf of the Republican ticket, Federalists prevailed. Rhode Island law also required the Governor to call the assembly into session to fill any vacancies which might result from election ties, death, resignation, or incapacity; none occurred. The electors met in Bristol. As in 1796 they voted "for two Persons one of whom for President and the other for Vice President."[50] They gave Adams 4 votes, Pinckney 3, and John Jay 1.[51]

For the first time, Virginians went to the polls to choose electors on a general ticket. The two parties had mobilized and prepared tickets. Republicans had promptly formed an all-star slate, designed to win popular support throughout the state. The *Virginia Argus* publicized their efforts and educated readers on the workings of the general ticket. It informed the public that in voting for electors the people were choosing Jefferson or Adams. Governor James Monroe appointed predominantly Republicans to serve as election commissioners, and Congressman John Dawson solicited help from German newspapers in neighboring Pennsylvania. When the polls opened on November 3, relatively few Virginians turned out. By November 21, the *Virginia Argus* and *Gazette of the United States* reported the decisive triumph of the Republican slate. The electors met at the capitol in Richmond and voted uniformly for Jefferson and Burr.[52]

North Carolina Governor Benjamin Williams attested on November 22 to the election of twelve electors in various districts. Republicans had reason to regret that they had not taken the advice of Charles Pinckney to move toward legislative appointment or to imitate Virginia and adopt the general ticket. For reasons which appear to have hinged on local circumstances, Federalists did better than expected. The electors met in the Commons Hall of the statehouse in Raleigh and gave Jefferson and Burr 8 votes each and Adams and Pinckney the remaining 4 votes each.[53]

Like neighboring Massachusetts, New Hampshire had changed its law directing how electors should be chosen by shifting from popular choice to legislative appointment. The new procedure added to Federalist strength. Appointed by joint ballot on November 27, the electors met at Concord and cast all votes for the Federalist ticket.[54]

Kentuckians went to the polls to choose their presidential electors on November 11. The four successful candidates met at the capitol in Frankfort on the appointed day and gave a unified vote to the Republican duo. Reports of their votes traveled very slowly to the rest of the country, but most political activists placed Kentucky in the Republican column. The same might be said for Tennessee. Generally considered Republican, word of exactly how it proceeded to choose electors did not reach many in the East until the end. Tennessee Governor John Sevier certified that the three electors had been chosen according to the Tennessee law of October 26, 1799. They met in Knoxville and gave their votes to Jefferson and Burr.[55]

In Pennsylvania Federalists and Republicans remained deadlocked. Possibly believing that the Federalists had more to gain by having Pennsylvania sit out the election completely, the Republican majority in the lower house of the legislature proposed on November 20 that each house nominate a certain number of persons for electors, from which a joint ballot would select fifteen. On the next day, the Federalist senators responded by suggesting that each house nominate eight candidates and the two houses vote for fifteen persons. This answer indicated that Federalists were trying to cancel out Republican votes; they did not intend to keep Pennsylvania from voting. The representatives countered with an offer that each house nominate nine. The tiny Federalist minority in the senate was winning the battle. On December 1, the house came around to the senate's proposal. On December 2, the majority in the joint vote got the small satisfaction of an 8-7 margin of Republican over Federalist electors. As Republican Nathan Penrose explained, that one vote could be the difference between victory and defeat nationally. Indeed, according to calculations which showed that Rhode Island had gone Federalist and Maryland had divided evenly, Jefferson then had 57 electoral votes to 58 for Adams, in which case the single vote could produce a tie. But many Republicans in Philadelphia and elsewhere were furious. Governor McKean reminded legislators of the need for a permanent law for electors, while Jonathan Roberts wrote his father to complain of an inexpedient compromise which abandoned principle and disguised inherent defects in the constitutional provisions for the election of President.[56]

The outrage also targeted intransigent Federalist senators. Republicans were determined to fasten on their opponents for all time the label of anti-democrats. For a bare Federalist majority of two in the upper house to frustrate a Republican majority of thirty-two in the lower meant a victory of sorts for the day but likely defeat in the long run. As McKean explained to Jefferson, "The thirteen are execrated by the Whigs[;] they will never have the power to perpetrate the like mischief again."[57] Indeed, in October Republicans had taken six of the seven senate seats up for election in which the stalemate over the choice of electors had been a principal issue. In 1801 Republicans won seventy-one of eighty-three seats in the lower house and all nine senate seats scheduled for elections, sweeping the Federalists out in devastating fashion.[58]

For the present, Governor McKean certified that on December 2 the legislature had chosen fifteen electors. Samuel Wetherille served as presiding officer when the electors met and gave Jefferson and Burr 8 votes and Adams and Pinckney 7.[59]

As reports from the various states trickled in, many Americans believed that all four candidates had sixty-five electoral votes and that South Carolina would determine the election. When the legislature met at Columbia on November 24, Charles Pinckney asserted his influence on behalf of the Jeffersonian cause and against those of his second cousin, Charles C. Pinckney. He had a substantial base of support among members from the upper country, which received a boost from a new pro-Jefferson group in the low country. A United States Senator and not a member of the legislature, the Republican Pinckney tried to secure the appointment of electors committed to both Jefferson and Burr, but he may have issued "feelers" to see if Federalist and uncommitted legislators might support Jefferson and Pinckney, a move designed to insure that Jefferson would be one of the top two in the national electoral count. In retrospect, it appears that the Federalists' best chance rested on an appeal to Republicans to support native son General Charles C. Pinckney, a member of the state senate, along with Jefferson. General Pinckney himself steadfastly denied authorizing such a pairing and maintained a public stance insisting on support for Adams and Pinckney or nothing at all. Caucuses, parliamentary maneuvers, and rumors served as symptoms of a political fever which spread from Charleston throughout the state and the nation. South Carolina's legislature on December 2 appointed eight electors, all of whom came from the straight Republican slate. They took their oath of office from Governor John Drayton, met at the statehouse in Columbia at eleven o'clock in the morning, and gave their votes to Jefferson and Burr.[60]

There were some last minute reports, false as they turned out to be, of electoral votes for Pinckney in South Carolina, which stirred desperate hopes among Federalists outside of the state. Had the state's electors given eight votes to Jefferson and Pinckney, what would have resulted? If Federalist electors in the rest of the nation voted for both Adams and Pinckney, then Pinckney would have tied Jefferson. The House of Representatives, in which Federalists had a numerical majority but controlled only half the delegations, would have had to choose between the two men. Given the actual difficulties endured in 1801 when the contestants were two Republicans, Jefferson and Burr, a choice between a Republican and Federalist would probably have been more bitter and intense. The possibility raises the interesting question of how Federalist supporters loyal to Adams would have behaved. No matter which became President and which Vice President, it is likely that complaints about the dual vote by the electors would have increased. But in reality, a Federalist elector in Rhode Island had thrown one vote away from Pinckney to John Jay. Thus a South Carolina vote for Jefferson and Pinckney would have made Jefferson President and Pinckney Vice President. Pinckney did not have a direct path to the first office.

Federalists were in shock, "thunderstruck," according to Lewis Morris. They blamed their defeat on a false sense of honor and a lack of sufficient partisanship. New York Federalist Abraham Van Vechten moaned, "We are all in the Suds."[61] On the other side, Thomas Jefferson received a report from South Carolina, which insured Republican success. The correspondent sent the letter after the legislature appointed the electors and on the eve before they voted. He wrote, "The Vote tomorrow I understand will be Thomas Jefferson 8. Aaron Burr 7. Geo[rge] Clinton 1. You will easily discover why the one Vote is varied." But, of course, the correspondent was wrong--dead wrong-- about the throwing of one vote to Clinton to establish Jefferson's precedence over Burr.[62]

There was some initial uncertainty about the uniformity of the Rhode Island vote, and the results from Tennessee and Kentucky reached the eastern states late. Then the South Carolina results sealed the Republican victory but did not clarify whether the two Republican candidates received equal votes. In due course, Americans came to believe that Thomas Jefferson and Aaron Burr had carried eight states. New York, the only uniformly Republican state outside of the South and West, joined Pennsylvania, Virginia, North Carolina, South Carolina, Georgia, Kentucky, and Tennessee. In addition, Jefferson and Burr divided Maryland equally with Adams and Pinckney. Adams and Pinckney prevailed in seven states: Massachusetts, New Hampshire, Vermont, Rhode Island, Connecticut, New Jersey, and Delaware. They also picked up additional votes in Pennsylvania, Maryland, and North Carolina. While South Carolina put the Republican ticket over the top, the sectional voting pattern underscored the importance of New York and Pennsylvania for parties based in either New England or the southern states, and of the two, New York, because it encouraged the winner-take-all method, was the great prize.[63]

9

The Contingency Election of 1801

Although Republicans had won the presidential election, they faced an unhappy surprise. In Virginia, James Madison had considered the wisdom of having electors support Jefferson unanimously and then to have all but one or two vote for Burr. But Virginians knew that they had deserted Burr in 1796 and that he had been principally responsible for bringing New York into the Republican column. Therefore they felt they must vote for him as well as for Jefferson. Although they had not gained commitments, Republicans expected their electors in some other states, like South Carolina and Tennessee, would throw votes away from Burr. In fact, Thomas Jefferson wrote to his running mate, expressing fears that too many second votes might be lost, which would open the door to a Federalist Vice President. Explaining that he could not with propriety be seen engaged in these arrangements, Jefferson conceded that matters had been badly handled. James Jackson, Governor of Georgia, knew of plans by his state's electors to cast two votes for George Clinton rather than Burr. At the last moment, however, communications arrived, urging a unanimous vote for both major candidates to foreclose Federalist chances for one of the two offices. Republican desires to avoid the division which led Federalist electors in 1796 to get Adams the top office while losing the second and insufficient attention to final details led to the likelihood of a tie vote, if the electors voted "fairly," a term which contemporaries began to use in 1800 to mean "faithfully" and in accordance with the expectations of those who had appointed them.[1]

The framers of the Constitution had anticipated the possibility of two or more candidates having an equal and majority vote, which the double vote of electors allowed. They provided that in such an instance, the House of Representatives, the branch of the legislature which stood closer to the people, should make the choice, but they required that the members of the House vote as state delegations with each state having one vote, thereby recognizing the important political and constitutional role of states in the republic and soothing the ruffled feathers of those small states which had reservations about the advantages enjoyed by large states in the electoral college. The successful candidate had to carry a majority of the states.

The Constitution placed in the existing House, elected in 1798 during war preparations, the duty to elect the President. The Federalists held a numerical majority of representatives but did not control a majority of the sixteen state delegations in the House. Two states, Vermont and Maryland, had even numbers of representatives who split equally along party lines. In the former, the prospect that Republican Matthew Lyon of "spitting" fame and Federalist Lewis Morris could agree on anything seemed remote. Whether Republican congressional delegations would vote consistently with their electors remained uncertain, for states generally chose representatives and electors in very different ways and for different purposes. How Federalist delegations, whose state electors had voted for Adams and Pinckney, would act became the central question. Timothy Pickering calculated that neither side could form a majority of states and observed, "It is a very singular state of things when that person whom neither party likes, is to become probably the President of the U.States."[2] While they could prevent the choice of Jefferson, Federalists could not put Burr in the White House without Republican acquiescence.[3]

The behavior of Republicans in Burr's home state showed that they were first and foremost loyal to the national party and to Jefferson. Initially, New York Republicans did not see a substantive difference between the two standard bearers. Robert Livingston expressed great pleasure at hearing South Carolina had voted equally for Jefferson and Burr and noted casually and without apparent concern that the House would have to choose between them. "It can be of small consequence to republicanism which is President or Vice-President," the *American Citizen* asserted; "they are both republicans, and have the full confidence of the people in that respect."[4] But as Federalists considered the prospect of picking between the two, the paper shifted ground. It continued to believe that Burr would make a good President and be a dependable republican, "but it is certain that it is not the will of the people that he should be President for the next four years." Those Federalists who opposed the election of Jefferson by the Congress "knowingly act against the expressed will of the majority, and are therefore culpable," it concluded.[5] The moderately Federalist *Daily Advertiser* published an essay by Aristides, who asserted that the people had a clear preference, the Virginian for President and the New Yorker for Vice President, but had been prevented from expressing their sentiments because of the peculiarities of the constitutional provision requiring electors to cast two votes for President. Aristides warned Federalists that the election of Burr would sicken rank and file members of their own party and leave Republicans unreconciled. Instead of Burr's serving to bridge differences between the two parties, he would become the source for widening the gap.[6]

Federalists could not help but notice the dismay of the victorious Republicans. Daniel Hale, who had served as secretary of state of New York since

1793, saw many complications in the House, which "will probably lead to a difficulty not provided for by the Constitution." But he believed the Republicans were "as mortified at the Idea of Burr's being the President as either Adams or Pinckney."[7] James McHenry, the former Secretary of War, found that the "Democrats in Congress are in rage for having acted with good faith, that they swear they will never do it again and virtually incriminate each other for having done so now."[8]

Thoughtful Federalists expressed concerns about a spiteful policy. For example, a correspondent writing to Congressman Henry Glen, wondered at the motives of Federalists who could support Burr, assuming that Burr would accept the office over Jefferson. How could they have any confidence in a man who turns 180 degrees to win an office? "If they do elect him," he added, "they must do it from motives of revenge, in order to disappoint the republicans of the man of their choice; and I confess I would be sorry to see so much littleness exhibited by the representatives 'of this great and enlightened nation.'"[9]

Hamiltonians had grave reservations. Robert Troup wrote Rufus King, "Perhaps you will be still more astonished to hear that a serious opinion is growing up among our friends at Washington that Burr ought to be preferred to Jefferson."[10] He cited Jonathan Dayton of New Jersey as a "warm advocate of this preference" but knew of many others greater in influence who desired the same end. Hamilton himself threatened to give up politics altogether should his party proceed on such a dangerous course.[11]

Republican Congressman Edward Livingston agreed that Federalists could not in good conscience elect Burr. The Federalists made a good show of supporting Burr, he believed, to conceal their real object, "a defeat of the Election & an usurpation of the Government by some creature whom they intend to designate by law."[12] Indeed, all through January and early February sensational rumors circulated, all of which assumed that Federalists would deny the presidency to both Jefferson and Burr. One suggested that the Federalists would elect no one and then have Secretary of State John Marshall act as President; a second, pointed to the President Pro Tem of the Senate, John E. Howard of Maryland, as the likely acting President, since his office, unlike that of the Speaker of the House, continued beyond March 4, 1801 when the current term of all House members ended; a third spoke of the Congress enacting a law to provide for a succession until a new election could be held in another year. It is not at all clear, however, that Federalists thought through the various options, agreed on a single one, and considered the political costs and benefits of succeeding or failing. Instead, they slid into the role of spoiler.[13]

Jefferson complained about Federalist machinations: "This tells us who are entitled to the appellation of anarchists with which they have so liberally branded others."[14] Having just adjourned but fearing a conspiracy to overturn the election results, the Virginia legislature asked Governor James Monroe to keep them apprised so that the members could reassemble to take appropriate action. Monroe then established a special express line of riders to bring reports from

Stephen T. Mason and Wilson Cary Nicholas in Washington to Richmond. Samuel Smith hoped that Jefferson as Vice President and therefore head of the Senate would prevent the selection of the President Pro Tem as President and that Jefferson and Burr together would convene the new Congress by their joint authority after March 4. James Madison considered that President Adams might veto any proposed bill to establish an interregnum, but he could not confidently predict how Adams would respond. The Pennsylvania legislature decided to remain in session until at least March 4 in a state of readiness throughout the political crisis. Governor McKean believed he had the reply to any Federalist scheme: since a Republican should be president, Jefferson and Burr should draw up an instrument in which one resigned the presidency. In private correspondence, some Virginians considered the withdrawal of the state from the union as the ultimate response. James Hillhouse of Connecticut heard some Republicans threaten disunion; New Jersey Congressman Aaron Kitchell could imagine disunion followed by war, a catastrophe for the republic.[15]

The presidential election law of March 1, 1792 stated that the returns from each state should be opened before a joint session of the Congress on the second Wednesday in February. On February 11, therefore, the Congress learned the official results of the election; Jefferson and Burr received 73 votes each, Adams 65, Pinckney 64, and Jay 1. Only after this count could the House proceed to balloting for Jefferson or Burr.[16]

In anticipation of the contingency election, the House of Representatives had prepared a code of "political etiquette" on February 9, 1801. The rules stipulated that if a quorum appeared on February 11, the House would proceed by ballot, and, if no choice resulted, the members should continue to succeeding ballots without interruption from other business. The House should not adjourn once balloting began. During the balloting, representatives were to sit as state delegations, and each delegation deposited duplicate certificates of its vote into two separate general ballot boxes, each of which would be examined by tellers representing the various states.[17]

On a snowy February 11, the House made its first attempt at an election. Jefferson won the votes of New York, New Jersey (whose electors had voted for the Federalist candidates), Pennsylvania, Virginia, North Carolina, Georgia, Kentucky, and Tennessee, but he fell shy of the required majority of nine. Burr gained the support of New Hampshire, Massachusetts, Rhode Island, Connecticut, Delaware--all of which had voted for Adams and Pinckney--and South Carolina, which had voted for Jefferson and Burr. Two states, Vermont and Maryland, divided. After seven ballots, the members took a break "for *one* hour to eat a mouthful."[18] New Jersey Congressman John Condit reported on the determination of Maryland Republicans as evidenced by the fact that they carried the very ill Joseph Hopper Nicholson into the House on a bed to cast his vote, after which he retired to an adjoining committee room to rest between ballots. Harrison Gray Otis of Massachusetts wondered at Nicholson's devotion. He admitted that he would not risk his own life for "any President on Earth, but being in good health & spirits & having nobody to lie with at house, I have no objection to staying here all night."[19] Eleven more ballots followed with no change in the 8-6-2 alignment, though some observers believed that Burr gained and Jefferson lost a few individual votes by the close of the day and evening. Though weary and under great pressure, the representatives proceeded calmly and without incident, and Speaker Theodore Sedgwick thought that "the greatest good humor & urbanity of manner prevailed."[20]

The Constitution's silence on what should happen if the House failed to make a choice in the contingency election left ample room for conjecture. Robert Troup criticized the obstinacy of both parties and feared a non election and consequent civil commotion. Still, he noted, "I hope a more fortunate issue--but I have many anxious moments on the occasion."[21] John Laurence wondered why the wise men who framed the Constitution had failed to provide for the prospect that no choice might be made. Indeed, the Constitution relied on the political process to work and expected the people to hold those who acted, or did not act, accountable. Laurence, too, concluded, "I cannot believe we shall be without a Chief Magistrate, after the 3d of March, notwithstanding the obstinacy which prevailed on the 13th Instant."[22] Harrison Gray Otis agreed, as did Albert Gallatin, floor leader for the Republicans.[23]

Republicans had to make certain that New Yorkers did not have a preference for one of their own over the Virginian. Maryland Republican Senator Samuel Smith observed David A. Ogden, addressing the New York delegation. Ogden "boldly represented, how much New York would be bene- fited, by having [Burr] for the President, urging a variety of other reasons, to induce them to join the high federal party in their *pretended attempt.*"[24] Jonathan Dayton, the New Jersey Federalist Senator and a supporter of Burr, collared James Linn, one of the state's representatives, and tried to put him in Burr's camp by asserting that Theodorus Bailey and Edward Livingston, two of New York's Republican Congressmen, and Samuel Smith secretly preferred Burr to Jefferson. Bailey himself did not know how such unfounded rumors could pass for truth. In spite of these maneuvers, whether authorized by Burr or not, and rumors of yet others, the Republicans in the New Jersey and New York delegations held firm.[25]

Republicans worked on other delegations, such as Delaware, where James Bayard as the sole Congressman determined the vote of the state; Maryland, where their Representatives Gabriel Christie, George Dent, Joseph Hopper Nicholson, and Samuel Smith evenly matched Federalists George Baer, William Craik, John Dennis, and John C. Thomas; and the New England states, which sided with Burr. Connecticut's all-Federalist delegation, elected on an at-large basis, felt the special attention given them. John Cotton Smith remarked on the civility with which Republicans courted the "poor Federalists." They expressed confidence that Smith and his colleagues preferred Jefferson and would in any event respect the wishes of the Republican Party and the popular majority. Smith then raised an interesting hypothetical question. If Federalists had prevailed in the election and Adams and Pinckney had tied in electoral votes, would Republicans in the House, especially those from the South, have been so accommodating to Federalist wishes and deferentially cast their votes for Adams? Surely Smith expected at least some Republican Congressmen to prefer Pinckney of South Carolina to Adams of Massachusetts. If his conjectures were correct, then the course taken by Federalists in the House assumes a less sinister appearance, while the Constitution's sparse provisions for the election of President, the lack of experience with contingency elections, and the newness of national political parties bear greater responsibilities for the impasse.[26]

The American public was treated to press reports about the contingency election and about the procedural and political calculation of partisans and the relative qualifications of Jefferson and Burr, as the people awaited a break in the stalemate. Interested readers had therefore a host of substantive, political, procedural, and personal factors to take into account, but they could hardly affect the decision of Congressmen in Washington, especially Federalists who surveyed "the pretensions of each [candidate], and their several and comparative demerits."[27]

Although William Cooper, the great landlord of western New York, had earlier asserted that "Burr or no President is the order of the day," New York Federalists, who had worked with and against Aaron Burr at closer quarters and for a longer period than their counterparts in other states, appeared much less enthusiastic about his candidacy and less militant in their opposition to Jefferson.[28] James Watson, for example, worried that Federalists would hold responsibility for a Burr administration, and he had little confidence that they could do so safely. He believed they could endure a Jeffersonian administration whose evils probably would be temporary. Moreover, the Federalists could retain their separate identity, remain united, and appeal to the voters at the next election. Instead, Federalists trapped themselves in a struggle in which the risks of failure were very great. Only a crack in Republican unity could bail them out.[29]

Back in Washington, the House proceeded from day to day and ballot to ballot without making progress. The tightening of lines since February 11 made it extremely difficult for either side to succeed in winning over any individual representative. As Uriah Tracy noted, "No man's reputation would be safe, should he now change."[30] While there were Federalists, like Samuel W. Dana, who believed that the Republicans could more readily accede to Burr, one of their own, than Federalists could accept Jefferson, Republicans dug in and refused to be bullied by their opponents.[31]

While Alexander Hamilton urged his Federalist colleagues to support Jefferson, a temporizer, rather than Burr, an opportunist, he had very little effect. Connecticut Senator Uriah Tracy believed that the approach of March 3 at midnight would put an end to the business but conceded that "whether it will be closed till then, becomes more doubtful every ballot."[32] Many members of the House must have been eager to leave Washington and go home. Harrison

Gray Otis told his wife, "The last week has fled rapidly, in spite of all the disagreeable and still unfinished business, in which we have been engaged, and my heart beats higher and my impatience increases as the day of my departure approaches."[33]

Amidst rumors of military preparations by Republicans in Virginia, Pennsylvania, Georgia, and elsewhere, Congress felt pressure to make a decision before March 4. Some Federalists believed that they had gained assurances from high places of Jefferson's intentions. Others had doubts about supporting Burr and even greater ones about the effects of an interregnum. They thought it likely that Jefferson would win the next election. Moreover, the firmness of Republican support for Jefferson and serious questions about the electability of Burr played on Federalist Congressmen. Finally, James Bayard, the sole Congressman from Delaware, pronounced his intention of voting for Jefferson rather than prolong the crisis.[34]

In a Federalist caucus, Bayard explained that he preferred Jefferson to destroying the Constitution, but a sufficient number of his colleagues refused to support him. A second caucus in which Bayard's position received sharp criticisms and provoked threats of political reprisal found the Delaware Congressman resolute. Though not happy with him, most of the other Congressmen agreed to vote alike. Yet William Edmonds of Connecticut insisted to the end that he would vote for Burr. Other New Englanders and Lewis Morris then withdrew. Benjamin Huger of South Carolina who had steadfastly voted for Jefferson also retired, and the various Federalist delegations acted in their own way to end the stalemate. On the thirty-sixth ballot on February 17, crucial Federalists abstained from voting, and Jefferson gained the votes of ten states. Delaware and South Carolina submitted blanks, and the previously divided delegations in Vermont and Maryland sided with Jefferson as the Federalist members abstained. Connecticut, Massachusetts, New Hampshire, and Rhode Island stayed with Burr.[35]

Jefferson became President in the House election without the vote of a single Federalist, and some took pride in this fact. Federalist Joseph Hopkinson of Philadelphia wrote to New York Congressman Henry Glen to complain of the sudden shift on the thirty-sixth ballot. He acknowledged that Burr probably could not win the Presidency and in that circumstance Hopkinson did not wish to prevent Jefferson's election. Still, he thought, "It was time enough to have given the point up at 5 minutes before 12 ocl[ock] of the night of the 3d of March."[36] Republicans would neither forget nor forgive spiteful Federalism.

10

The Electoral College in 1801

Historians as well as contemporaries viewed the election of 1800 as a critical, even revolutionary, event. Many saw the triumph of Jefferson and the Republicans as a restoration of key ideological components of 1776, such as the insistence on limited central government; separation of financial, mercantile, and imperial interests from the administration of government; opposition to standing armies; adherence to civil liberties; and trust in local authorities. Others stressed the importance of political parties, the establishment of a legitimate opposition, and the peaceful transfer of power from the party in power to the one out of power as a consequence of a free choice. Indeed, these observers saw 1800 as a "swing" election. But in addition, the contest between Federalists and Republicans in 1800 sharply defined the course of electoral college development.

By 1800 Federalists and Republicans understood that state elections, even those occurring several years before presidential ones, affected crucial decisions about how electors should be chosen and for whom they should vote. Persons were chosen electors because they could be counted on to represent the wishes of those who appointed them. Even in 1789 all electors knew that they were going to vote for George Washington; the only uncertainty was who would come in second. The fact that electors met on a particular date to cast votes assumed that they would not sit around at length and deliberate on candidates and strategies, and the existence of contingency procedures meant that they did not have to remain in session until the results were known. By 1792 many electors were "fixed" on their candidates well before they met. In 1796 parties which lost referred to electors as puppets whose strings were pulled by party organizations. Of course, when their candidates won, the parties praised such behavior by electors as fair and faithful.[1]

Presidential elections had also shown that the electors in small states, like Delaware, New Jersey, and Connecticut, voted as a unit, in part because they were appointed by the dominant party in the legislature and in part because of their greater homogeneity of interests when compared to large states. They thereby made maximum use of the extra power given them by the assignment of two electors for their Senators. The fact that all three were Federalist states led Republicans to argue loudly in favor of district elections as a more democratic alternative. In contrast, the large states of Massachusetts, Pennsylvania, and Virginia had the potential before 1800 of casting split votes for the opposite reasons--their particular mode of popular election and greater diversity of interests. The large states had to reconsider the way they chose electors if they expected to outweigh small states. Pennsylvania, in particular, learned this lesson the hard way. If the electoral college came to advantage the large states over the small, it is because the small state taught the large the advantage of unified voting.[2]

Each elector formally cast two votes for President as the Constitution stipulated. But electors who had strong views of which person they wanted for President and which for Vice President had no way they could make their preferences known except by casting all of their votes for the former and fewer votes for the second. Difficulties with this practice lurked in the depths of the elections of 1789 and 1792, then surfaced in 1796. Political leaders and newspaper editors had no trouble identifying Adams and Jefferson as rivals for the presidency and Pinckney and Burr as contestants for the vice presidency, and the selection of the two highest electoral vote getters created an anomalous situation. Trying to insure the presidential election of John Adams, Federalists threw so many votes away from Thomas Pinckney, their Vice Presidential candidate, that the Republican candidate for President, Thomas Jefferson, finished second in the electoral vote. This distressing outcome caused concern, even alarm, among Federalists about the wisdom of the existing electoral college method of choosing the executive.[3]

George Cabot of Massachusetts approved of having a Federalist for President but bemoaned the success of Jefferson because of the "exertion among agents of a foreign nation to secure his election."[4] Although the office of Vice President possessed little power and Jefferson might be expected to behave respectfully toward John Adams, Cabot could not get over his fear that Jefferson "will have an influence that may be unpropitious."[5] On the Republican side, Jefferson told his close friend and ally, James Madison, that he had no difficulty accepting a position subordinate to John Adams. "I am his junior in life, was his junior in Congress, his junior in the diplomatic line, his junior lately in the civil government," he explained, and he saw Adams as "the only sure barrier against Hamilton's getting in."[6] Hard-line Federalists found little consolation in Jefferson's graceful acceptance of second place. And 1800 could mean a much sterner test--the peaceful transfer of power of the entire executive branch from a party which had always controlled the national government to an opposition party.

The deepening political divisions between Federalists and Republicans in the atmosphere of the Quasi War and the Alien and Sedition Acts led to proposed constitutional amendments from Federalists in Massachusetts, Connecticut, and Maryland to ensure that only native born Americans served in the executive and legislative branches of the national government. These Federalist initiatives reinforced the party's nativist image and its penchant for exclusiveness and intolerance, while Republicans stood for pluralism and an open society, one receptive to immigrants. They showed that while holding the Constitution in high regard Federalists had no reservations about altering the text to promote what they considered to be necessary improvements and refinements.[7]

The presidential election of 1796 also prompted Federalist initiatives for designation. For example, New Hampshire in 1798 coupled its support for a citizenship restriction with a call to have presidential electors designate which of their two votes is cast for President and which for Vice President. It required a majority of the electors to elect both officers--another significant change from existing practice. If no one had a majority, then the Senate selected from the top five candidates. That Senators were to vote as state delegations was yet another change. A majority vote of all the states decided the winner. Kentucky Federalist Humphrey Marshall moved adoption of an amendment for designation on January 24, 1798, in the United States Senate, and New Hampshire Federalist Abiel Foster introduced a similar motion in the House of Representatives on March 2, 1799 without success. The Vermont legislature adopted a resolution for designation on November 5, 1799 and sought support from other states. South Carolina also offered amendments for designation, whereby it would not matter if candidates for the vice presidency won more votes than those for the presidency; they would gain election to the office which voters had intended for them. Such a reform would also guarantee the majority party control of both executive offices. As expected, Republicans objected to this belated slap in the face to Jefferson, opposed designation as unnecessary, and countered with demands for district election of electors, especially to break Federalist blocs in New York, Connecticut, New Jersey, and Delaware.[8]

While some states received designation with interest, Rhode Island's General Assembly rejected it in June of 1800, and its rationale served as an amber light to those who pressed for adoption. A committee of the legislature studied the idea and reported that designation would diminish the influence of small states and encourage deals among the large states to form electoral majorities. The committee anticipated that a state might offer support for a presidential candidate from another state in return for an immediate pledge to its own vice-presidential candidate or a presidential candidate in the next election. The double vote for electors frustrated these backroom deals and gave the small states the balance of power. The large states with open frontiers will increase in power with population growth, while the smaller, well-settled states will grow more slowly. Finally, the committee decided that separate ballots for the two offices would lessen the chances of quality persons being chosen for the vice presidency. The legislature supported the committee recommendation unanimously.[9]

Republicans had other alternatives. It is significant that over the spring, summer, and early fall of 1800, political leaders throughout the nation considered an idea, mainly Republican in origins, of a constitutional amendment to require district election of presidential electors and representatives to Congress. Maryland's legislature adopted such a proposal on December 9, 1800 and circulated it to other states. Connecticut Federalists saw this as a partisan measure aimed squarely at their state, which had elected uniformly Federalist Congressmen on a general ticket and allowed legislative appointment of electors. In May of 1801, Federalists in the Connecticut legislature pointedly rejected the idea and offered an extensive rationale. First, it argued for diversity among states and opposed any imposed uniformity. Second, it claimed that states' rights were essential in a republic, and legislative voice in the appointment of electors buttressed these rights. Third, it believed the proposed change degraded state sovereignty by leaving legislatures with only the administrative task of dividing the state into districts. Fourth, Connecticut Federalists protested that the change would tamper unnecessarily with the Constitution when any state which wished to adopt the district mode could do so already.[10]

In spite of Federalist resistance, Wilson Cary Nicholas believed that the framers of the Constitution intended to secure presidential electors from the influence of parties and foreign governments and that the best way of attaining that goal was to prevent legislatures from appointing electors. He preferred direct election, but, if that proved impractical, he considered district elections the alternative that was most consistent with republican ideals. Praising Virginia for implementing this mode in 1789, 1792, and 1796, he regretted the departure for the general ticket in 1800, which was necessitated "upon the reasonable ground of putting this State upon the footing of other States who elected by a general ticket or by a legislative appointment."[11]

In March of 1800 Congressman John Nicholas, a Republican from Virginia and an able speaker on the floor, recommended that the House in which Federalists had a numerical majority consider such an amendment to the Constitution just when his home state decided to adopt the general ticket to guarantee all the electoral votes for the Republicans. The timing was not right and this reform collided with political hardball.[12]

Later, speaking for a select committee which studied the idea, Nicholas made a report to the House on January 22, 1801. He started with the generally popular proposition that no change should be made in the fundamental law of the land unless a greater good could be expected. The Constitution permitted wide latitude in the selection of electors, and practice indicated that methods fell under two broad categories: election by popular vote or legislative appointment. But Nicholas saw that these categories contained variations within. Thus, some states created districts, and qualified voters chose a single elector in each district, while other states allowed for a general vote. In the latter, voters chose electors at large, or selected electors distributed in districts statewide. Several states were prudent in anticipating death, absence, or other disability which might prevent an elector from attending the meeting of electors, and in such cases they provided a means for filling the vacancies. Many states took no precautions at all. Under legislative appointment, some states followed a joint ballot of the legislature. Sometimes the electors were taken at large and in other instances from a restricted list or taken in certain proportions by each House. Regardless of the particular method used, Nicholas and his committee believed the states' actions all fell within the legitimate construction of the Constitution, and the Congress had sanctioned them by admitting the votes at every presidential election.

Nicholas posited that the framers of the Constitution chose their words purposefully. They expected diverse applications and chose not to favor one method and to allow experience to test the theory. At some future day, the people might reach a consensus on the best mode based on experience. But according to Nicholas, evidence indicated that there was no general agreement at that time.

The committee did not believe it necessary to go into the relative merits of every method used by the states but saw serious liabilities in prescribing one and only one mode. To implement district elections, every state would have to be divided into units and those subdivided again for the convenient collection of votes, and officials would have to be appointed at all levels to conduct the elections. Reliance on such a large number of officials assumed their integrity and competence. Even then, errors would likely occur and absolute conformity to the law could not be assured. Officials would reject the votes of some qualified to vote and admit that of others not so qualified, and their judgment might be the result of error, design, or corruption. Such decisions would lead to election disputes between rival candidates for elector.

The gathering of the polls from the subunits at a central place in the district for comparing the results provided additional opportunities for mistake and intrigue. Nicholas knew of instances of disputed elections which turned on such points, and, fortunately, legislative bodies provided avenues of redress in these cases. But whereas many contested elections could be resolved in legislatures having the time and means, disputes in elections for electors had no such remedies. Those declared winners in the first instance would have to serve as electors regardless of the basis for challenge, for there was no time to settle all controversies. The absence of a remedy might actually tempt the unscrupulous to take advantage. After deliberation, the committee determined that it was "inexpedient" to alter the Constitution to provide district election of electors.

Nicholas rested his arguments against a mandatory district election for presidential electors on pragmatic arguments, but he must have known that many Republicans no longer were committed to district elections, which did not serve either the party's interest or promote its understanding of majority rule. Like so many of his contemporaries, he classified the modes for selecting presidential electors into two--legislative appointment and popular election--and subdivided the latter into choice by districts and general ticket. Yet, Republicans had been moving away from this view and responding to political realities. Surely many Virginia Republicans recognized this. John Dawson, for example, sought James Madison's advice on the proposed constitutional amendment for district elections of electors, and he acknowledged that "it is an intricate subject."[13]

It is evident that Dawson, like Charles C. Pinckney of South Carolina, thought that Republicans in Virginia and North Carolina should consider legislative appointment of electors as a necessary defensive response to Federalism. Wilson Cary Nicholas put it more directly in a letter, a copy of which went to Jesse Franklin of North Carolina.

> It can never be fair that a minority shou'd be counted in one State against the opinion of the Majority, and not in another. Test this principle by what may happen by the const[itution] to the same number of votes each. You elect by districts and shou'd [you] be divided 7 for one and 5 for the other candidate[,] you will only have one sixth part of the weight of N. York. Her 12 votes will be counted when in fact but two of yours will count in favor of the man that a maj[orit]y of the people wou'd wish to see elected and what wou'd make this more unreasonable is that your majority may be greater than the majority in New York.[14]

No one was more astute in this regard than Thomas Jefferson. He had particularly rich experience with the workings of the electoral college. In 1792, for example, those interested in urging him to run for Vice President thought they discovered an obstacle in pairing him with another Virginian--George Washington. Many Virginia electors used their second vote that year to support George Clinton for Vice President, not to challenge Washington for President. In 1796 when the returns were exceedingly close and appeared for a time to be leading to a tie with Adams, Jefferson realized that a contingency election in the House might not lead to a choice and the Constitution said nothing about what should happen in that event. In part to avoid entering such uncharted waters, he made it known that he would gladly defer to the New Englander, his senior in every respect. By early 1800 Jefferson could see the way Federalists and Republicans prepared furiously for the presidential election by modifying the way electors were chosen, leaving only Rhode Island, Maryland, Virginia, North Carolina, and Kentucky with popularly chosen electors, and of these Rhode Island and Virginia used the general ticket. As presiding officer of the Senate, he also listened to discussions about Senator James Ross's proposal to have a grand committee canvass the electoral votes.[15]

Demonstrating that he was not one to cling to abstractions, Jefferson saw that it came down to making the necessary majorities to win the presidency. As he put it,

> All agree that an election by districts would be best, if it could be

general; but while 10. states chuse [*sic*] either by their legislatures or by a general ticket, it is folly & worse than folly for the other 6. not to do it. In these 10. states the minority is entirely unrepresented; & their majorities not only have the weight of their whole state in their scale, but have the benefit of so much of our minorities as can succeed at a district election. This is, in fact, ensuring to our minorities the appointment of the government.[16]

He noted that in essence the choice was either to divide the nation into 16 states or 137 districts for choosing electors. Surely, he knew that in theory the two paths could produce different results, but he recognized that the key to success was to create majorities, whether by the route of forming majorities or pluralities in enough states, or the alternative of winning in the nation. The essential question was not how the people chose electors but where the electoral votes were aggregated. He perceived that the real distinction, therefore, was between those states which allowed for legislative appointment and popular election on a general ticket, both of which could mean a winner-take-all system, on the one hand, and district elections, which probably meant proportional votes for all candidates, on the other. Under the circumstances, he wished to keep his own and his party's options open and not to close prematurely in favor of mandated district elections.[17]

Nonetheless, Federalists and Republicans, especially the latter, having perceived so much at stake in the 1800 election and beset by controversies in many states, saw problems with the Constitution's provisions for presidential electors. James Madison, a principal framer of the Constitution, admitted that the text was not as full as it might have been in prescribing the election of the executive officers and thought an amendment rather than a law the appropriate remedy. Even before the electoral votes had been cast, the *American Citizen* regretted the confusion and ambiguity which clouded the "true meaning and intention of certain clauses in the constitution" and generated "heated disputes and virulent animosities" in the Congress and in state legislatures. "Why are not measures taken to settle with intelligible precision certain constitutional clauses, and give to them a definition which cannot be controverted," the paper asked?[18] In characteristic Republican fashion, the editor urged, "In cases, that are doubtful, a construction ought always to be given favourable to the rights of the people, and protective of the true principles of republicanism." The *Aurora* saw the Pennsylvania experience as evidence of the folly of giving an aristocratic party the power to interpose between the rights of the people and the presidential electors who spoke for popular will. The *American Citizen* came to see a pattern in the behavior of states: "In almost every instance, the right of election on the part of the people has been contended for and carried into effect where republican legislatures exist, and where aristocratic legislators have been chosen, the people have been deprived of this right of suffrage."[19]

A True Republican submitted to the *Aurora* an essay with the thesis "that the Federal Constitution is materially defective in its provisions respecting the election of President."[20]   Drawing upon the Pennsylvania record, the writer sought to prevent state legislatures from setting aside the clear wishes of the majority of the people. The solution appeared to be a constitutional amendment which would provide "that the Presidential Election be held on the same day throughout the Union, and the choice be made *immediately by the People, without the intervention of Electors.*"[21]   The nation could no longer tolerate the "puerile and circuitous mode" prescribed by the framers. The delegates in the Philadelphia Convention had been good men but excessively cautious to avoid "some imaginary evils" of the kind practiced only in a petty British corporation. "By the simple and happy expedient of *ballots* and *small districts*, every citizen gives his individual vote for Chief Magistrate, without tumult and without difficulty. If in one state the sense of the great body of citizens is thus easily collected, why not in all the states?"[22]

Experience with the contingency election in 1801 did nothing to alleviate Republican concerns about existing constitutional procedures. To the contrary, it strengthened Republican demands for reform.

III

SHUFFLING THE DECK

11

Partisan Principles and Interests

On March 4, 1801 Thomas Jefferson was inaugurated as the President of the United States and Aaron Burr as Vice President. Jefferson knew that he had become President in the contingency election without a single Federalist vote, and he read Federalist congressional actions as "a declaration of perpetual war." He predicted that rank and file Federalists would join Republicans to maintain the Constitution, democratic principles, and the union against the ultra-Federalists. Believing that Federalist conduct in the House during the week of balloting and on the final vote met such strong public condemnation as to leave the party elite isolated from the people, Jefferson made the favorable reading that Republicans had gained more from the actions of their rivals than from two or three years of a conciliatory Republican administration.[1]

Meanwhile, Jeffersonians enjoyed the good fortune of a Europe at peace and took measures to strengthen their hold on Americans. Federalists in the states had to cope with a hostile national administration for the first time. Jefferson's patronage decisions, based on party loyalty as well as merit, disturbed Federalists who may have thought that Jefferson had given assurances of moderation during the days preceding his election in the House. Those with a past history of service to the Revolution and with no record of corruption found their displacement difficult to accept. Reports of removals filled in a picture of outright partisanship by the administration.[2]

But Republicans took action in many other areas besides patronage. Federalist Gouverneur Morris lamented the Jeffersonians' successful attempts to repeal the Judiciary Act of 1801; they also cut back the armed forces and repealed excise taxes. Republican Edward Livingston was pleased to find Federalists reduced to the rhetoric of despair: they had come to the "mortifying conviction that [their] power of deceiving and oppressing the people is forever lost."[3] The imbalance between Federalists and Republicans still posed some prospective problems, such as overconfidence and factional disputes within Republican ranks, which invited Federalists to take sides as a way to regain influence.[4]

In New York, Governor John Jay submitted to the legislature a resolution from Maryland proposing a constitutional amendment which would require that after March 3, 1801 those qualified to vote for the most numerous branch of the legislature in each state should choose presidential electors and Representatives to the Congress in districts. The Republican-controlled assembly agreed to the Maryland initiative and sent it up to the senate on March 5. On the same day, Assemblyman Jedidiah Peck moved adoption of a plan for another amendment to implement designation. The assembly postponed action, perhaps because it looked forward to adjournment within weeks and because the next presidential election was almost four years away. In the meantime, the senate on March 6 received and deferred action on the Maryland proposal, probably for the same reasons.[5]

When it reconvened in early 1802 a Republican house of assembly and a Federalist senate considered a dual constitutional amendment relating to presidential elections. Interest in such reforms rose among Republicans after the experience in 1800 and 1801. Treasury Secretary Albert Gallatin believed that the party had to anticipate re-election in 1804. For that purpose, he thought that friends in New York and elsewhere should press for district election of electors. In addition, he advised the party to screen Vice Presidential candidates. If Republicans nominated Burr for Vice President, Federalist electors could cast votes for the New Yorker, and their votes together with those of Republican electors would make him President. Those Republican electors who tried to prevent such an outcome by scattering their second votes risked giving the second office to the Federalists. The Constitution needed to be amended to provide a remedy against such a travesty, but the chance of doing so appeared uncertain. Jefferson conceded that Gallatin had "a remedy to a certain degree."[6] He then suggested that a different reform, essentially what has come to be known as the automatic plan, would accomplish the same end. Jefferson saw that eliminating the office of elector and allowing the candidate with the plurality of votes to take all the electoral votes of the state worked as well. His understanding of how to leverage pluralities into winner-take-all operations marked him as a very shrewd student of the electoral college. It also indicated that Jefferson considered a range of solutions to the problems that Gallatin foresaw and that he was not committed to the district election option.[7]

In the slightly Federalist state senate, DeWitt Clinton moved on January 26, 1802 for adoption of an amendment with two parts, the first providing for district elections of electors and the second for designation. While the senate considered this proposal, Governor George Clinton communicated to it resolutions from North Carolina for an amendment proposing the same two changes. After the senate agreed to provide that the districts in each state once established should not be altered until the next federal census, the senate adopted the plan, and the Republican house followed suit. Soon thereafter DeWitt Clinton won the vacant U.S. Senate seat, and he then helped carry the proposed constitutional amendment from New York to Washington.[8]

During 1802 the U.S. House of Representatives saw a flurry of proposals to amend the Constitution, especially regarding the mode of electing the executives. On February 1, Lewis R. Morris of Vermont presented his state's resolutions, which were read and placed on the table. On February 15, Congressman Benjamin Walker of upstate New York introduced the New York resolutions of January 30 to the House. Four days later, the Representatives came to resolutions for both district election and designation. They sent them, along with the New York resolutions, to the Committee of the Whole on the State of the Union. By the next day, John Stanley of North Carolina presented parallel resolutions adopted by his state on December 15.[9]

Alexander Hamilton in a series of letters to Federalist friends in the Congress expressed his views of the New York proposal. He did so at a time when he was reeling from criticisms over his role in the demise of the party in 1800 and 1801 and stood helpless at the Jeffersonian attack on the judiciary. He came out in support of both designation and district elections as good policy, which would reduce the arts of intrigue at which the Republicans excelled and would limit the influence of state governments in the choice of President.[10]

Having played the game of trying to manipulate the two votes each elector cast for President in every presidential election from the adoption of the Constitution through 1800, Hamilton knew the difficulties which the electoral system posed for him. Although a member of the minority party in state and nation since 1800, he put aside the argument which many Federalists now made in opposition to designation. Hamilton had reason for being appalled at a procedure which had almost made Aaron Burr President and invited civil disturbances. As for district elections, he had played both sides of the street throughout the 1790s and in 1800, and he now took a position which might help the Federalist minority to gain proportional representation in the electoral college. He also returned to the position he had taken in the Philadelphia Convention in favor of having electors chosen in districts. His goals at both times were executive independence and national authority, and his means were democratic.

Hamilton returned to these themes in a letter to James A. Bayard, Federalist Congressman from Delaware. Bayard replied that he agreed wholeheartedly with Hamilton on the propriety of the amendments. Hamilton seemed to be a pillar of reason in recommending a long-term position for his party, but his influence had diminished to the point where he could not count on many Federalists following him.[11]

On Saturday, May 1, 1802 Philip Van Cortlandt, the veteran New York state legislator and Congressman, moved that the Representatives form into a Committee of the Whole to consider constitutional amendments. South Carolina's Benjamin Huger thought Van Cortlandt was joking, for the House was at that moment about to adjourn. Abiel Foster, a New Hampshire Federalist, likewise protested. He reminded Van Cortlandt that New Hampshire had previously submitted resolutions similar to those of New York, and those had been deferred because they came late in the session. He expected the New York proposals to receive the same treatment. Thomas T. Davis of Kentucky and James Mott of New Jersey joined in the outcry, while Lucas C. Elmendorf of Kingston, New York, supported Van Cortlandt with the argument that the proposals were so plain that it would not take much time to act upon them.[12]

Bayard indicated that he had always been puzzled by the framers' provision for the election of President and was inclined in principle to support both designation and district election of electors. But he protested that any amendment to the Constitution should be examined carefully and not be voted upon in haste. Nonetheless, the sparsely attended House then voted 38-30 in favor of Van Cortland's motion.[13]

In the Committee of the Whole, Bayard wanted to examine district election, a course that would complicate discussion and probably prevent any action before adjournment. New York Representative Samuel L. Mitchill chided Bayard for wanting more time for study given how prominent a role the Delaware Federalist had played in 1800 and 1801. He claimed that the historical record was clear:

> Wise and virtuous as were the members of the Convention, experience has shown that the mode therein adopted cannot be carried into operation; for the people do not elect a person for an elector who, they know, does not intend to vote for a particular person as President. Therefore, practically, the very thing is adopted [that is] intended by this amendment.[14]

Hence the reform ought to be implemented. Mitchill supported a change which could prevent the embarrassment of the tie in the 1800 election, but he did absolutely nothing to alleviate the fears of many that a contingency election could lead to stalemate with no President chosen.

Samuel W. Dana, an old school Federalist from Connecticut, refused to allow the New Yorker's claim that the choice was plain and simple. He asserted that if the House opened the subject of altering the Constitution, he wanted to discuss whether the nation needed a Vice President at all, for the office had been created solely to service the mode of electing the President. Moreover, he wished the Congress to consider representation, whether on the basis of white population or white and slave, and the decision on this question would affect the allocation of electors to each state. South Carolina's Huger indicated that he probably supported designation but feared that adoption of that reform alone would result in the failure to secure district election. Evidently, Federalists wanted to delay the vote by opening the door to a host of other amendments. The committee voted in favor of designation by 42-22, one vote shy of two-thirds. The Committee therefore reported to the House that it opposed the amendment.[15]

The House then rejected the negative recommendation of the committee by a 24-48 vote. The House proceeded to a third reading of the amendment and the engrossed resolution was brought in and carried 47-14. The 14 negative votes came from the Federalist side of the aisle: James A. Bayard, Thomas Boude, Manasseh Cutler, John Davenport, Roger Griswold, Archibald Henderson, Benjamin Huger, Lewis R. Morris, Nathan Read, John Stanley, Benjamin Tallmadge, Samuel Tenney, George B. Upham, and Lemuel Williams.[16]

Earlier in the Senate, on April 12, DeWitt Clinton had put forward a constitutional amendment, which no longer contained the districting provision and centered on designation, which clearly advanced Republican interests. His motion was seconded and ordered to lie for consideration. On April 16, Senator Stephen R. Bradley of Vermont recommended a separate amendment requiring that electors be chosen by voters in districts.[17]

On Monday, May 3, 1802, the day the Congress had chosen to adjourn, the Senate received the House proposal. The text was short and did not reveal where and how the words would fit into Article II: "That in all future elections of President and Vice President the persons voted for shall be particularly designated, by declaring which is voted for as President and which as Vice President."[18] The Senate tabled the measure for consideration later in the afternoon when without much discussion it voted 15-8 in favor of the House proposal, just one vote shy of the mandatory two-thirds. The aye votes included southern and western Senators Robert Wright of Maryland, Stevens T. Mason and Wilson C. Nicholas of Virginia, Jesse Franklin of North Carolina, Thomas Sumter of South Carolina, Joseph Anderson and William Cocke of Tennessee, Abraham Baldwin and James Jackson of Georgia, John Breckinridge and John Brown of Kentucky, and from north of the Delaware River George Logan of Pennsylvania, DeWitt Clinton of New York, and Christopher Ellery and Theodore Foster of Rhode Island. The nay votes came from Dwight Foster of Massachusetts, Simeon Olcott of New Hampshire, Uriah Tracy of Connecticut, Gouverneur Morris of New York, Aaron Ogden of New Jersey, William H. Wells of Delaware, John E. Howard of Maryland, and David Stone of North Carolina, a Republican with a key vote on this occasion and again in the next session when the Eighth Congress revisited the proposed amendment.

Morris later felt compelled to explain to New Yorkers the reasons for his position. Having been a principal figure in the Philadelphia Convention which created the system of presidential electors, Morris reviewed the delegates' efforts to follow a procedure least likely to invite intrigue and corruption and most likely to consist with the people's voice. The Convention had anticipated all the criticisms recently leveled at the electoral college but had found that every other mode had equal or greater liabilities. Designation would mean that presidential candidates would offer the second office as bait, which would attract persons of lesser stature and abilities than the present system.[19]

Morris explained that the Philadelphia Convention had imagined the possibility that two candidates would have an equal majority of the votes of electors, and one of these might be a person of great talents and integrity while the other had fewer qualifications. Moreover, factional interests in the House might lead the Representatives to select the latter. If they did so, they would soon learn the valuable lesson that they should always vote for the best candidate. The Constitution encouraged such behavior and made fraud and corruption difficult.[20]

In many respects it is remarkable that the two houses of Congress moved with such dispatch on amending the Constitution in the late spring of 1802. Given the much more elaborate debate on designation that was to follow, particularly with respect to how designation would fit with other portions of Article II, this action appears in retrospect to have been hasty and ill advised.

These preliminary skirmishes with constitutional amendments did not mean that Federalists determined the course of events; Republicans occupied the driver's seat. Fundamental trends in the 1802 state elections left Federalists with little to celebrate. President Jefferson could claim with pride and confidence, "We have gained ground generally in the elections," and "we have lost ground in not a single district of the US except Kent county in Delaware."[21] The *National Intelligencer* published an essay which compared the relative strength of the Republican and Federalist parties in 1800 and in 1802 and concluded that the former had gained at the expense of the latter. Given congressional reapportionment in accord with the 1800 census, which augmented the electoral weight of Jeffersonian states, the present composition of state legislatures which appointed electors, and the existing mode of selecting electors, the analyst determined that Republicans would win a landslide victory if the presidential elections were held at the close of 1802.[22]

But there were signs of division among the Republicans. At the national level, the election of 1800 had opened suspicions among Jeffersonians about Burr's intentions, and nothing in the first years of the administration alleviated tension. Samuel Osgood praised President Jefferson for placing Republicans in several New York City positions but informed him that New York's real Republicans feared that these new appointees were more friendly to Burr than to Jefferson. Jefferson subsequently wrote to George Clinton for patronage advice, saying that "there is no one whose opinion would command with me greater respect than yours," and he pointedly refused to proffer an office to Matthew L. Davis, a loyal Burrite.[23] In early 1802 Burr as President of the Senate broke a tie vote and sent the bill to repeal the Judiciary Act of 1801 back to committee, a temporary setback in early 1802 but one which reverberated through the Republican Party.[24]

One sign of things to come in New York was the way the Livingston and Clinton interests combined to push Aaron Burr and John Swartwout out of the directorship of the Manhattan Bank, whose charter Burr had secured from the legislature in 1799. Eventually Swartwout accused DeWitt Clinton of trying to destroy Burr, and in reply the combative Clinton charged Swartwout of being a liar. The allegations led to a duel between the two men on July 31, 1802, an unseemly event for prominent politicians, but it did not lessen popular support for Clinton as some Federalists and Burr's friends had hoped.[25]

More serious were charges leveled against Aaron Burr by James Cheetham of the *American Citizen*, the journalistic voice of DeWitt Clinton, whose cousin, David Denniston was Cheetham's partner. Cheetham published "The Narrative of the Suppression by Colonel Burr of the History of the Administration of John Adams," which led to a series of other pieces alternately in defense of Burr and then attacking him. Ambrose Spencer thought this pamphlet war together with his intrigues for the presidency would destroy Burr's public standing. Federalist District Judge Egbert Benson observed the increase in the numbers of "honest men" as the internecine fighting among Republicans continued. But he believed the Clintonians, composed of the old antifederal elements and "Apostate or Renegade Federalists," held the advantage over Burr, who would not be able to create a third or neutral party which was "neither federal nor antifederal."[26] Gouverneur Morris also recognized that this was not a fight between equals. He fully expected the Clintonians to preponderate. What he was witnessing was a purge, not a civil war. And Federalists had to be careful of jumping on the losing side once again.[27]

In 1803 Congress returned to the matter of constitutional amendments, although no one knew for sure who the Republican floor leader in the House would be. Since William B. Giles's absence due to illness, John Randolph, Samuel Smith, and Joseph H. Nicholson all showed interest, but none had established a claim. The substantial Republican majority needed competent leadership to maintain unity, and experienced legislative leaders knew that a small majority could be disciplined more readily than a large one. Republicans would not have traded places with the Federalist minority, but they faced tests in trying to stay together on strategy and on key votes. Representative Benjamin Huger of South Carolina revived discussions on amendments when he moved on February 1, 1803 that the Senate and House come to a resolution for district election of presidential electors.[28]

On February 8, James Bayard of Delaware asked that the House assume its role as a Committee of the Whole to take up a proposal for an amendment that had lain on the table since January 3. He hoped to avoid the rush and confusion of the last session by examining the issue while there was plenty of time before adjournment. Republicans, like Samuel Smith of Maryland and Andrew Gregg of Pennsylvania, objected. Smith believed the House had to examine a report on discriminating and countervailing tariff duties, while Gregg pressed for settlement of outstanding issues related to the District of Columbia. Several Federalists disagreed and urged immediate action. Kentucky Republican Thomas T. Davis with tongue in cheek wondered what accounted for the change among those who did not want to be rushed last March but were in a hurry now. He surmised that opponents of the amendment had decided that given the composition of the House and the predilections of those in attendance, a vote on the amendment would fail. Bayard replied that he did not understand why some Representatives argued for time when so many of them had declared in the last session that they were ready to vote. But on the question to give precedence to the constitutional amendment over other issues on the agenda, the House defeated Bayard.[29]

On February 9 Roger Griswold, Federalist from Connecticut, urged that the House assume its role as a Committee of the Whole to consider the proposed constitutional amendment. The House refused. John Dawson of Virginia then asked that the Committee of the Whole be discharged from considering amendments so late in the session and moved that further discussion be deferred until the first Monday in November. The House agreed.[30]

Republicans in the House may have been waiting for more propitious times. John Taylor of Virginia hoped that in the interim Republicans could focus on designation and not be distracted by other constitutional reforms, which might disrupt the unity necessary to carry the reform effort. As John Quincy Adams had previously observed, Republicanism

> had obtained and preserves an irresistible preponderance in thirteen of the sixteen State legislatures, and the resistance in the three others scarcely maintains its ground. In both houses of Congress the majority is already decisive, but at the ensuing Congress, will be much larger. The division in the Senate is now nearly equal. But for the next two years, there will be nearly two thirds of the partizans [sic] of the present government.[31]

Adams's calculations had very weighty implications for the future of any constitutional amendment. Republican initiatives, like the repeal of the Judiciary Act of 1801, required only a simple majority in each house. The impeachment of a justice and the ratification of a treaty demanded a two-thirds majority in the upper house. But a constitutional amendment needed the approval of two-thirds of both houses and then of three-fourths of the states, and advocates of an amendment had to be mindful of the composition of Congress and of the state legislatures. James Hillhouse realized that Republicans desired postponement until the next session "under an Idea that the amendments will then be readily agreed to, and may be got through a sufficient number of the Legislatures of the individual states in the course of the Next Winter."[32]

Federalists appeared powerless to stop the deluge of Republican measures. Though they had pockets of influence in the Carolinas and Maryland and again in the small states of Delaware and New Jersey, they held a formidable competitive position only in New England. Republican Caesar Rodney's victory over James Bayard in Delaware's congressional election and an impending Republican victory in legislative elections in New Jersey deepened worries about future control of these previously stalwart Federalist states. Through 1802 and 1803 they fought a defensive struggle to preserve what they could of the system they had built in the 1790s.[33]

While the war against the judiciary reflected the present power and disposition of the Jeffersonian administration, the acquisition of Louisiana spoke to the perpetuation of Republicanism into the future. The prospect of further diminution of Federalist and New England influence, the creation of an agrarian empire linking West to South, and the willingness of the Republicans to adopt a loose interpretation of the Constitution to justify the incorporation of Louisiana prompted a vigorous reaction from the Federalist minority. In "The Connecticut Address" citizens of the "first respectability" defended state institutions against encroachment by Republicans seeking "to subvert the system of our state government."[34] In New York the *Evening Post* published a series of articles refuting the pro-Republican essays of Algernon Sidney, Publius, and Greene as direct attacks on the federal system, and reprinted "The Mirror, The Government of the United States Not a Democracy" to show that the Constitution had established a republican and federal government, which sought to keep watch over and restrain the democratic part. The desire to provide correct instruction about the Constitution linked all of these separate pieces.[35]

Christopher Gore of Massachusetts realized that the eastern states had almost no impact on public policy at the national level. Because of Republican ties to the West, the Jefferson administration had no need to heed critics. New England Federalists, like Fisher Ames and Timothy Pickering of Massachusetts and William Plumer of New Hampshire, contemplated the secession of the Northeast. In the plans of the Essex Junto, New York played an important role, for the inclusion of this crucial middle state would add greatly to their effectiveness. To execute such a cooperative venture, however, required victory at the polls, and for this purpose some placed their hopes on Aaron Burr.[36]

The loss of power for Federalists and the Northeast also concerned Rufus King, who was no friend to secession plots. He realized that the Republican zeal for constitutional change, evidenced not only by the attack on the judiciary but in the drive for a designation amendment, should not be encouraged. But the likelihood of Federalist failures and the threat of Republicanism gaining a permanent hold on the national government led King to struggle with the suggestion of Pickering and other New Englanders for a Federalist amendment which would attack the basis of Southern power, the three-fifths clause. Such a change would restore to New Englanders equality with Southerners and diminish the influence of the Jeffersonian coalition of the South and West.[37]

While Republicans welcomed the advancing tide of democracy and delighted in the ebb of Federalism, they did not feel secure. They suspected that New England and Federalists, demoralized and resenting their diminished capacities, could play the role of dissidents--willing to be the spoiler at best and disunionist at worst. Unable to elect their own presidential and vice presidential candidates, Federalists retained the power of choosing between the two Republican candidates for President and thereby wreak havoc with the best laid plans of the Jeffersonians. Had the Federalists a competitive potential, they would support their own candidates and their electors would vote for the party ticket, as they had done in every previous election. Only when Federalist chances became hopeless did it become attractive for their electors to choose a Republican.

Republicans in New York, having watched the Federalists in the state playing just such a mischievous role in the continuing dispute between Clintonians and Burrites, understood as well as any how difficult it was to maintain unity and to press on with their political agenda under such conditions. Republicans sought a guarantee against Federalist machinations, and they were willing to amend the Constitution to secure this goal.

12

The House Initiates an Amendment

The *Aurora* informed its readers that there were two principal items of business on the agenda for the Eighth Congress. The first dealt with the purchase of Louisiana and the second with a constitutional amendment to safeguard the republic against the recurrence of the 1801 crisis, when Federalists sought to make Burr President. *The United States Chronicle*, on the other hand, noted that the President called this session to "secure his Seat, during his own pleasure" and left for the people only "submission."[1]

On Monday, October 17, 1803, when the House began the first session, Republicans held an advantage of 96-38 votes and easily selected for Speaker Nathaniel Macon of North Carolina, a Republican admired by many Federalists for his fairness and impartiality. Virginia Congressman John Dawson offered the designation amendment, and the House resolved itself into a Committee of the Whole to consider it. Joseph H. Nicholson raised an important point: the relationship between designation and the remainder of Article II of the Constitution required further explication. He made an initial attempt:

> The person voted for as President, having the greatest number of votes, shall be the President, if such number be a majority of all the Electors appointed; and if no person have such majority, then from the five highest on the list of those voted for as President, the House of Representatives shall immediately choose by ballot one of them as President. And in every case, the person voted for as Vice President having the greatest number of votes, shall be the Vice President. But if there should be two or more who have equal votes, the Senate shall choose one of them for Vice President.[2]

The debate within the Committee now began in earnest. Representing Virginia, one of the larger states in the Union, John Clopton expressed reservations about the resort to the five highest on the list in the contingency election. With designation, Clopton thought that five might contribute to the selection of one without substantial support in the country. He recommended reducing the number to two and suggested that the same apply in the contingency election for Vice President.[3]

On Thursday, October 20, 1803 Nicholson asked that the House create a committee of seventeen, consisting of one Representative from each state, to work out the details of the amendment. The House concurred and named John Dawson of Virginia, Silas Betton of New Hampshire, Manasseh Cutler of Massachusetts, Joseph Stanton, Jr. of Rhode Island, Samuel W. Dana of Connecticut, James Elliot of Vermont, John Smith of New York, John Smilie of Pennsylvania, Caesar A. Rodney of Delaware, Joseph H. Nicholson of Maryland, Thomas Sandford of Kentucky, William Blackledge of North Carolina, George W. Campbell of Tennessee, Richard Winn of South Carolina, David Meriwether of Georgia, Jeremiah Morrow of Ohio, and William Lattimore of the Mississippi Territory.[4]

Federalist Benjamin Huger then reminded the House that the current proposal for designation had originated in New York and had been submitted to the Seventh Congress. New York had also asked for the district elections of presidential electors, and in part out of respect for that state he proposed to add this provision to the proposed amendment. The select committee of seventeen received his proposal, totally ignored it, and allowed it to die.[5]

On October 23, John Dawson reported a designation resolution with several changes from the committee of seventeen:

> The person having a majority of all the Electors appointed shall be the President; and if there shall be no such majority, the President shall be chosen from the highest numbers, not exceeding three, on the list for President, by the House of Representatives, in the manner directed by the Constitution. The person having the greatest number of votes as Vice President shall be the Vice President; and in case of an equal number of votes for two or more persons for Vice President, they being the highest on the list, the Senate shall choose the Vice President from those having such equal number, in the manner directed by the Constitution.[6]

The House referred the report to the Committee of the Whole.

Perhaps the clearest explanation of why Republicans favored designation came from Virginian John Clopton. Clopton worked through a hypothetical example for his colleagues. Given four candidates, A, B, C, and D, 95 electors cast their first votes for A for President and divide their second vote, 75 for C and 20 for D for Vice President. The remaining 81 electors cast their first votes for B for President and divide their second vote, 25 for C and 56 for D for Vice President. Under the present system, Clopton calculated that C would become

President, though no elector wanted C for that office.   Clopton played on memories of 1801 when Federalists had tried to foist on the people a person few wanted for President. With designation, A would become President and C Vice President.   Hence the wishes of the ninety-five electors, who comprised a majority of the electors, would prevail in both instances.[7]

What Clopton described made sense in 1803. It probably reflected the thinking of most members of the House and indicated that they lived in a political world different from that of the framers. Although the framers expected George Washington to be the sole candidate for President in the first election, they had projected beyond a Washington presidency. In so doing, they erred on at least three points. First, they did not make sufficient allowance for the way the election of Washington would set precedents which would influence later developments. In 1789 and again in 1792, the electors used one vote for Washington for President and the second vote for a Vice President. By 1796 many Americans thought of this practice as natural. Second, the delegates in Philadelphia in 1787, with the notable exceptions of James Wilson and Abraham Baldwin, underestimated how quickly the new federal government would generate national political figures capable of winning widespread popular support. The device of the double vote was not needed to procure majorities. Third, the founding fathers, though alert to the role of political parties at the state level, did not anticipate how quickly two parties, inchoate as they were, would form on the national level. These parties wanted victory for their tickets. Clopton's model and the conclusions he drew from it would not have made much sense to them in 1787; they were based on the working assumptions of politicians developed within fifteen years of ratification.

On Monday, October 24, the Committee of the Whole engaged in an extensive debate on the report. The major dispute involved the number of candidates to be considered in a contingency election, which affected small states differently than large states and Federalists differently than Republicans. Dawson began with the moderate position that any amendment should leave as much of the original language and intent of the Constitution as possible. Since Article II had allowed for five names in a contingency election, the committee decided to couple designation with three candidates for President and two for Vice President.[8]

When Republican Joseph H. Nicholson of Maryland argued that there was no harm in the House's reviewing all candidates who received electoral votes, Federalist Calvin Goddard of Connecticut rose in support. As a representative of a small state, Goddard claimed that the entire thrust of the designation amendment diminished the influence of the small states and enhanced that of the large states whose candidates were likely to prevail in the selection of both executive offices. Limiting the number in the contingency election further depleted the power of small states. But Congressmen from all the small states did not rally to this position. When the members took a vote on Nicholson's proposed change, they defeated it soundly by 29-77.[9]

Republican Congressman Smilie of Pennsylvania then offered to substitute the number five for three in the committee resolution to test House sentiment. Goddard spoke predictably in favor. He rejected any suggestion that the will of the people was synonymous with the will of Virginia, New York, and Pennsylvania, all states which were not only large but Republican in sympathy. But before the matter could be pursued further, the Committee rose to review issues related to Louisiana, another matter of great constitutional import and partisan interest in the House.

On Wednesday, October 26, 1803 the Committee of the Whole returned to examine the resolution, which included the words *not exceeding three*, which was read twice, amended, and agreed to by the House. But on Thursday, October 27, the House briefly revisited the debate of the previous day, and Joseph Clay, a Pennsylvania colleague of Smilie, wanted to strike out *three* and insert *five*. After a brief flurry of predictable statements for and against this change and efforts to accommodate as many House members' wishes as possible in order to maintain the momentum for designation, the Committee agreed to the change. The House then turned its attention to the Louisiana Treaty.[10]

James Hillhouse thought that advocates of amendment had not yet agreed among themselves on what they wanted, and he was on the mark. But already he sensed that it was only a matter of time before the Republicans concerted their efforts, and he placed his hopes on deliberative state legislatures to check the Republican Congress. He believed that the Constitution should be placed high above ordinary law and be protected from partisan tampering. The fact that the proposed amendments "are publickly avowed to be intended to operate upon the next Presidential Election" was by itself sufficient reason for rejection. "No amendment to the Constitution ought ever to be adopted with a view of aiding or influencing a *particular* Election."[11] Indeed, other Federalist Representatives and Senators began to portray the amendment as a clearly partisan measure, which differed in this respect from all previous amendments to the Constitution. Even more important, Hillhouse and other Federalists began to argue that the Constitution as a higher law possessed an almost sacred quality; people should revere it and prevent its despoliation. Republicans had to be careful that their repeal of the judiciary act of 1801, the acquisition of Louisiana, impending impeachment proceedings against Federalist judges, and advocacy of the designation amendment did not make them vulnerable to this charge.

Finally, on Friday, October 28, 1803 the House took up the proposed amendment to the Constitution, and a grand debate occurred, most of it relating to the large-versus-small state issue. Federalist speakers presented a historical view of Article II. Federalist Gaylord Griswold of New York, a Yale graduate, lawyer, and native of Connecticut, and Benjamin Huger, a rice planter from South Carolina, asserted that compromises between the large and small states allowed for the formation of the Constitution. Huger went so far as to claim that the Constitution created a union of large and small states, not of the people. The large states wanted to elect the President by direct popular vote, while the small states insisted on an equal vote for every state. The delegates created the present system as a compromise: the large states had the advantage in the election by electoral votes and the small states gained the edge in contingency elections in the House. According to Huger, the larger states are compelled by the double vote of electors to pursue one of three options: (1) give an equal number of votes to two candidates and let the House choose the President, (2) cast very large portions of votes to them in the hope of having them finish first and second but making it possible for small states to reverse the order, or (3) concentrate behind one candidate and allow others to choose the second officer.

It followed that the smaller states, by which Griswold and Huger meant Federalist states, had an interest in seeing elections determined in the House, not by presidential electors. Designation eliminated one of the avenues to House elections. These two Congressmen did not share with Alexander Hamilton any enthusiasm for the proposed amendment. By the same token, Republicans had nothing to gain from any of the scenarios preferred by Griswold and Huger.[12]

The next speakers drifted to other topics. Seth Hastings, Representative from Massachusetts, continued the Federalist offensive by predicting that designation would denigrate the office of Vice President. In the future, electors would use only one vote for a candidate qualified for the Presidency and the other would go to a person qualified to preside over the Senate. Hastings also suggested that, if the Congress was going to look seriously at correcting flaws in the existing Constitution, it should focus on the three-fifths clause which affected the allocation of electors. John C. Smith of Connecticut tried to provoke Republicans to respond by asking, "whether the present resolution had not grown out of an overweening anxiety to secure, at all hazards, the re-election of the present Chief Magistrate?"[13] When the Speaker of the House ruled that it was inappropriate to introduce the President into the debate, Smith replied that he meant no disrespect. Still, he would ask that no change should be made in the electoral provisions while the incumbent is a candidate for re-election.

After a few final exchanges by New England Congressmen Eustis, Hastings, and Dana over whether Representatives were to obey mandates from state legislatures, Republican Matthew Lyon of Kentucky, formerly of Vermont and notorious for having spat on Roger Griswold in an earlier encounter, got in a final word. He denounced the introduction of the "hackneyed" topic of the three-fifths clause as reflecting ignorance of blacks who as slaves were much more useful and beneficial than those who were free. He considered that whenever this subject came up it was "brought up, as mere matter of exclamation, and intended to create popular murmur and discontent."[14] With that Republican blast and with no substantive Republican speech, the Republicans spoke with their votes at two-thirty in the afternoon. They passed the resolution by the requisite constitutional majority, 88-39, and brought what they thought would be an end to their role in framing the Twelfth Amendment on October 28, 1803. But they had reckoned without the Senate![15]

13

The Senate Adopts a Different Plan

On October 17, 1803, DeWitt Clinton wrote to his wife from Washington, D.C., indicating that he expected "a speedy conclusion as to those points that demand my presence here and of course a speedy return to my family."[1] He may have relied on the 24-9 Republican advantage in the Senate, but his confidence was ill founded. On behalf of the New York legislature, Clinton moved for adoption of a carelessly drawn designation amendment in the United States Senate on October 21. His proposal included a provision that

> The person having the greatest number of votes for President shall be President, if such number be a majority of the whole number of Electors appointed, and if there be more than one who have such majority, and have an equal number of votes, then the House of Representatives shall immediately choose by ballot one of them for President; and if no person have a majority, then from the___highest on the list, the said House shall, in like manner, choose the President.[2]

When the Senate began its review of this amendment on Saturday, October 22, Clinton sought to move expeditiously. If the Senate required three separate readings of resolutions on three separate days, he requested that his motion be read a second time now so that it would be ready for a third reading on Monday. The Senate might then send the amendment to the state legislatures, two of which, Tennessee and Vermont, were then in session. President Pro Tem John Brown determined that the rules and proceedings of the Senate did not require that a resolution in which the concurrence of the other house was necessary should be read three times on separate days, and cleared the way for prompt action.[3]

Fellow Republican Senator Stephen R. Bradley of Vermont moved to strike out the embarrassing section referring to candidates having equal and majority votes, an impossibility after designation. Seconded by Clinton, the motion carried. Bradley also wished to require a majority vote of the electors to select the Vice President in the first instance and of the Senate to make the choice in the second. Clinton replied that he had not anticipated this motion, but considered it justified. Then Republican Pierce Butler of South Carolina, signaling that his vote should not be placed in his party's column yet, recommended that in future elections for President no one should be eligible more than four years in any period of eight years. Jonathan Dayton of New Jersey moved that the Clinton resolution and the various proposals for amendments be sent to a select committee instead of being debated on the floor. Butler agreed on proceeding carefully, and his formal motion for a committee carried by a bare 16-15 vote. The Senate then named Butler, Bradley, Clinton, Wilson Cary Nicholas of Virginia, and Samuel Smith of Maryland to the committee.[4]

On Sunday, October 23, the select committee prepared a report, which it printed and distributed that evening to Senators at their boarding houses. William Plumer, Federalist from New Hampshire and no friend of Clinton, noted that the designation proposal had been approved by the New York legislature for two successive years and introduced by Clinton with assurances that he had thought about the resolution often. Yet within a matter of few hours of discussion, Clinton seconded a motion to strike a part of it and then voted to add a whole new principle to it.[5]

On Monday, October 24, Butler reported on behalf of the committee. Dayton, the Federalist and Burrite from New Jersey, and Clinton, the anti-Burrite Republican from New York, then engaged in a verbal skirmish. The former proposed striking out any reference to the Vice President, since designation removed any useful purpose for the office. Elimination of the office made designation moot. Uriah Tracy of Connecticut seconded the motion. Clinton replied that Dayton sought to distract the discussion from the main point and wanted delays which would make it difficult for the amendment to reach legislatures at convenient times. Dayton countered that Clinton "arraign[ed] motives instead of meeting arguments."[6] Wilson Cary Nicholas opposed Dayton's motion; he saw no way that the elimination of the vice presidency could be examined now. Focusing on what was the overriding Republican concern, he reported that over the next two to three months, the legislatures of two-thirds to three-quarters of the states would be in session. It was imperative that Congress submit a designation amendment in timely fashion.

Several other Senators, including Republicans Pierce Butler and Thomas Worthington of Ohio, moved for postponement so that they could have adequate time to think about the subject. A stalwart Republican supporter of designation, James Jackson of Georgia, on this occasion supported the Federalist from New Jersey partly because he liked the idea of abolishing the Vice Presidency, which was "the fifth wheel to a coach." After declaring, "I am not for doing business on horseback," he asked, "were the State Legislatures all about to die?"[7] Surely, they could be reconvened if Congress submitted an amendment to them. The question for postponement lost by a narrow 15-16 vote. Then Dayton got in the final word, attacking Clinton's "rudeness and indecency of language" and declaring that "there would be a fitter time and a fitter place for taking that notice of it which it merited."[8] Now the Senate adopted a motion for adjournment.

This clash involving "warm expressions" between DeWitt Clinton and Jonathan Dayton served as a reminder of the hostilities between Clinton and Dayton's political ally, Aaron Burr. Dayton, who must have been aware of the earlier Clinton-Swartwout duel, suggested that Clinton's denial of reading other people's motives amounted to an accusation that Dayton was a liar. According to Plumer, Dayton dispatched the Senate doorkeeper to Clinton that evening to ask for an explanation, and Clinton replied through a friend that both he and Dayton should make concessions. Dayton, however, insisted on an answer to his note. At eleven o'clock, he sent Pierce Butler to visit Clinton and gave him authority to accept an honorable reply or to issue a challenge to a duel. Clinton readily complied with a letter of apology. One copy went to Dayton and a second to Robert Wright of Maryland.

Intermediaries for the two, General Samuel Smith and Wright, worked out a satisfactory resolution and no formal challenge was ever issued. Clinton, in the meantime, took leave of the Senate. Wright, who read Clinton's statement, explained that the reason for pushing so hard for prompt action resulted from the desire of Clinton, the mover of the motion, to be present for the completion of the task before he returned to New York. But since others requested time, Wright thought it proper to provide it. Wilson Cary Nicholas of Virginia applauded Clinton's handling of the affair and expressed regret that the New Yorker had withdrawn from the Senate, where his talents were very much needed. William Plumer, on the other hand, had no regrets at the departure of one he described as bitter, vindictive, insolent, and haughty. Clinton's enemies in New York took delight in what they portrayed as a hasty and cowardly retreat from Washington.[9]

On November 4, 1803 Clinton formally resigned from the Senate to assume the post of Mayor of New York City. From the final days of October when the House passed its version of the designation amendment through mid November, the Senate occupied itself with other matters, such as the Louisiana Treaty. Timothy Pickering hinted at another reason for the leisurely pace. For four or five days in a row, most members of Congress joined other residents of Washington and nearby Maryland and Virginia to attend the race track, located several miles from the Capitol. William Eustis also noted that during the racing week portions of the ceiling in the Senate chambers collapsed, "a part of which had like to have killed Dayton," and necessitated recessing.[10] On Friday, November 11, Senator Thomas Worthington of Ohio reported that he had received a resolution from his state urging adoption of a designation amendment, but even that prompting did not end the hiatus in proceedings. On November 14, William Wells of Delaware urged resumption of work on designation, which elicited from John Taylor, William Cocke, and Robert Wright the defense that they did not have all of their supporters present. William Plumer told his brother that the Senate was tinkering with the Constitution for which the House had already agreed "to rivet a patch of *paper*" over a hole it had found.[11]

On Wednesday, November 16, 1803, the Senate decided to make the designation amendment the order of the day for Monday, November 21. Dayton wrote to Burr, informing him of the schedule and the full and free discussion likely to take place. Dayton advised, "You would do well to loiter on your way so as not to reach this place before Wednesday."[12] Indeed, Burr had no desire to preside over the Senate on an occasion when so many references would be directed to his office and to the election of 1800.

On November 23, the Senate began in earnest to consider the amendment, but in so doing it took no official notice of the House resolution for designation. Instead of working with the House text, making amendments, and then working to gain concurrence, the Senate proceeded on its own.[13]

President Pro Tem John Brown's inquiry whether the two-thirds vote required for passage of a constitutional amendment applied to all votes or only the final vote precipitated a lengthy, exasperating argument on procedure, a portent of things to come. The Senate went further afield in argument over whether the Vice President could vote on issues related to a constitutional amendment should there be a tie among the Senators. On the question of whether two-thirds was required on all votes, the Senate decided in the negative, with John Quincy Adams showing some independence from his Federalist colleagues by voting with the majority. Pierce Butler then inquired whether that question could be settled short of a two-thirds vote, and Brown replied that it could.[14]

When the Senators proceeded to the substance of the resolution, they rejected Dayton's motion to strike out all references to the Vice President. Then they moved to introduce three elements absent in the House version: (1) requiring a majority vote of the electors, instead of a plurality, for election of the Vice President, (2) reducing from five to three the number of candidates placed before the House of Representatives in a contingency election, and (3) providing for the eventuality should the House fail to elect a President by March 4.[15]

In the course of discussions on November 23, Stephen Bradley indicated once again his displeasure with the clause that allowed a Vice President to be chosen by less than a majority vote. He favored the majority requirement for an officer who might succeed to the top office on the death, disability, or resignation of the President. Otherwise, designation would diminish the second office, which "would be hawked about at market, and given as change for votes for the Presidency," a charge often made by opponents of designation.[16] Robert Wright of Maryland reminded the Senate that the resolutions from Vermont on November 5, 1799, and those of Massachusetts on March 4, 1800 endorsing the Vermont proposals recommended designation and a majority vote of electors for the election of the Vice President. The Senate majority agreed with Bradley and Wright.

The Senators engaged in the most extensive and most repetitive debates over the question of numbers, whether three or five, and their arguments were linked closely to the supposed claims of the large and small states. The Federalists and a few Republicans argued for the larger number as the Constitution presently allowed. Republican Pierce Butler, a member of the committee of thirteen at the Philadelphia Convention, conceded that intrigues in previous presidential elections had been troublesome, but he considered the circumstances of 1800 and 1801 to be highly unusual and not likely to recur. Designation could provide a safeguard, but at the cost of "putting into the hands of four of the large States the perpetual choice of President" and, for that matter, Vice President. He could not in good conscience depart from the decisions reached in Philadelphia solely to prevent a Federalist Vice President. He asked, "When we were as Republicans out of power, did we not reprobate such conduct?"[17]

On November 24, John Quincy Adams said he thought five was acceptable to Massachusetts as well as to many small states. He reminded Senators that the House seemed attached to it. On November 29, Adams explained that his preference for the larger number derived also from his concern for preserving the federative character of the office of President. The change to three attacked this principle in favor of a more popularly elected President by giving numerical majorities among the people, rather than the balance between the people and the states, the deciding voice.[18]

Republican speakers tried to minimize the allegedly antagonistic positions of large and small states. Samuel Smith thought the whole issue grossly overblown. He saw Maryland, once belonging to the larger states but now ranking among the intermediate states, as neither large nor small. The framers intended to make the chief officers of the national government as immediately accountable to the people as possible, he claimed. Accepting three in a contingency election accorded with the goal of respecting the wishes of the people. Retaining five would serve as an incentive for minor candidates to enter the contest, weaken the discipline of two major parties, and result in most presidential elections going to the House for resolution.

Most of all, Smith wanted to avoid the trauma of 1801, when a minority sought to impose on the nation a candidate not of its original choice. That failing, the minority expressed a willingness to resort to the creation of a President by law, depriving the people of their choice for President. Smith did not want to depend totally on the good will of a future House or the integrity of future electors to vote only for candidates of their own party. Designation would head off most contests from ever reaching the House, where the votes of nine states with but one-fifth of the population of the nation could decide. For Smith the essential question was majority rule and minority compliance, not large states versus small, and this view accorded well with Republican principles.[19]

William Cocke of Tennessee protested that the issue involved not the protection of small states but the self-interests of a minority Federalist Party. Some accused the sponsors of designation of trying to make sure that no Federalist

Vice President would be elected. Showing no sympathy for the plight of Federalism, Cocke asserted that this was precisely the point.[20]

John Taylor of Caroline County, Virginia, spoke more dispassionately, yet firmly, against the small state argument. Declaring himself opposed to any classification of states designed to foment jealousies and anxieties which would threaten the peace of the country, Taylor maintained that Senators should realize that the matter of numbers related directly to contingency elections. If they wanted to keep elections out of the House, where many states are represented by a tiny handful of Representatives, they should support designation, which would encourage electors to make the selection.[21]

On Friday, November 25, Senators could read the printed version of the amended resolution, but they chose to defer substantive discussions because of an illness to Joseph Anderson of Tennessee. On Monday, Anderson remained incapacitated. Some anxious observers deplored the delay and attributed it to Pierce Butler, who seemed to be insisting on support for another amendment to place term limitations on the President. He may also have been taking out his frustrations with the administration for personal slights on patronage matters. But the delays resulted more from the need by Republican leaders to have a two-thirds vote on hand; they could not spare a single vote.[22]

On November 29, 1803 the question was called to put in *five* and it failed. The question was then put to insert *three*, and it passed. The Senate spent most of the next day in recursive debate. Plumer believed that the Republican majority hoped to take a final vote, but he realized by late afternoon that pushing too hard might antagonize some wavering colleagues and drive them to join the Federalist minority. Hence, Republican senators agreed to adjournment.[23]

The Senate proceedings through November revealed as much about strategy as about substance. The Republican majority had to remain firm enough to resist Federalist obstructionism without antagonizing those Republicans who had reservations with one feature or another of the complex resolution, while Federalists had constantly to woo wavering Republicans by appealing to arguments on the high ground, those based on the sanctity of the Constitution and the delicate balance between large and small states, and by seeking delays and complicating amendments. Although most Republicans agreed in principle on the need for designation, they differed among themselves over details and language. Because the final two-thirds vote would be close and there were a few Republicans, like Butler, who might desert, proponents had to be alert to attendance of all their members and keep tabs on the vote count. On November 25th and again three days later, the absence of Senator Anderson occasioned postponement of further consideration. John Taylor was eager to get to a final vote on November 30, for he feared that John Condit of New Jersey would have to leave soon to attend to an ailing daughter. The desire to proceed swiftly led the Republican majority on some days to refrain from responding to minority arguments, and this silence provoked Federalists to bait them with tough, hard-hitting, sometimes personal, attacks.[24]

The Senators re-engaged in earnest on Thursday, December 1, when Timothy Pickering introduced a motion which sent the Senate scurrying. He wanted a provision stating that the President should be chosen by law, if the House in a contingency election should fail to make a choice within twenty-four hours. In reply to Uriah Tracy who asked for elaboration, Pickering explained, "The States might choose by lot or by ballot in a box, which the President might collect; or a number of names might be put in a box from which the Speaker might draw one."[25] Samuel Smith suggested throwing the dice to fill the Executive Chair. It seemed that opponents were determined to do everything which parliamentary procedure allowed to stall and block passage of designation.[26]

Republicans were getting impatient with Federalist tactics. Smith reiterated that if the Congress had defied popular choice and elected a President by law in 1801, "the person, whoever he might have been, would have met the fate of a usurper, and his head would not have remained on his shoulders twenty-four hours."[27] Fellow Marylander Robert Wright questioned the seriousness of the amendment's foes, who were willing to turn to a lottery to choose the President.[28]

After Timothy Pickering changed his motion to provide for election by law in the event that Congress failed within forty-eight hours after March 4 to make a choice, the Senate voted and rejected it by voice vote. Adams put forward a variant of the Pickering motion, which consumed time and delayed further progress. But Republicans, for all their exasperation, realized that they had to make provision for the failure of the contingency process. Wilson Cary Nicholas, for example, had privately expressed fears of just this kind of national crisis.[29]

On Friday, December 2, John Taylor proposed and Robert Wright seconded a motion:

And if the House of Representatives shall not choose a President whenever the right of choice shall devolve upon them, before the 4th day of March next following, then the Vice President shall act as President, as in case of the death or other Constitutional disability of the President.[30]

Clearly Republicans sought a reasonable compromise. Since the ascension of the Vice President to the presidency occurred in the context of a designated electoral vote, this person most likely would represent the majority party. The Senate accepted the motion.[31]

Adams proposed an additional change to take care of the eventuality of a vacancy in the vice presidency on March 4 by having the Congress prepared to act. Republicans had so far treated Adams gently because he had initially expressed support for designation, but they must have become increasingly certain of having a two-thirds vote by the sharpness of their reactions to his remarks. After chiding Adams for conjuring up such an improbable scenario, James Jackson reminded the Massachusetts Senator that one-third of the Senate seats would be vacated after March 4, and the remaining two-thirds would be dispersed. Robert Wright pointed out that an even more serious difficulty was the non-existence of the House of Representatives after March 4. Adams did not shine in his attempts to answer Jackson and Wright, and his amendment was voted down without a division.[32]

December 2 became a marathon session, starting at eleven o'clock in the morning and finishing near ten at night, as one Senator after another delivered lengthy orations prior to the final question on the resolution. Adams thought that Uriah Tracy for the opposition and John Taylor for the proponents excelled, but most speakers gave good civics lessons on this occasion.[33]

Tracy, who held a bitterly antidemocratic philosophy, gave a summation of the minority position and launched into a major address, notable for its care, balance, and thoroughness, subject only to the criticism that it was more than the subject required. Later reprinted and circulated throughout the Northeast in pamphlet form, Tracy's argument provided the best single statement of the Federalist position. In what must have consumed several hours, Tracy entered into an extensive discussion of the amendment. He began with the major premise that the amendment would dilute the influence of the small states and strengthen that of the large ones. He included all except New York, Pennsylvania, Virginia, North Carolina, Georgia, Ohio, Kentucky, and Tennessee as small states.[34]

Tracy believed that the text of the Constitution and the testimony of the framers made clear that the document was primarily a compromise between large and small states. Central to this compromise was the "federative principle," which he defined as the equality of the states. This principle operated most conspicuously in the selection of the President. The allocation of presidential electors took into account both popular and federative elements, and in the contingency election in the House the equality of states prevailed. Of course, the composition of the House and Senate also reflected the balance of rival interests. The proposed amendment to the Constitution would move the nation in the direction of a consolidated, simple republic.

He found the operation of the existing electoral system to be mystical and wonderful. The electors' job required them to nominate two persons for President though they could not know which would gain election. The absence of certainty encouraged them to vote only for those best qualified to serve. Small states benefitted because their electors could choose from the candidates submitted by electors from the large states and make one of them President; or, should the electors from large states anticipate such behavior and scatter their second votes, the small states could secure the Vice Presidency for one of their own. Tracy's account of large and small states made political sense in the world of 1803 only by substituting South and West for large and North and East for small, or, better still, majority and Republican for large and minority and Federalist for small. He asserted that designation and the limitation to three candidates in the contingency election both had the effect of diminishing the influence of the small states.

Moreover, Tracy feared that designation was but the beginning of a wave of alterations to the Constitution, "the bulwark of the feeble members of the Confederacy."[35] Experience offered no justification for tampering with the Constitution and attempting an innovation whose consequences could not be fully anticipated. In the previous election, the House voting by states made a choice, and the person selected was the candidate of the great states. This decision was rooted in the federative principle, for more Representatives voted for Burr than for Jefferson. He knew of no intrigue by either candidate and absolved Aaron Burr of any conspiracy to steal the election. The public will had full expression in the votes of electors who cast two votes for President; thereafter the Constitution prescribed that the federative will of the House determine who should be President and who Vice President. The large states exceeded their proper powers in trying to make this distinction, for the Constitution intended that the Vice President should be discovered only in the process of electing the President.

Tracy recollected that when the electors cast their votes, there were expectations that Burr might receive a vote or two in one of the eastern states. Had he gotten such a vote, he would have been elected President without the intervention of the House. The majority party in the future could avoid such a prospect by having their electors scatter their second votes instead of coalescing around one person. That course would open prospects for the minority party to elect a Vice President. Designation, however, and the requirement that each executive officer must have a majority of the electoral votes to win meant that the same party would take both. Tracy was right on the mark.

Admitting that the present system might put an occasional election in the House, Tracy remained confident that no reform was necessary. He believed that electors could be more easily corrupted than members of the House of Representatives because the former worked outside the public purview, while the Congress operated in the open. On this point, Tracy seems to have disagreed with many framers of the Constitution. He repeated the prediction of Federalist colleagues that designation would produce inferior Vice Presidents. Future Vice Presidents would come from large states capable of delivering electoral votes for presidential candidates.[36]

Tracy moved toward his conclusion by turning to the requirements for a two-thirds vote in each House in order for a constitutional amendment to proceed. He insisted that the true meaning of two-thirds of both Houses meant two-thirds of all the members, or in the present case 23 of the 34 Senators and 91 Representatives. He feared the consequences of a ruling that two-thirds of those present at any time could propose an amendment, for such would make it easier to change the Constitution.[37]

John Taylor took the floor and described all the rhetoric of the opposition as fanning hostilities and suspicions of the small states against the large, the people against changing the Constitution, and Senators against other Senators.

According to Tracy and his Federalist philosophy, the Constitution vested the minority with the right to rule. Taylor found that to be false. The Constitution gave the majority of the people and the majority of the states the power to govern.[38]

Hence the issue was not one between large and small states, but between the people and the House of Representatives. Designation and the reduction of candidates in the contingency election to three increased the likelihood of the people's making the choice (assuming that the electors spoke for the people more immediately and specifically in this matter than Representatives) and reduced the chances of a House election. These changes also ruled out a Federalist Vice President, and Taylor approved of this result. It would be unwise to have a "minor monarchical faction" choose the Vice President, who could succeed to the first office. Taylor scored partisan points, while he focused on preventing a recurrence of the 1800 and 1801 political crisis. He wanted to confine reform to these points and not to open the door to wholesale changes in the Constitution. In this way, he and the Republican majority showed their respect for the work of the framers and tried to shield themselves from charges of tinkering with the fundamental law.[39]

At 7:50 P.M., the question was called for inserting the number *three* into the proposed amendment. It carried 21-11. Dayton believed that the question could not be called on the designation amendment before examining other matters in the committee report, including the proposal to limit the number of terms of the President. Pierce Butler agreed. The Senate did not.[40]

In spite of the lateness of the hour and the mounting impatience of the members, Senators engaged in a last go-around, clearing the air of what they claimed were misstatements and misinterpretations of their positions. John Quincy Adams, Samuel Smith, Uriah Tracy, James Breckinridge, and Pierce Butler spoke alternately against and for the resolution. Then the question was finally called, and the ayes prevailed 22-10. The majority was composed of Christopher Ellery and Samuel J. Potter of Rhode Island, Stephen Bradley and Israel Smith of Vermont, Theodorus Bailey of New York, John Condit of New Jersey, George Logan and Samuel Maclay of Pennsylvania, Samuel Smith and Robert Wright of Maryland, Wilson Cary Nicholas and John Taylor of Virginia, Jesse Franklin and David Stone of North Carolina, Abraham Baldwin and James Jackson of Georgia, John Smith and Thomas Worthington of Ohio, Joseph Anderson and William Cocke of Tennessee, and John Breckinridge and John Brown of Kentucky. The acquiescence of Stone, who had cast the decisive vote against an earlier version of the designation amendment in March of 1802, provided the margin of victory. The minority consisted of John Quincy Adams and Timothy Pickering of Massachusetts, James Hillhouse and Uriah Tracy of Connecticut, Simeon Olcott and William Plumer of New Hampshire, Jonathan Dayton of New Jersey, William H. Wells and Samuel White of Delaware--all Federalists--and Pierce Butler of South Carolina, the lone Republican to oppose the amendment, who was castigated as a traitor like Burr to Republican orthodoxy.[41]

Uriah Tracy pleaded that twenty-two ayes did not suffice to meet the criterion of two-thirds of the Senate which consisted of thirty-four members from seventeen states. The President ruled, however, that the vote conformed to the Constitution and previous usage in the Senate; hence, he declared the question carried. Thus on December 2, 1803, the Senate concluded its work on the amendment.

On the next day, Wilson Cary Nicholas wrote to his former colleague, DeWitt Clinton, to apprise him of the status of both the quarrel with Dayton and the amendment. On the former he assured Clinton of a good outcome. There continued to be a delay only because of the unintended absence of General Smith. On the latter, Nicholas reported passage around ten o'clock at night on December 2. He took credit for securing the assent of David Stone of North Carolina, whose reservations were overcome. All in all, Nicholas considered the task from beginning to end to be "the most arduous work we ever engaged in, persevering and artful enemies in our front, with insincere friends in our own ranks; we deserve some credit for our success."[42]

Federalists, particularly those from New England, believed the amendment augured ill for the future. James Hillhouse feared a wholesale attack on the Constitution, which deserved to be treated as an inviolable text. William Plumer of New Hampshire agreed. He was convinced that the desire to assure the re-election of Jefferson motivated the change of the Constitution, and Federalist New England could do nothing to stop it. At the root of Republican power, he thought, was slavery and the three-fifths clause, which secured Jefferson's election in 1800 and which provided the additional Congressmen needed to pass the amendment in the House of Representatives. As a result, Republicans held the power to destroy the federative principle and, should they be successful, Republicans would unleash a democratic fury.[43]

14

The House Concurs

On Tuesday, December 6, 1803 the House received the Senate proposal for a constitutional amendment and resolved itself into a Committee of the Whole. William Plumer anticipated that there might be some resistance there because the proposal is "very different from the one they sent to us," and several Congressmen expressed annoyance with the Senate and sought postponement. But Republican managers could not afford to have challenges to or alterations in the Senate text, for some Republican Senators had left Washington to attend to personal affairs and escape the reclusive life in the new national capital. They could not afford further delays.[1]

Roger Griswold of Connecticut then asked that the House discharge the Committee of the Whole from considering the Senate proposal, which lacked the constitutional two-thirds vote of the entire Senate. Whatever the merits of Griswold's question, it had the intended effect of creating a lengthy diversionary debate. David Thomas of New York found in the 1789 Journals of the Senate that only sixteen of twenty-two members were present. Yet, the Senate acted on recommendations from the House to amend the Constitution with "two-thirds of the Senators present concurring therein."[2] John Smilie of Pennsylvania chided Federalists by asserting that, if the opponents had their way, the Bill of Rights would be ruled invalid for want of a proper two-thirds. Massachusetts Congressman Samuel Thatcher, however, refused to accept these arguments; regardless of how many Senators were in attendance, he reasoned, the vote in support of an amendment may have constituted two-thirds of the whole number.

Caesar Rodney tried to strengthen the Republican position by shifting attention forward from 1789 to the 1802-1803 session. He noted that in 1802 the House consisted of 106 members, two-thirds of which amounted to 71. Yet the House passed an engrossed resolution for a designation amendment by a vote of 47-14. In the current session, the membership amounted to 140 with 94 making two-thirds. Yet the designation amendment had passed on October 28 by an 88-31 vote. Finally, Federalist Benjamin Huger of South Carolina called the question at about 4 o'clock in the afternoon, and Griswold's motion to challenge the legitimacy of the Senate vote went down to defeat. Having devoted the entire day to this sparring session, the House adjourned. John Quincy Adams, who had come to listen to the debate, must have been amused to find a replay of the contentious debate and parliamentary wrangles which he had experienced in the upper house.[3]

On Wednesday, December 7, 1803 the House tried to launch into a major debate. Huger sought to delay action until the House incorporated his proposal for district elections of electors into the Senate resolution. The legislatures of New York and South Carolina had favored such a change, and, in a former Congress, John Nicholas of Virginia had put it forward, he pointed out. New York Federalist Gaylord Griswold knew that his state legislature had favored both district elections and designation, and he wondered why it did not institute this reform.[4]

Republican Samuel L. Mitchill of New York felt compelled to unravel the history of his state's position on designation and districting. That legislature had proposed two changes, and he himself had introduced them to the House of Representatives. The House acted on designation, which the Senate rejected; the House did not act on the other at that time. Mitchill had advised the House that he was not bound to the recommendations of his state's legislature and that he had come to the conclusion that an amendment for district elections was unnecessary. He could not have been totally ignorant of the report on district elections submitted by John Nicholas in January of 1801 or of the views of Thomas Jefferson on this subject.[5]

The House defeated Huger's motion for coupling district elections with designation, and it formed a Committee of the Whole to read the Senate resolution. The members reviewed first the provisions relating to the Vice President. Vermont's Federalist Representative James Elliot believed firmly in designation but maintained that allowing the Vice President to become President, if the House in a contingency election failed to make a choice by March 4, was inconsistent with designation. It became clear that proponents of the amendment had to deal with a few Federalists and almost all Republicans who wanted designation unadorned by the additional provisions in the Senate resolution, other Federalists who might accept designation if coupled with district elections, and still other Federalists opposed to any form of designation. Somehow, they had to secure a two-thirds majority behind the package of satisfactory, if not ideal, terms in the Senate resolution and get approval in time for submission to the states prior to the 1804 presidential election.

Connecticut Representative Samuel W. Dana sought to enlarge on Elliot's motion by striking out all references to the Vice President, and Roger Griswold supported this preemptive strike against designation. Federalists, who spoke often about defending the sanctity of the Constitution against Republican tinkering, offered wholesale changes as a strategy for delaying and perhaps defeating designation. But the House defeated both Elliot's and Dana's motions.[6]

Before the Republican majority could move ahead to the main question, William Chamberlain of New Hampshire asked to strike out the words *persons having the highest number not exceeding three* in the Senate resolution. Goddard wondered why the Senate had ignored the earlier House version calling for five. He was more puzzled by the meaning of the phrase than the number itself. Did *the highest number, not exceeding three* mean only persons having three votes, he asked?[7]

After Congressmen spoke at length and attempted to determine whether the three referred to persons or votes, proponents of the amendment tried to minimize the importance of the number. Smilie explained that he preferred five but could live with any reasonable number in return for designation. But Griswold fastened to the grammatical usage and poked away. Did the words mean that "persons not having precisely three votes, cannot be elected?"[8] He hoped the Congress would not submit to the states a resolution that was either absurd or obscure. Elliot was not sure who was the best grammarian, but he believed it made a difference whether or not the amendment provided for a maximum of three candidates in the contingency election.

In this labyrinth, a first term Connecticut Congressman, Simeon Baldwin, took the floor. The Yale educated lawyer who would soon become an associate justice of the state Supreme Court, Baldwin took a customary, legal reading of the words *not exceeding three*. Whether three referred to persons or numbers, this phrase intended to limit the greater number but did not preclude taking a smaller number.

> It is an expression of frequent occurrence in our Statutes; persons may be fined *not exceeding* a certain sum, or may be imprisoned *not exceeding* a certain number of years. Whenever the expression is thus used, a sum, or a number less than the excess limited, may be assumed; and by provision under consideration the choice of President may consistently, with the expression, be restricted to two persons, or to two classes of numbers.[9]

He believed the House should use language which consisted with its intent, such as "from the *three persons* having the highest numbers" or "from the persons having the *three highest numbers*," as the Representatives desired.[10]

Otherwise Baldwin expected that Congress could face an awkward problem in determining how many candidates should be considered. Although actual balloting for President would be by states, all other questions would be determined in the usual way, and members from Virginia, Pennsylvania, New York, and Massachusetts counted for seventy-four members, or a majority of the present House. They could limit the number of candidates to two and exclude a candidate who enjoyed strong support in the other thirteen states. He advised that the language to be placed in the Constitution should be plain and clear.   After further argument, the Committee ignored Baldwin's remarks, passed the main amendment, and rose to report to the House.

Timothy Pickering listened to the Representatives from a seat in the gallery, and his skepticism about the wisdom of the proposed amendment deepened. He had already concluded that the phrase *not exceeding three* was obscure; now he found it "altogether *unintelligible.*"[11] Thinking that he had at least understood the intent of these words, Pickering was stunned to hear Baldwin raise a point that was totally novel to him and probably to all the other Senators who had voted on the resolution. Yet, "when mentioned, it was not attended to."[12]

Representatives whose motions had been frustrated by the majority in the Committee had the opportunity to try again in the House. Further time was taken up as the Republican majority voted down attempts to abolish the vice presidency and to alter the numbers specified in the Senate resolution. Speaker Nathaniel Macon then put the question to the whole resolution. The House majority agreed to the entire resolution and ordered that it be engrossed for a third reading.

Roger Griswold recommended that the House give the measure a third reading the following day, for the members had already sat for more than eight hours. He thereby spun another mini-debate on a procedural question. Advocates of postponement had lost all the votes but had succeeded in delaying action. Many supporters of the amendment were stretched to the limit of patience and pressed for the third reading immediately. But weariness and frustration led to heated charges of logrolling techniques against the majority. Nonetheless, the House gave the resolution its third reading, and the question became, "Shall the same pass?" A correspondent for the *American Citizen* reported that opponents of the amendment had raised every conceivable kind of objection, including grammatical and arithmetic ones, but every attempt to accommodate these critiques spoiled and weakened the substance. It was already six o'clock and with the mail scheduled to leave in a few minutes, he could not provide any information about the final outcome.[13]

The House remained in session well into the night and listened to several lengthy speeches. Tempers flared. John Randolph's suggestion that the minority had resorted to unreasonable attacks and dilatory tactics angered Elliot in particular. This eruption brought a motion from Republican John Smilie of Pennsylvania for adjournment, and the ayes carried at about nine o'clock. John Quincy Adams, who had listened to the debate until four o'clock, seemed amazed that the House had continued for so long and not taken the final vote. Congressman Thomas Dwight of Massachusetts complained that the debate had turned into an endurance test in which "our dinner was to be eaten at that late hour, after which it would hardly be advisable however fatigued, until eleven o'clock or after to resort to the bed--and going to bed this late, if advisable it is not probable that we shall rise very early in the morning."[14]

On the following day, December 8, the House resumed consideration of the amendment and presented the climactic debate on the resolution. Republicans fleshed out their view of the history, constitutional theory, and political thought which argued for designation. Andrew Gregg of Pennsylvania began with an able, reasoned, and well-modulated defense of the resolution. He recalled that a Federalist from New Hampshire first introduced the idea in the Congress and later another from South Carolina expressed interest. More recently Republicans from Pennsylvania and Virginia brought the idea forward. Meanwhile, legislatures in New York, Vermont, Tennessee, Ohio, and Kentucky expressed support. Every region of the country and both parties advocated designation. He favored it without reservation and wished the resolution before the House had confined itself to that.[15]

Gregg viewed the argument over the effects of the amendment on small states as both oversimplified and confused. He believed the nation would continue to have two major parties for a long time and that each would have an interest in selecting the most able person for President, regardless of the state of origin. Instead of large states arraigned against the small, he perceived loose associations or coalitions of states rooted in regional interests. Finally, while the Constitution recognized the federative principle, it did not do so at the expense of the democratic principle.

George W. Campbell of Tennessee developed the Republican position in more partisan terms. He viewed the Constitution as the creation of the people and not the states, for the text began with "We the people," and from this premise sprang the most basic spirit of the fundamental law. In the election of the President, the framers intended the people to make their choice through their electors, not the states through their Representatives in the House. They provided for the eventuality of a non-election by electors, but in so doing they did not contradict their commitment to a popularly chosen executive. Anything which contravened these elemental suppositions, Campbell felt, should be altered, and anything which worked to reduce the chances of a House election should be adopted.

Campbell had heard that the small states accepted the contingency election in the House in return for rights which they surrendered to the large states elsewhere. He could not help but be skeptical. "If the small States considered it so, they must have esteemed those rights and powers thus surrendered of very small importance indeed," he noted.[16] The contingency election would occur infrequently, perhaps once in a century. In 1801 the small states did not form one united interest; neither did the large states. Even in a House election, Campbell wondered, what were the chances that a candidate from a small state would be one of those submitted to the House. He admitted that small states could choose among the candidates from large, but Campbell considered it highly improbable that the small states of the different geographical regions of the nation would combine. Like Gregg, Campbell knew that loyalty to political parties governed the actions of those who represented the states in Congress and in the electoral college.

James Jackson of Georgia in a partisan, fighting, and effective speech declared, "As the Constitution at present stands it has, in a great measure, placed the election in the hands of a minority--in the hands of political enemies-- and out of the control of the majority."[17]   Joseph Stanton of Rhode Island reminded any who needed reminding of the perils of the last election and thought that Federalists like Roger Griswold must have been out of the country or out of their senses to say now that there had been no crisis.

Federalists did what they could to deflect these criticisms. Trying to get Congress to assume a position above the fray, Thomas Lowndes of South Carolina wished to postpone action until after the presidential election, when it could be considered without the appearance of party motives. Of course, postponement under the circumstances was just as partisan as moving ahead with designation. Roger Griswold and John Dennis spoke for a complex republic. The Constitution established a federal government, and its friends, Griswold said, were federalists who had to guard against any measure which would unduly increase the powers of the large states or diminish those of the small. Dennis agreed that the will of the majority should prevail in so far as this rule applied to individual states, but he denied that majority rule lay at the heart of the Constitution. A federal spirit permeated the provision for presidential electors, who were not chosen to get the sense of the majority of the people but of the plurality of people and of the states.[18]

Finally, John Randolph provided a summation of the majority position. He noted the objections to the three innovations of the Senate resolution. He dismissed as relatively trivial the dispute over the number three. As for the elevation of the Vice President to the Presidency after March 4, he heard one critic complain that this provision undermined designation while at the same time another critic opposed designation itself. How could these members both vote against the resolution, he asked?[19]

Designation will prevent problems such as those which plagued the last election. That election had been difficult enough when the House had to choose between two men whose views differed only in shade. What would have happened had the choice been between two members of rival parties? Randolph conjectured that there would have been no election. He knew for himself that he would have continued voting through March 4.

Designation will also have a beneficial effect on the Vice Presidency, he asserted. Given his known position against this office, Randolph took a most benign view of this matter, probably because he was summing up for the Republicans and not just speaking for himself. Under the present system, electors voted solidly for the person they wanted for President and scattered their second vote, leaving the vice presidency very much in doubt. He did not provide actual evidence from previous elections to show that this had happened. With designation, electors could concentrate their votes for Vice President as well as President and thereby choose a person of quality.

Before concluding, Randolph indicated that five states could stop passage of this amendment. Rhode Island, Delaware, Ohio, Tennessee, and Georgia, the smallest of states from different regions of the country, could vote nay. Based on the number of Congressmen, these states had about one-twelfth of the population of the nation. It is, of course, also true that Massachusetts, New York, Pennsylvania, Virginia, and North Carolina could block passage. At various times, members suggested both possibilities, but Randolph saw that as the best reason to expect that neither group would unite in this fashion. He finished his remarks without sharp partisanship and covered each major area of the resolution competently.

William Eustis, one of the Republicans in the minority, attempted to do for the opponents what Randolph had done successfully for the advocates. Eustis analyzed the three separate parts of the resolution: designation, which only modified the rules of the Constitution; reduction of candidates in a contingency election from five to three in ambiguous language; and the elevation of the Vice President on a non-election of the President. Eustis maintained his consistency by saying he believed in the House resolution of October 28 which provided for designation and the retention of five candidates, a proposal for which both he and Representative Randolph had voted. He could not follow the Virginian into accepting the Senate version simply on the basis that the Senators will not recede from their resolution. Eustis took time to disagree with two of his Federalist cohorts from Massachusetts on the matter of amending, which he saw as constitutionally sanctioned and perfectly proper. Thus Eustis concluded with a relatively brief, moderate, and bipartisan address, designed to win over any wavering Republicans rather than to affirm Federalist views.[20]

The question was now called, and the House voted 83-42. At this point, Speaker Nathaniel Macon declared for the majority and created the final 84-42 result without a vote to spare. Only seven Republicans voted with the Federalists.[21]

The Federalists did not have the one-third plus one votes to block House or Senate acceptance of the resolution, and the alignment in both followed closely along party lines. Simeon Baldwin, already unhappy with life in isolated Washington, wrote to his wife to share his political woes: "Our little band of Federalists foiled in all our measures by the weight of numbers--are well united--but are reduced to the only consolation left us a consciousness of acknowledged superiority of Talents & Dignity--but they are of little effect here."[22] Fellow Connecticut Federalist Benjamin Tallmadge also acknowledged that his party had possessed only marginal influence on the course of the debates and resorted to proposing alterations, seeking delays, provoking Republicans, and postponing the inevitable.[23]

On Monday, December 12, 1803 the House agreed to a motion "that the President of the United States be requested to transmit to the Executive of the several States copies of the article of amendment proposed by Congress."[24] The House ordered the clerk to carry the resolution to the Senate for concurrence. There Uriah Tracy moved that the amendment should be sent to the President for his approval, but the Senate disagreed 7-24 with only Adams, Hillhouse,

Olcott, Pickering, Plumer, Tracy, and White voting aye, and the Senate passed the House order. The ordeal of Congressional debate was over with hardly a vote to spare in either House, and the fate of the Twelfth Amendment rested in the hands of the states.[25]

IV

WINNER-TAKE-ALL

15

Ratification of the Twelfth Amendment

On Christmas day, 1803, seven-time New York Governor George Clinton surveyed the political scene. He believed that the cause of Republicanism had never been stronger since the close of the Revolutionary War. The only cloud on the horizon formed from this very success, for it was natural that the party would relax when at the zenith of power: "Our superior strength of itself has already dissolved one of our strongest ties--*Common Danger*."[1] He received support for his assessment from President Jefferson, who observed that the two of them had marched straight forward for twenty-eight years without turning to the right or left and that they might soon be able to retire from the world of political strife. But first Republicans had to gain passage of the Twelfth Amendment, which would give them control of presidential elections and win vindication for Thomas Jefferson.[2]

The President's insistence on adoption made ratification a matter of party principle and personal loyalty. Jefferson had taken a proper public position in the contingency election of 1801 by stating that he would have cheerfully accepted the elevation of Burr, but he determinedly resisted usurpation. Yet privately, he had become furious at the extent to which Federalists were willing to meddle with the free choice of the voters; Madison had told him that only the absence of a standing army prevented Federalists from overturning the 1800 election altogether.[3]

When Congress adopted the designation amendment and submitted it to the states, Jefferson recalled that the Federalists had promoted it after the 1796 election to strike at him and opposed it now for party motives. Federalists fought it, for they recognized that designation meant "neither a Presid[en]t or Vice President can ever be made but by the fair vote of the majority of the nation, of which they are not."[4] He then made clear that ratification of the amendment would amount to a vote of confidence in him:

I am a friend to the discrimination principle; and for a reason more than others have, inasmuch as the discriminated vote of my constituents will express unequivocally the verdict they wish to pass on my conduct. The abominable slanders of my political enemies have obliged me to call for that verdict from my country in the only way it can be obtained, and if obtained it will be my sufficient voucher to the rest of the world & to posterity and leave me free to seek, at a definite time, the repose I sincerely wished to have retired to now.[5]

Federalists tried to deny ratification in the states in part by having Uriah Tracy's speech in the Senate reprinted and circulated. Timothy Pickering spent the period from mid-December to New Year's Day writing lengthy letters to Federalists and moderate Republicans who might be amenable to persuasion. Simeon Baldwin and James Hillhouse circulated Tracy's speech to their correspondents. Tracy himself sent a copy to Rufus King with a cover letter in which he lamented in coarse language that the Republicans were breaking down many institutions. But invective did not substitute for votes in the state legislatures. Hillhouse held faint hopes and expected that "the same party views which influenced the two houses of Congress will operate [there]."[6] Even the indefatigable Tracy regretted that the amendment had "arrested so little attention" and despaired "of calling up anything like the operation of common sense on that or any other subject."[7]

By late January and early February of 1804 North Carolina, Kentucky, Ohio, Virginia, Maryland, and Pennsylvania had voted for ratification, and in these states there was little debate and little opposition. North Carolina's house of commons received from Governor Jonathan Turner the text of the proposed Twelfth Amendment to the Constitution after 4 P.M. on December 20, 1803 and promptly prepared a bill to ratify and sent it to the senate, and the upper house notified the commons of its concurrence all before the close of the day. Final action on the bill took place on December 21, when the house voted 91-18 in favor. Kentucky acted with similar dispatch and without extensive debate, when the legislature adopted an act to ratify and the measure became law on December 27, 1803. Just to the north, Governor Edward Tiffin informed the Ohio General Assembly of the proposed amendment on Christmas Eve, Saturday, December 24. By Monday, a joint committee reported a bill to the senate, which adopted and sent it to the house. After a day of working out kinks in the bill, the house voted 28-0 on December 28 in favor of new language, which the senate accepted on the same day. On December 30, Ohio joined the ranks of ratifiers. Virginia's house of delegates agreed to a similar act by a 128-8 margin on December 28 and the senate concurred on the December 31.[8]

The Maryland senate received the proposed amendment on December 19, and a committee prepared a bill on the next day. On December 22 the senate passed the bill unanimously and sent it to the house, which accepted it 40-26 two days later. With executive approval, the measure became law on January 7,

1804. In Pennsylvania Governor McKean approved and signed a comparable bill to ratify on January 9 after the house had passed it 74-9 and the senate 23-1. Matthias Barton thought the members of the Pennsylvania legislature gave only cursory attention to the amendment as "many of them appear to consider the proposed Amendment of as little importance, as if it was a Question whether the Electors of Pennsylvania should vote by *written* or *printed* Tickets!!!"[9] Being familiar with the issue of designation unencumbered by other major innovations and aware of the imminence of the presidential election, Republican legislatures had no need for extensive debates and engaged in none. They had only to vote affirmatively or negatively to the text submitted to them.[10]

Delaware with its long history of Federalist dominance offered another story. Republicans had succeeded in electing David Hall to the statehouse and showed growing strength in the legislature. Hall told the legislature on January 6, 1804 that he supported the amendment because in a republic the voice of the majority should prevail. Republicans prepared an able defense of the amendment. First, they paid homage to the Constitution as the best which the world had yet seen but asserted that the ablest minds of the ages could not draft a perfect document. The framers themselves realized that experience would show flaws in their work and had made provision for amendments. Without that feature, the Constitution would not have received the endorsement of the requisite number of states and would not have been ratified. Delaware supported the addition of the Bill of Rights and later the Eleventh Amendment, and had also modified its state constitution. Hence all innovations of the Constitution were not dangerous.[11]

Second, the history of designation demonstrated that this alteration had bipartisan support. Republicans pointed to the Vermont initiative for designation when Federalists controlled the legislature. That same proposal received the approbation of the Federalist-controlled Massachusetts General Court. The New York legislature, with Federalists in the majority in one house, recommended the same change. Republicans scolded Federalists who at this late date promoted partisanship by opposing what they themselves had originated.

The Republicans did not see the small states as jeopardized by this constitutional reform. Since there were many more small states than large and alteration of the Constitution required the assent of two-thirds of the Senate and three-fourths of the states, the small states could take care of themselves just as they had in uniting with many large states against Federalist measures.

They rejected the conclusion that the amendment diminished the influence of small states. To the contrary, they believed that a precise reading of the amendment showed advantages for the small states. The words in the Constitution referred to the five *persons* highest on the list, whereas the amendment spoke to the three highest *numbers*, which might include a dozen people. Moreover, the framers of the Constitution intended that elections in the House of Representatives be the secondary, not primary, mode for electing the President. They wanted electors to make the choice.

Designation impinged on the rights of neither the small states nor the minority. In any legitimate democratic government, the majority must rule. The majority may err, but it cannot be claimed that "the minority are less subject to intolerance than the Majority."[12] That Thomas Jefferson would be the beneficiary of the reform made no difference; designation was justified under any circumstance and with any candidate. The Republicans in the Delaware legislature concluded that Congress had passed the amendment with constitutional majorities of the same type that had approved the first eleven amendments to the Constitution.

Though they had the better of the argument, the Republicans could not overcome the Federalist advantage in numbers. They did not even obtain permission to introduce their arguments formally on the record. The Federalist majority provided a rationale for rejection, which appeared in various newspapers across the country. They reiterated the points which opponents of designation had made in the congressional debates: (1) constitutional innovations are dangerous, especially when motivated by immediate partisan interests, (2) every change proposed favors the large states, (3) the reduction from five to three candidates in the contingency election hurts the small states, (4) the amendment reverses the original Constitution's intent to give the small states a voice in the choice of President and Vice President, (5) the amendment tips the political balance in favor of the numerical majority against the minority, (6) the existing arrangements recognize the fallibility of the majority and the occasional insights of the minority, and (7) the amendment did not receive the two-thirds vote of the whole numbers of each house of Congress. The house voted 9-6 in favor of this position on January 13, and the senate concurred on January 19. Delaware thus became the first state to reject the amendment.[13]

Then came Vermont, a state where Federalists had been the stronger party throughout the 1790s and where they made an effort to defeat the Twelfth Amendment. In so doing, they ignored the fact that as recently as 1799 they had been mainly responsible for getting the state legislature to adopt a resolution in favor of designation. Republicans, having recently become the majority (taking control of the legislature for the first time in 1801), did not intend to be passive and complacent. They knew that Federalists had circulated Senator Tracy's speech throughout the state and hoped to stir up the anxieties of the small states against the large. As John White, Jr. put it, "Should the Federalists be able by their incessant labours to prevent it from gaining the assent of only one republican state, the whole might/should be lost, and this might be effected by the absence of a single member [from the legislature]!"[14]

Governor Isaac Tichenor submitted the proposed amendment to the legislature on January 26, 1804. In committee, Henry Olin challenged the legitimacy of the congressional resolution because the 84 votes in the House and the 22 in the Senate did not constitute the required two-thirds vote of their respective full houses. After a lengthy discussion, the committee rejected this view and after a few more days of deliberation the house voted 93-64 to declare Vermont's assent. The measure became law on the 30th.[15]

Massachusetts joined Delaware in refusing ratification. George Cabot conceded that in the abstract one could make the case for reform. He and others had favored it at one time when it seemed indispensable to preserve government "in good hands" and to keep the nation out of "the fangs of France." Republicans now seized on designation to advance their own partisan agenda. To continue to support the reform would be to become "Dupes of our own virtues."[16] On February 2, 1804, the delegates rejected the amendment 79-131 and the senate did the same by a 13-19 tally. Cabot and the Federalists were no less partisan than the Republicans; yet they believed, as did their hated rivals, that they spoke to the best interests of the country.[17]

New Jersey, once reliably Federalist, became the eighth state to ratify. One Jersey Federalist told Timothy Pickering that Uriah Tracy's speech "ought to have weight, I am well convinced--that it will, I have little or no Hope at present."[18] Indeed the state's council and assembly easily ratified on February 22, 1804, making eight states in favor and two against the Twelfth Amendment.[19]

Meanwhile, as a precaution against the outside possibility that ratification would not take place prior to the vote of electors in December of 1804, Republicans in Congress passed a law in March. It stipulated that if presidential electors had not received official word of ratification or if they met less than five days after newspapers in the state published an account of ratification, they were to vote in accordance with the original Constitution without designation and then vote a second time with designation. Only the votes consistent with the Constitution in force on the day the law required electors to meet would be opened.[20]

On January 31, 1804 Governor George Clinton delivered the traditional opening message to the New York legislature and urged adoption of the proposed Twelfth Amendment. He reminded the legislature that it had recommended a similar amendment for two successive years and voiced optimism that "so desirable and salutary an improvement will meet with your early sanction."[21]

Although Clinton and the Republicans had previously linked designation with district elections, they said little about the latter now. An assembly committee had reported a bill in 1803 to divide the state into districts and offered a constitutional justification for this change. Though the assembly made progress on the reform, it ended its session without final action. Republicans maintained their stance as friends of democracy, but a substantial number of them clearly had second thoughts about complicating their own quest for power in New York and in Washington. On the bases of consistency and principle, many continued to espouse district elections, but they held back from implementing a reform which might diminish New York's clout in presidential elections by dividing the electoral vote. Republicans could not have failed to see that Federalists in the state senate had supported the proposed national constitutional amendment for designation and district elections primarily because of the inclusion of the latter, while most of their partisans had become more attached to the former. They must also have had access to Jefferson's views, which were shrewd and practical, not rigidly linked to every democratic change. Republican control of government was essential to protect and advance the principles of 1800 and should not be undermined by a foolish consistency.[22]

As for the chances of designation in New York, the composition of the legislature told all that was necessary: there were 25 Republicans, 6 Federalists, and 1 Burrite among the senators, and 82 Republicans, 16 Federalists, and 2 Burrites among the assemblymen. On February 3, former Federalist Ezra L'Hommedieu brought in a bill in the senate to ratify the Twelfth Amendment. On February 8, the Senate voted 24-4 to ratify. The house received the senate bill later that day, and on February 9 the Committee voted to recommend adoption by a 79-14 vote. New York became the ninth state to ratify.[23]

Rhode Island had gone on record in 1800 against designation, when both houses unanimously rejected it. Now Federalist papers in Providence and Newport gave extended coverage to Uriah Tracy's speech, defended the Connecticut Senator against attacks that he favored a British form of monarchy, and reported the Delaware resolutions. There were also rumors of a dispute between Rhode Island Republicans and the Jefferson administration over patronage. Allegedly, the former insisted on removals of all Federalists, especially collectors at Newport and Providence, as a precondition for acting positively on the proposed amendment, and the latter resisted. William Plumer may have been referring to this rumor when he noted that he had a "tale" about Rhode Island's ratification. But the Republican-controlled legislature stayed on course and adopted designation on March 1, 1804. The minority then proposed in vain that the amendment be submitted to the voters.[24]

South Carolina and Georgia became the eleventh and twelfth states to accept. South Carolina held a special session of the legislature to make certain that it could register its support prior to the regular session in November, by which time the presidential election would be upon the nation. On May 15 the two houses of the legislature agreed to the language of a resolution to ratify and the following day jointly asked the Governor to communicate word of ratification to the President of the United States. Georgia Governor Jonathan Milledge called for a special session of the legislature to deal with the amendment prior to the upcoming presidential election, and on May 14, 1804 the two houses agreed to the creation of a joint committee to report on appropriate measures. By May 16, the house approved a bill, and within two days the senate had concurred and sent the bill to the governor, who signed the measure on May 19.[25]

Connecticut joined Delaware and Massachusetts in rejecting the Twelfth Amendment. On May 11, Governor Jonathan Trumbull, a stalwart Federalist, delivered a message to the legislature in which he expressed his unwavering support for the venerable Constitution and his equally firm opposition to the spirit of experimentation which animated advocates of the amendment. The legislators agreed overwhelmingly. The lower house repudiated a resolution for ratification by a vote of 77-115.[26]

New Hampshire offered an anomalous situation. The legislature had received communications from the Jefferson administration including the resolution of Congress for a constitutional amendment on December 29, 1803 but postponed consideration until the next session of the General Court. John T. Gilman, Governor from 1794 to 1805, belonged to the Exeter Junto. As a state treasurer, he had attempted to keep tax revenues at levels above expenses "to habituate the people to paying them," and "his many ponderous public statements as governor overflow[ed] with old-school didacticism, preaching patience, restraint, and order to the people, honesty, firmness, benevolence, and public service to their natural rulers."[27]

When it reconvened in June of 1804, the New Hampshire house of representatives chose Republican John Langdon, recently defeated by Gilman in the contest for the statehouse, to be speaker. Gilman's message of June 12 warned that reasons for altering the Constitution must be clear and compelling, free of tendencies to perpetual changes and other unforeseen disadvantages. In its courteous reply, the house paid homage to the Constitution but pointedly observed that experience showed imperfections in any human creation. The representatives followed words with action on June 15, adopting two measures: the first condemned the press for abusing Jefferson and expressed "fullest confidence in the justice, benevolence and wisdom of the President of the United States," and the second adopted the Twelfth Amendment.[28] The votes were 85-72 for the former, and 81-73 for the latter. The senate by identical 7-5 votes supported both on June 13 and 15.[29]

Governor Gilman then took an extraordinary step. He vetoed the legislature's ratification and rejected the carte blanche praise for the national administration. Claiming that he had a right and duty to express his position on acts and resolutions of the house and senate, Gilman made explicit his objections to designation. The proposed amendment weakened the position of the small states in the choice of both the President and Vice President, diminished the stature of the second office, and undermined the role of the Constitution "as a permanent rule."[30] Neither house could muster the necessary two-thirds vote to override the veto. New Hampshire's status vis-a-vis the amendment became murky.

Tennessee, however, provided an unchallengeable thirteenth state, when it adopted in late July. At a special session, the legislature went on record in favor of the amendment on July 27. In the end only Delaware, Massachusetts, and Connecticut, the most steadfast Federalist states, voted against the amendment. On September 24, 1804 James Madison in his capacity as Secretary of State informed the Governor of New York that the Twelfth Amendment to the Constitution had been ratified. Hence its provisions would apply to the presidential election in December, and that, in turn, meant that Federalists had no chance to affect the outcome for either President or Vice President. The Republican ticket was a shoo-in.[31]

16

The Election of 1804

Rufus King, a potential Federalist candidate, had no illusions about the probable outcome of the presidential election: "there can be no doubt that the Pr[esident] will be reelected--a vice President of the same Politics is also sure to be chosen, if the amendment of the Constitution takes Place of wh[ich] there can scarcely be a doubt."[1] Timothy Pickering concurred and added sourly that with designation Jefferson could be re-elected for life.[2]

On February 25, the Republicans held their congressional caucus in Washington and considered candidates for their ticket. They had no difficulty in nominating Jefferson for President. After considering prospective running mates, the caucus gave George Clinton 67 votes, John Breckinridge 20, Levi Lincoln 9, John Langdon 7, Gideon Granger 4, and Samuel Maclay 1. The results disappointed Breckinridge and his western supporters, who believed Virginia should look westward rather than eastward for the vice presidential nominee. Perhaps the most resounding vote, however, was the zero for Aaron Burr.[3]

Clinton, who had refused a chance for an eighth term as Governor of New York on the grounds of age and disability, accepted the nomination which was tantamount to election to an office which had eluded his grasp several times earlier. He justified his decision to Pierre Van Cortlandt, Jr., saying that he had looked forward to retirement but expected that the vice presidency "will leave me a portion of Time for exercise & recreation which I conceve [sic] essential to my Health[,] impaired as it is by the incessant Care & confinement which the one I now hold has imposed on me."[4] Vermont Federalist Martin Chittenden saw reason behind the choice of "poor old George": "Because from his age & infirmities he never will become a rival or stand between Virginia & the Chief magistracy of the nation."[5] It is true that designation identified Clinton as the candidate for the second office, but the fact remains that after the election of 1804 Clinton would have assumed the duties of chief magistrate, if Jefferson vacated the presidency for any reason.

Some Republicans guessed as early as July of 1803 that Charles C. Pinckney and Rufus King would be Federalist candidates for President and Vice President, and they inveighed against them. But the Federalists held no official caucus. In March several Federalist newspapers recommended Pinckney and King, but the party made no formal public statements about their candidates. "The authoritative" Federalist paper, the Boston *Columbia Centinel*, flatly declared on October 3, "The proper personages to be voted for as President will be the inquiry of electors after they are chosen. The Federal Republicans believe it to be their duty to select the wisest and most patriotic citizens for electors. They are not tied down to two candidates."[6]

The Republican sweep in the 1800 and 1802 elections which had set the table for prompt ratification of the Twelfth Amendment in the states also meant that Jeffersonians controlled most state governments. If they wished, Republicans could change the mode of choosing electors to advance their principles as well as their interests in the upcoming presidential contest. But of the seventeen states participating in the presidential election, only four chose district elections. Those which switched from legislative appointment usually turned to elections by general ticket.[7]

In Massachusetts, Federalists still controlled state government, but Republicans posed formidable challenges. The Federalists had taken punishing body blows for having rejected popular participation in the choice of presidential electors in 1800. Republicans hammered at them for mistrust of the people and lack of confidence in native son Adams to carry the state in a fair contest. They insisted that the legislature return the right to choose electors to the people in districts. Although their partisans in Virginia, New York, Pennsylvania, and elsewhere found legislative appointment or general ticket election perfectly acceptable and although their Senators and Representatives in Congress refused to support a constitutional amendment to require district elections of electors, Republicans in the Bay state struggled to get a proportional voice in the presidential election. The Federalists in the General Court calculated that the party's interest would suffer either by retaining legislative appointment or returning to the mode of the 1790s which opened the door to minority representation in the electoral college. Believing that the state should speak with a unified vote so that it would not be outweighed by small states and counting on converting their diminishing majority in the state into a winner-take-all advantage, Federalists opted for popular election on a general ticket with at least one elector chosen from each congressional district.[8]

Republicans tried to make the Federalists pay for past and recent political sins. In a broadside, Barnabas Bidwell reminded citizens that Federalists stood for monarchy, pointed to Hamilton's speeches in the Philadelphia Convention and to John Adams's *Defense*, denounced repressive taxes, sedition acts, and standing armies, and tied all of this historical baggage to the Essex Junto and Governor Caleb Strong. Bidwell warned that the re-election of Strong and the Federalists would lead to the loss of popular voice in the choice of presidential electors. On the other side, an anonymous pamphleteer defended Federalists against the tyranny of Virginia imperialism. The author justified the general ticket and legislative appointment as consistent with the Constitution which sought to give to each state "the full effect of an undivided vote."[9] District elections, to the contrary, negated the power of Massachusetts:

> The votes of a single District, united with the votes of other States, might, and frequently would decide an Election, contrary to the vote and sense of all the other Districts in the same State; and thus the State would become absurdly instrumental in defeating, instead of promoting its own views.[10]

Both parties prepared and distributed tickets of their candidates for electors to insure the presence of one person from each congressional district and proper spelling of the names to avoid later disputes. The state's attorney general ruled, however, that votes must be handwritten, and he forced both parties to improvise. Ironically, the vote on November 5 produced a Republican victory. The electors met in December and gave all their votes for Jefferson as President and for Clinton as Vice President.[11]

New Hampshire had followed Massachusetts in going from a complex, combined system for choosing electors in the 1790s to legislative appointment in 1800. With Republicans in control, the legislature opted in June of 1804 for popular selection by a general ticket. Those chosen were to meet on the first Tuesday in December in Concord at which time the legislature by joint ballot could fill any vacancy. The electors gave their votes for Jefferson and Clinton.[12]

Connecticut stood fast as a Federalist state. It relied on legislative appointment. The electors met at Hartford and voted for Pinckney as President and King as Vice President.[13]

Rhode Island continued with election of electors by the general ticket, which it had tried for the first time in 1800. Governor Arthur Fenner certified that the people had chosen four men. They met at the state house in Bristol, where each elector signed a ballot previously prepared in a common hand. The ballot stated, "I vote for Thomas Jefferson Esqr (the present President of the United States) for President of the United States to commence the 4th March 1805" and "I vote for George Clinton Esqr (late Governor of New York) for Vice President of the United States to commence the 4th March 1805."[14] Rhode Island electors did not write in any other names.

In Vermont, Republican Governor Isaac Tichenor told the state legislature that existing law provided for legislative appointment and asked whether it was not time "to refer it to the great body of our freemen in districts, or through the state at large?"[15] The legislature, reflecting a Republican majority which had supported ratification of the Twelfth Amendment just months before, deferred any action on this question. On November 3, in a grand committee, the house and council with the governor in the chair chose electors. Tichenor certified the selections, and the men met at the dwelling house of Elisha Taylor in Woodstock on the appointed day and gave their votes for the Republican ticket.[16]

The middle states reflected the national strength of the Republican Party. In New York, Federalists were resigned to the outcome. The April elections for the assembly demonstrated an awesome Republican advantage: in the one-hundred member assembly, Republicans could count on eighty-three members, Federalists on fourteen, and Burrites on three. In the senate, the former stronghold of Federalism, Republicans had twenty-nine members, Federalists two, Burrites one. A Federalist newspaper from the mid-Hudson area saw the upcoming presidential election as a fait accompli. The *Hudson Balance and Columbian Repository* characterized the electors generically as "the merest machines, the simplest blockheads on earth." They did not have to be persons of wisdom, discretion, and honesty, "For the plain fact is, the president and vice-president are already chosen; and nothing is wanting but a little specious formality and childish mummery, to make the work complete."[17]

On November 9, the legislature met to choose electors. The Federalist minority slate consisted of some of the most prominent figures in the state, but these notables stood no chance of appointment where majority control meant total victory for the winning ticket of electors. The *Albany Register* remarked with approval the decision of the legislators: "The electors, we have no hesitation in saying, will be decided friends of JEFFERSON and CLINTON for the two first offices in the Union, agreeably to the arrangements made by the Republicans in Congress."[18] In this brief sentence, the editor described how far the organization of national political parties had come since the framers had created the electoral college.

Before concluding this short fall session, the legislature adopted a bill "relative to the election of president and vice-president." This measure provided for the eventuality that illness, accident, or some other cause prevented one or more of the electors from reaching Hudson on the day for balloting. Those duly appointed by the legislature who were present by three o'clock at the proper site could by majority vote choose alternates.[19]

On the first Wednesday in December, the electors met to cast their votes according to law. The *Hudson Balance and Columbian Repository* satirized the event:

> It is rumored that there was a very singular exhibition of *Puppets* in this city on Wednesday last. As we have not seen any person who was an eye-witness, we cannot pretend to give a very accurate account of it. But it is said that the figures were nineteen in number, generally of the full size of men, and some of them tolerably well executed. It is also said, that though no wires could be perceived, still it was plain to be seen that all the movements were governed by somebody behind the curtain.[20]

In leveling such attacks on the institution of the electors who, had they been Federalists, would have performed in the same way, this newspaper and other Federalist sources denigrated the office of presidential elector and contributed to the creation of the modern image of the electoral college.

The Republican *American Citizen* reported with satisfaction that the electors had gathered in Hudson. They appointed William Floyd chairman of the New York electoral college and proceeded to their peculiar duties. The electors sent a packet of materials to Washington, D.C. These included a list of all the presidential electors and a certificate recording their votes in accordance with the Twelfth Amendment to the Constitution. All the ballots for President were counted, and these showed 19 votes for Jefferson. Then all the ballots for Vice President were counted, and these provided 19 votes for Clinton.[21]

New Jersey, now under Republican control, shifted from legislative appointment of electors to election on a general ticket. This change accorded with democratic ideals of popular participation and with the advantages of the winner-take-all system, allowing Republicans to have their cake and eat it too. Together with the Twelfth Amendment, this reform eliminated any chance for the Federalist minority to confound majority wishes in the state. The election in September for electors, occurring at the same time as for Congressmen, produced a Republican rout. *The True American* reported that the eight candidates on the Republican ticket received between 13,039 and 13,119 votes. Federalists may not have formed a ticket; the highest Federalist candidate got only 19 votes. The electors met at the statehouse in Trenton on the first Wednesday in December and voted for the Republican pair.[22]

Pennsylvania moved to prevent a recurrence of the bitter and embarrassing struggle to vote in 1800. In 1802 the Republican majority in the legislature passed a general election law applicable in 1804 and every four years thereafter. The law stipulated popular election on a general ticket. Republicans also provided that if there were any absentees among the electors on the day they met to vote, the legislature by joint ballot could fill the vacancies.[23]

By 1803 Governor Thomas McKean reported that all eighteen Representatives and both Senators from the state were loyal Republicans and that Jefferson could count on twenty electoral votes. Indeed, the elections in the fall of 1804 produced victories for the Republican slate. On the appointed day for voting, they missed William Montgomery. The legislature accordingly filled the vacancy by appointing his son, Robert. McKean later referred to the twenty as "my sincere friends," and they faithfully cast their votes for the Republican candidates.[24]

Delaware remained a tiny Federalist principality. Its legislature appointed electors, who met at Dover and gave their votes for Pinckney and King.[25]

Within the South, Maryland stayed with district election of electors, which held the potential of a divided vote for President. The relevant legislation divided the state into nine districts, seven of which chose one elector each and two of which chose two, for a total of eleven electors. The governor notified the electors of the ratification of the Twelfth Amendment, and they proceeded to vote "by separate and distinct ballots for one person as President and one person as Vice President" in accordance with the new rules.[26] Jefferson got 9 votes for President to Pinckney's 2, and Clinton received 9 votes for Vice President to King's 2.[27]

Virginia stayed with the general ticket, even though Federalists posed absolutely no threat to Republicans in 1804. A law adopted in January of 1804 divided the state into twenty-four districts, each of which was entitled to an elector. Qualified voters went to the polls on the first Monday in November and turned in a ballot with twenty-four names, one from each district in the state on one side and the voter's name on the other. The legislature, if in session, could fill any vacancies which appeared on the day before electors cast their votes; otherwise, the governor with the advice of the council performed this task. Republicans did not have to put together a star-studded slate since Federalist resistance was only token, and they won handily. The electors met in Richmond and voted for the party ticket.[28]

North Carolina Governor James Turner reported that elections had been held in fourteen districts in each of which voters chose one elector. State law provided that the General Assembly by joint ballot could fill vacancies as long as it made sure that alternates came from the districts in which vacancies occurred. Their electors, solidly Republican, met in Raleigh and complied with the Twelfth Amendment by signing one sheet of paper indicating the choice for President and a second sheet for Vice President.[29]

South Carolina stayed with legislative appointment as prescribed in a law of 1792. Governor James B. Richardson certified the appointments, and the electors cast a unified vote for the Republican ticket[30]

Georgia Governor John Milledge indicated that the General Assembly by a joint ballot on November 14, 1804 chose electors. From Louisville, the electors reported that they had given all their votes for Jefferson and Clinton. The same handwriting on all twelve ballots suggests that the use of the ballot was a mere formality.[31]

Among the newer western states, Kentucky chose electors by elections in a combined district-general ticket arrangement. The legislature divided the state into a northern and southern district, in each of which the qualified voters chose four residents to serve as electors. The electors met at the statehouse in Frankfort on the appointed day and gave their votes to Jefferson for President and to Clinton for Vice President.[32]

Governor John Sevier of Tennessee reported that voters in district elections chose electors, and they in turn gave their votes for the Republican candidates.[33]

Ohio participated in a presidential election for the first time. In his annual message to the legislature on December 5, 1803, Governor Edward Tiffin asserted that the people's representatives should decide whether it was better to appoint electors by the joint ballot of the legislature or to elect them by a general ticket. Pointedly, he did not recommend district elections as one of the choices. The legislature opted for a general ticket election for three electors on the first Saturday in November. Choice by lot took care of ties. The electors met at the courthouse in Chillicothe, where each elector indicated for which person he voted for President and for Vice President. They went solidly Republican.[34]

On the second Wednesday of February 1804, the Congress gathered in the Senate chambers in Washington, D.C. They were attended by the teller from the Senate and two tellers from the House. The President of the Senate, Aaron Burr, announced the receipt of packets of electoral votes and certificates according to law. "You will now proceed, gentlemen, said he, to count the votes as the constitution and laws direct."[35] Seeing no set order for the packets, he chose to open ballots by regions, beginning with the northern states. He broke the seals of the envelopes and handed them to the tellers through the clerk, Samuel Smith. Then the Senate teller read aloud the returns and the attestation of appointment of the electors, and Joseph Clay and Roger Griswold, the House tellers, checked him with duplicates of the votes and attestations. At the conclusion, Smith informed the Vice President of the results, which Burr announced. There were no objections and no challenges to the votes.

Epilogue

The mid-term elections in 1802 gave Republicans a two-thirds majority in both the House (102-39) and the Senate (25-9) and clear control of legislatures in three-fourths of the states. Federalists had only New England and perhaps New Jersey and Delaware, where they clung desperately to power, and Republicans challenged them even there. They had no chance of winning the presidency in 1804. None. But with no opportunity to elect one of their own, they posed a new danger which differed from that of 1801: Federalist presidential electors representing a small minority of the people might mischievously cast one vote for a Federalist and the second vote for whoever was paired with Jefferson on the Republican ticket. These votes together with those of Republican electors would give this person more votes than Jefferson and thus defeat the Virginian. The Republican Party proposed a constitutional amendment to close this gaping hole in the electoral college method for choosing the President.[1]

On this issue, Jefferson showed himself more of a shrewd politician than a consistent theoretician. He did not press for district elections of electors, which Republicans had favored when they had been out of power and which would have created a very different electoral college from the one we have today. Now that he was in office, legislative appointment or general ticket election of electors, both of which promised winner-take-all outcomes, looked just fine. Having succeeded in getting control of the national government by using the existing system effectively, he and his party thought the time was not right to alter that system in a way which would make it more difficult for themselves to win re-election. Their experience told them that forging national majorities was no easy task, and their battles with Federalists were so bitter and of such recent memory that they could not give any quarter now. Jefferson put district elections on the shelf. He did the same with proposals to abolish the office of elector and with direct popular vote. Instead, he chose the option that most advantaged his party, hurt his rivals, and simplified the choices to be given to state legislatures--designation and designation alone. Nothing else would serve so clearly as a mandate.[2]

Jeffersonians also rejected the ingenious counterproposal of Federalist Senator Jonathan Dayton of New Jersey. Dayton recommended abolishing the office of Vice President; electors would cast only one vote for President. But Jefferson and his followers must have understood that the vice presidency was a politically useful office. Presidential candidates could offer the second spot to help secure their nominations and win the general election. In Jefferson's case, it meant Virginia making an alliance with a northern state, like New York, to bring national support behind the ticket. The choices Jefferson rejected and the reasons for rejecting them were, therefore, significant for the future of the electoral college.[3]

Jefferson got his wish when the Twelfth Amendment was sent to the states just prior to the 1804 election with the obvious intent to guarantee the election of the Republican ticket. It is no accident that the amendment modifying the electoral college had a partisan motive and in effect recognized the existence of national political parties by allowing the majority party both executive offices, a winner-take-all result in a new sense. Party choices were to prevail, not the two best candidates for President as the framers of the Constitution had envisioned.

Already the Constitution's provision for presidential electors assumed its modern aspect. Electors voted faithfully, not independently. They met to vote, not to deliberate. Although a few states still adhered to district election of electors, most saw the advantage of the winner-take-all system and relied on either legislative appointment or election by general ticket. Jeffersonians did nothing to alter this trend. The winner-take-all feature, with all of its pluses and minuses, came to be one of the strongest supports for the federal system which the framers had created in that it required presidential candidates to win the majority or plurality of votes in state after state rather than the numerical majority of voters or electors in the single consolidated district of the United States. Electors cast separate votes for President and Vice President, and the second office became a tool for winning the nomination and the election. This innovation denigrated the Vice Presidency, just as the critics had predicted. Unlike those in the past who sought the presidency and came in second, politicians of a lesser sort filled the post. On the other hand, designation reduced the chances of elections going to the House, and Republicans saw the wisdom of determining elections in the first instance by an electoral vote majority and avoiding contingency elections.

A national political party with an organization capable of nominating presidential candidates and offering a program and philosophy that attracted support across the country made archaic the Constitution's provision for each elector to cast two votes for President. Assisted by party loyalists at the state level, who pressed legislatures for a mode of choosing electors which would aid the national effort, Republicans and Federalists demonstrated that they could secure majorities for their candidates without the assistance of the dual vote. Indeed, the double vote created an awkward situation in 1796, perplexed both parties in 1800, and gave Federalists the opportunity to play the spoiler in 1804. In spite of Federalist protests that the Twelfth Amendment intended to diminish their influence, they would probably have done the same thing if circumstances had placed them in the shoes of the Republicans. After all, they had initiated talk of designation in the aftermath of 1796 and had speculated then about the Republicans' playing the spoiler in the future. That it was the liberal and democratic party which accepted the electoral college helped to legitimize it and allowed it to put on its modern face.

In all these ways, partisan political parties defined the institution created by the framers. Americans discovered that political parties were useful, even necessary, institutions, to help them define goals, select candidates, and convert popular pressures into actions. Presidential electors and major political parties developed in tandem, each supporting the other, with the viability of the latter affecting the efficacy of the former.

In Jefferson's second term, international events interfered with continued domestic reform and made the further alteration of the electoral college an item of low priority. If such a dominant majority party and its leaders--philosophically comfortable with democratic principles and positioned in the right places and at the right time in 1803 and 1804--refrained from bolder moves, then perhaps it is understandable why the electoral college continued to develop the way it did. Succeeding administrations felt like constraints: the pressure from international affairs or a domestic agenda, the knowledge that it gained power by playing the existing game better than its rival, the desire to retain control and to keep the opposition at a disadvantage. Few, if any, of them had numerical advantages in both houses of Congress and in state legislatures or the depth of partisan motives to allow them to press forward with electoral college reform in quite the way the Jeffersonians had.

Congress continued to receive proposals for constitutional amendments with the express purpose of reforming or abolishing the electoral college, and, during the Era of Good Feelings when party conflict at the national level temporarily subsided, there was renewed public discussion of the subject. Nonetheless, Congress never acted positively to alter the institution after 1804. Why not? First, party politics as played by the major parties acquired a stake in the preservation of this system, and Americans gradually became accustomed to its existence. A third candidate or party might still affect the outcome by taking enough popular votes in individual states to allow one of the others to win the state by a plurality, or winning some states outright and depriving major party nominees of a majority of the electoral vote. In the latter case, it is likely that one of the two major parties holds the advantage in the House of Representatives. Thus, it remains exceedingly difficult for a third candidate to win the presidency, a political desideratum for the major parties.[4]

Second, the large states learned quickly that they would not have the impact on presidential elections that small states had if their state electoral vote divided. Virginia, Pennsylvania, and Massachusetts all came around to this point of view by 1804. The winner-take-all method gave them greater clout than small states, and they saw little to be gained by giving this advantage away. Third, small states, like Delaware, New Jersey, and Connecticut, discovered that they carried disproportionate political weight with presidential electors than with any alternative method of election because they received electors according to federal numbers and not population. Large and small states worked the constitutional provisions to their respective advantage and acquired their own stake in the electoral college as it had developed. The electoral college became systemic and difficult to modify or abolish.

The experience of the early republic shows that neither the framers of the Constitution nor those who implemented it in the early republic were all-wise and all-knowing when it came to the election of a President. They made mistakes in the process of creating the electoral college, but they also experienced successes. In the process, they demonstrated that the Constitution takes life as Americans try to fit it to their needs and interests; its definition derives as much from practice as from the text or the intent of the framers. It is, after all, active citizenship which determines the course of political history in a republic.

APPENDICES

Table A.1
Electoral Vote 1792

	Washington	Adams	Clinton	Jefferson	Burr
Connecticut	9	9	0	0	0
Massachusetts	16	16	0	0	0
New Hampshire	6	6	0	0	0
Rhode Island	4	4	0	0	0
Vermont	3	3	0	0	0
Delaware	3	3	0	0	0
New Jersey	7	7	0	0	0
New York	12	0	12	0	0
Pennsylvania	15	14	1	0	0
Georgia	4	0	4	0	0
Maryland	8	8	0	0	0
North Carolina	12	0	12	0	0
South Carolina	8	7	0	0	1
Virginia	21	0	21	0	0
Kentucky	4	0	0	4	0
Totals	132	77	50	4	1

Source: Svend Peterson, *A Statistical History of the American Presidential Elections*, p.11.

Table A.2
Electoral Vote 1796

	Adams	Pinckney, T.	Ellsworth	Jefferson	Burr	Clinton	Others
Connecticut	9	4	0	0	0	0	5
Massachusetts	16	13	1	0	0	0	2
New Hampshire	6	0	6	0	0	0	0
Rhode Island	4	0	4	0	0	0	0
Vermont	4	4	0	0	0	0	0
Delaware	3	3	0	0	0	0	0
New Jersey	7	7	0	0	0	0	0
New York	12	12	0	0	0	0	0
Pennsylvania	1	2	0	14	13	0	0
Georgia	0	0	0	4	0	4	0
Maryland	7	4	0	4	3	0	2
North Carolina	1	1	0	11	6	0	5
South Carolina	0	8	0	8	0	0	0
Virginia	1	1	0	20	1	3	16
Kentucky	0	0	0	4	4	0	0
Tennessee	0	0	0	3	3	0	0
Totals	71	59	11	68	30	7	30

Source: Svend Peterson, *A Statistical History of the American Presidential Elections*, p.12.

Table A.3
Electoral Vote 1800

	Jefferson	Burr	Adams	Pinckney, C.C.	Jay
Connecticut	0	0	9	9	0
Massachusetts	0	0	16	16	0
New Hampshire	0	0	6	6	0
Rhode Island	0	0	4	3	1
Vermont	0	0	4	4	0
Delaware	0	0	3	3	0
New Jersey	0	0	7	7	0
New York	12	12	0	0	0
Pennsylvania	8	8	7	7	0
Georgia	4	4	0	0	0
Maryland	5	5	5	5	0
North Carolina	8	8	4	4	0
South Carolina	8	8	0	0	0
Virginia	21	21	0	0	0
Kentucky	4	4	0	0	0
Tennessee	3	3	0	0	0
Totals	73	73	65	64	1

Source: Svend Peterson, *A Statistical History of the American Presidential Elections*, p.13.

Table A.4
Electoral Vote 1804

	Jefferson	Pinckney, C.C.
Connecticut	0	9
Massachusetts	19	0
New Hampshire	7	0
Rhode Island	4	0
Vermont	6	0
Delaware	0	3
New Jersey	8	0
New York	19	0
Pennsylvania	20	0
Georgia	6	0
Maryland	9	2
North Carolina	14	0
South Carolina	10	0
Virginia	24	0
Kentucky	8	0
Ohio	3	0
Tennessee	5	0
Totals	162	14

Source: Svend Peterson, *A Statistical History of the American Presidential Elections*, p.14.

Notes

INTRODUCTION

1. For basic information about presidential electors, see Congressional Quarterly, *Presidential Elections Since 1789*, 4th ed., 1987; I. H. Wheeler, *A Letter in Regard to the Electoral Votes 1789 to 1873* (Washington, D.C., 1876); W. J. McDonald, *The Action of the Senate and House of Representatives 1789-1873* (Washington, D.C., 1876); John Holcombe, *The Electoral College* (Washington, D.C., 1913); Joseph Jackson, *Survey of the Electoral College* (Washington, D.C., 1945); Staff of the Subcommittee on Constitutional Amendments of the Committee of the Judiciary, United States Senate, *The Electoral College: Operation and Effect of Proposed Amendments to the Constitution of the United States* (Washington, D.C., 1961). Competent traditional studies of presidential elections include J. Hampden Dougherty, *The Electoral System of the United States* (New York, 1906); David A. McKnight, *The Electoral System of the United States* (Philadelphia, 1878); Charles A. O'Neill, *The American Electoral System* (New York, 1887); Eugene Roseboom, *A History of Presidential Elections* (New York, 1959); Edward Stanwood, *A History of the Presidency from 1788 to 1897* (Boston, 1912).

2. Examples of modern analyses of electors are John D. Feerick, "The Electoral College--Its Defects and Dangers," *New York State Bar Journal* 40 (August, 1968):317-330; Joseph E. Kallenbach, "Our Electoral College Gerrymander," *Midwest Journal of Political Science* 4 (May, 1960):162-191; Allan P. Sindler, "Presidential Election Methods and Urban-Ethnic Interests," *Law and Contemporary Problems* 27 (Spring, 1962):213-233; Thomas M. Susman, "State of Inhabitancy of Presidential and Vice Presidential Candidates and the Electoral College Vote," *Texas Law Review* 47 (May, 1969):779-792; John H. Yunker and Lawrence D. Longley, "The Biases of the Electoral College: Who Is Really Advantaged," and Max S. Power, "Logic and Legitimacy: On Understanding

the Electoral College Controversy," in *Perspectives on Presidential Selection*, edited by Donald R. Matthews (Washington, D.C., 1973), pp. 172-203, 204-237.

3. Classic commentaries on electors begin with James Kent, *Commentaries on American Law* vol. 2 (New York, 1826); Joseph Story, *Commentaries on the Constitution of the United States* vol. 3 (Boston, 1833); James Bryce, *American Commonwealth* vol. 2 (London, 1890), 2d ed.; and M. I. Ostrogorski, *Democracy and the Organization of Political Parties* (New York, 1910), 2 vols. Modern critics include Joseph E. Kallenbach, *The American Chief Executive: The Presidency and the Governorship* (New York, 1966); Lawrence D. Longley and Alan G. Braun, *The Politics of Electoral College Reform* (New Haven, Conn., 1972); Neal R. Peirce and Lawrence D. Longley, *The People's President: The Electoral College in American History and the Direct Vote Alternative* (New Haven, Conn., 1981); John P. Roche, "The Electoral college: A Note on American Political Mythology," *Dissent* 8 (Spring, 1961):197-199; Lucius Wilmerding, Jr., *The Electoral College* (New Brunswick, N.J., 1958). A compilation of commentary by scholars, politicians, and others is Julia E. Johnsen, comp., *Direct Election of the President* (New York, 1949). Those more favorably disposed to the electoral college are Judith Best, *The Case Against Direct Election of the President: A Defense of the Electoral College* (Ithaca, N.Y., 1971); Alexander M. Bickel, *Reform and Continuity: The Electoral College, the Convention, and the Party System* (New York, 1971); Martin Diamond, *The Electoral College and the American Idea of Democracy* (Washington, D.C., 1977); Wallace S. Sayre and Judith H. Parris, *Voting for President: The Electoral College and the American Political System* (Washington, D.C., 1970).

4. Lolabel House, *A Study of the Twelfth Amendment to the Constitution of the United States* (Philadelphia, 1901), remains the only monograph; Richard P. McCormick, *The Presidential Game* (New York, 1982), offers a brief, provocative modern interpretation.

1. ORIGINS OF THE ELECTORAL COLLEGE

1. Max Farrand, ed., *Records of the Federal Convention* (New Haven, Conn., 1911), 2:584.

2. Jonathan Elliot, ed., *The Debates in the Several State Conventions on the Adoption of the Federal Constitution* (Philadelphia, Pa., 1836), 2:511.

3. James Madison to Thomas Jefferson, New York, 24 Oct. 1787, in Farrand, ed., *Records*, 3:131-136.

4. Charles C. Thach, Jr., *The Creation of the Presidency 1775-1789, A Study in Constitutional History* (Baltimore, Md., 1969), pp. 13-75; Edward S. Corwin, *The President, Office and Powers*, 3rd edition (New York, 1948), pp.

1-38; Joseph E. Kallenbach, *The American Chief Executive*, pp. 30-67; Shlomo Slonim, "The Electoral College at Philadelphia: The Evolution of an Ad Hoc Congress for the Selection of a President," *Journal of American History* 73 (June, 1986):35-58.

5. James Madison, *Notes on the Debates in the Federal Convention*, edited by Adrienne Koch (Athens, Ohio, 1966), p. 310.

6. Alexander Hamilton, *The Federalist*, no. 72, edited by Edward Mead Earle, (New York, 1937), pp. 468-474.

7. Farrand, *Records*, 2:32, 56-57.

8. Figures are based on the federal census of 1790. See *Historical Statistics of the United States to 1957* (Washington, D.C., 1960), pp. 12-13.

9. Farrand, *Records*, 1:80, 85.

10. Clinton Rossiter, *1787: The Grand Convention* (New York, 1987), pp. 250-251; Madison, *Notes*, pp. 93, 361, 369; Lolabel House, *A Study of the Twelfth Amendment*, pp. 9-18.

11. Farrand, *Records*, 1:77, 2:51, 57-59; and Madison, *Notes*, p. 328.

12. Farrand, *Records*, 1:81; Madison, *Notes*, p. 330.

13. Charlene Bangs Bickford and Kenneth R. Bowling, *Birth of the Nation: The First Federal Congress 1789-1791* (New York, 1989), pp. 55-60.

14. Madison, *Notes*, pp. 328-329, 356.

15. Charles Sydnor, *Gentlemen Freeholders, Political Practices in Washington's Virginia* (Chapel Hill, N.C., 1952), pp. 120-134; Bernard Bailyn, *Origins of American Politics* (New York, 1967), pp. 96-101; Gordon Wood, *Creation of the American Republic 1776-1787* (Chapel Hill, N.C., 1969), pp. 475-483; Michael Kammen, *People of Paradox, An Enquiry Concerning the Origins of American Civilization*, Reprint (New York, 1973), pp. 225-249; Robert E. Shalhope, *The Roots of Democracy, American Thought and Culture 1760-1800* (Boston, Mass., 1990), pp. 27-52.

16. Madison, *Notes*, p. 297.

17. Farrand, *Records*, 1:79, 2:32, 58, 101, 121. Slonim, "The Electoral College," makes the argument that the rivalry between the large and small states became the most important factor in shaping the final provisions for the electoral college.

18. Farrand, *Records*, 2:121.

19. Ibid., 2:84, 89, 98, 3:587-589.

20. Ibid., 2:399, 401-403.

21. Ibid., 2:399.

22. Ibid., 2:481, 493-494, 500-502; Madison, *Notes*, p. 575.

23. James Madison to Henry Lee, Montpelier, 14 Jan. 1825, *Records*, edited by Farrand, 3:464. A motion by Daniel Carroll and Gouverneur Morris to provide specifically for popular election of electors had been voted down as recently as August 24.

2. THE RATIFICATION DEBATE

1. Elliot, ed., *Debates*, 2:511.

2. Hamilton, *The Federalist*, no. 68, pp. 441-445.

3. Elliot, *Debates*, 3:484. See also 2:407, 4:314; *New Hampshire Gazette*, 14 Aug. and 18 Sept. 1788, and *Connecticut Journal*, 6 Aug. 1788.

4. Morton Borden, ed., *The Antifederalist Papers* no. 71 (East Lansing, Mich., 1965), pp. 205-206.

5. Merrill Jensen, ed., *The Documentary History of the Ratification of the Constitution by the States* (Madison, Wisc., 1978), 3:426, 459.

6. Columbian Patriot, "Observations on the New Constitution," in *Pamphlets on the Constitution of the United States, published during its discussion by the people 1787-1788*, edited by Paul Leicester Ford, (Brooklyn, N.Y., 1888), p. 12.

7. Jensen, ed., *Documentary History*, 3:240.

8. Ibid. See also Richard Henry Lee, *Letters From The Federal Farmer to the Republican*, no. 14, edited by Richard Harwell Bennett (University, Ala., 1977), p. 92. In 1792, the number of electors increased to 135 and Georgia's share declined to 4. Svend Peterson, *A Statistical History of the American Presidential Elections* (New York, 1963), p. 11.

9. Jensen, ed., *Documentary History*, 3:426; Elliot, *Debates*, 3:488-489.

10. Elliot, *Debates*, 3:492.

11. Borden, ed., *The Antifederalist Papers*, no. 72, p. 207.

12. Elliot, Debates, 4:288, 3:493; Borden, ed., *Antifederalist Papers*, no. 51, p. 148.

13. Elliot, *Debates*, 2:531.

14. Bennett, ed., *Letters*, p.16.

15. Cecelia Kenyon, ed., *The Antifederalists* (Indianapolis, Ind., 1966), p. 305.

16. Borden, ed., *The Antifederalist Papers*, no. 71, p. 303.

17. Elliot, *Debates*, 4:104.

18. Kenyon, ed., *The Antifederalists*, p. 305; Elliot, *Debates*, 3:488-489; Lee, *Letters From the Federal Farmer*, no. 14, p. 92; Jensen, ed., *Documentary History*, 3:241.

19. Elliot, ed., *Debates*, 2:482.

20. Ibid., 2:512.

21. Jensen, ed., *Documentary History*, 2:142, 565.

22. Jensen, ed., *Documentary History*, 3:532.

23. Elliot, ed., *Debates*, 2:253. See also Hamilton, *The Federalist*, no. 68, pp. 441-445.

24. Elliot, ed., *Debates*, 3:486.

25. Ibid.

26. Ibid., 3:103, 104, 4:315; and Farrand, ed., *Records*, 3:354.

27. Citizen of America, "An Examination into the leading principles of the Federal Constitution," in *Pamphlets*, edited by P. L. Ford, p. 35; Hamilton, *The Federalist*, no. 68, pp. 441-445.

28. Bennett, ed., *Letters*, no. 14, p. 92, and no. 3, p. 16. See also "The Letters of Fabius on the Federal Constitution," no. 2, in *Pamphlets*, edited by P. L. Ford, pp. 171-172; Jensen, ed., *Documentary History*, 3:532; Elliot, ed., *Debates*, 2:511, 3:494-495.

29. Citizen of America, "An Examination," in *Pamphlets*, edited by P. L. Ford, p. 35.

30. "The Letters of Fabius," no. 2, in *Pamphlets*, edited by P. L. Ford, p. 172.

31. Elliot, ed., *Debates*, 3:486, 4:104-105. See also Bailyn, *Origins*, pp. 79-95; J. G. A. Pocock, *The Machiavellian Moment, Florentine Political Thought and the Atlantic Republican Tradition* (Princeton, N.J., 1975), pp. 506-552.

32. James DeWitt Andrews, ed., *The Works of James Wilson, Being the Public Discourses upon Jurisprudence and the Political Science* (Chicago, 1896), 1:64. See also Elliot, ed., *Debates*, 2:512, 4:305, 315.

33. Elliot, ed., *Debates*, 2:439; Jensen, ed., *Documentary History*, 3:246; Citizen of America, "An Examination," in *Pamphlets*, edited by P. L. Ford, p. 35.

34. Elliot, ed., *Debates*, 4:105.

35. Ibid., 2:512; Andrews, ed., *James Wilson*, 1:64.

36. James Madison, to the contrary, believed that district elections by the people most closely reflected the intention of the framers. See Donald O. Dewey, "Madison's Views on Electoral Reform," *The Western Political Quarterly* 15 (March, 1962):140-142.

37. Elliot, ed., *Debates*, 2:511.

38. Farrand, *Records*, 2:501.

39. Ibid., 2:113, shows that in later July, Hugh Williamson had suggested giving each voter three votes with only one being allowed for someone from his own state. He may also have seen this step as a way to enhance the weight of smaller states in the selection of the President. Gouverneur Morris refined this idea by suggesting that each person vote for two persons, at least one of whom should be a resident of another state.

40. Farrand, *Records*, 2:513.

41. Slonim, "The Electoral College," pp. 53-54; Farrand, *Records*, 2:514-515, 524-525.

42. John Adams to Abigail Adams, 19 Dec. 1793, in *The Works of John Adams*, ed. by Charles Francis Adams (Boston, Mass., 1850), 1:460.

43. Paul Boller, *Presidential Campaigns* (New York, 1984), p. 4; George Clinton to Pierre Van Cortlandt, Jr., Albany, 30 Jan. and 10 Mar. 1804, in Pierre Van Cortlandt, Jr., Papers, Rare Books and Manuscript Division, New

York Public Library (hereinafter cited as NYPL), Astor, Lenox and Tilden Foundations.

44. Slonim, "The Electoral College," pp. 35-36, 57-58.

3. THE FIRST PRESIDENTIAL ELECTION

1. Wood, *Creation*, pp. 499-518; Richard B. Hofstadter, *The Idea of a Party System* (Berkeley, Calif., 1969), pp. 40-73.

2. Merrill Jensen and Robert A. Becker, eds., *Documentary History of the First Federal Elections* (Madison, Wisc., 1976), 1:90.

3. Ibid., 1:132-133.

4. *Connecticut Journal*, 22, 29 Oct. 1788, and 7 Jan. 1789, and *Connecticut Courant*, 20 Oct., 15 Dec. 1788, and 12 Jan. 1789.

5. *Public Records of the State of Connecticut* (Hartford, 1945), 5:495-496.

6. Electoral Vote of 1789, Connecticut, Legislative Division, National Archives (hereinafter cited as NA).

7. Ibid. See also *Connecticut Courant*, 9 Feb. 1789; *New Haven Gazette*, 11 Feb. 1789; *Connecticut Gazette*, 13 Feb. 1789; and *Connecticut Journal*, 18 Feb. 1789.

8. Jensen and Becker, eds., *First Federal Elections*, 1:777-778, 779; *New Hampshire Gazette*, 19 Nov. 1788; *The Laws of New Hampshire*, 5:331-333.

9. *Early State Papers of New Hampshire*, 21:336, 348-349, 369, 372, 374-376, 434, 436-437; Jensen and Becker, eds., *First Federal Elections*, 1:816, 823-824.

10. *Early State Papers of New Hampshire*, 21:440, 442-445; Jensen and Becker, eds., *First Federal Elections*, 1:816-823; Electoral Votes 1789, New Hampshire, NA.

11. Jensen and Becker, eds., *First Federal Elections*, 1:438, 440-441, 443.

12. Ibid., 1:464-466.

13. Ibid., 1:476-477, 481-482.

14. Ibid., 1:485-488.

15. Ibid., 1:491, 498-503; *Acts and Laws of the Commonwealth of Massachusetts, 1788-1789*, (Boston, 1788), c. 49, 20 Nov. 1788.

16. Jensen and Becker, eds., *First Federal Elections*, 1:531-536; *Acts and Laws of Massachusetts, 1788-1789*, c. 10, 6 Jan. 1789.

17. Jensen and Becker, *First Federal Elections*, 1:536-539, 744-763.

18. Ibid., 1:542; Electoral Votes of 1789, Massachusetts, NA.

19. Jensen and Becker, eds., *First Federal Elections*, 1:147-149; Jackson Turner Main, *Political Parties Before the Constitution*, Reprint (New York, 1974), pp. 268-295.

20. South Carolina, *Statutes At Large, 1787-1814*, (Columbia, 1839), no. 1427, 4 Nov. 1788.

21. Jensen and Becker, eds., *First Federal Elections*, 1:152-169, 201-203.

22. Gordon DenBoer, Lucy Trumbull Brown, and Charles D. Hagermann, eds., *The Documentary History of the First Federal Elections* (Madison, Wisc., 1984), 2:427-430, 434-437, 440-441.

23. Ibid., 2:441-442; Electoral Votes of 1789, Georgia, NA.

24. DenBoer, Brown, Hagermann, *First Federal Elections*, pp. 101-104, 107.

25. *Laws of Maryland made and passed at a Session of Assembly* [3 Nov.-23 Dec. 1788] (Annapolis, 1788), c. 10, 22 Dec. 1788; DenBoer, Brown, Hagermann, eds., *First Federal Elections*, 2:123, 128, 136-140.

26. DenBoer, Brown, Hagermann, eds., *First Federal Elections*, 2:161-169, 175-180, 185, 191, 194, 202.

27. William Tilghman to Tench Coxe, Chestertown, 2 Jan. 1789, and Henry Hollingsworth to Levi Hollingsworth, Elkton, 5 Jan. 1789, in *First Federal Elections*, edited by DenBoer, Brown, Hagermann, 2:180, 186.

28. Ibid., 2:192-193.

29. Ibid., 2:180-182, 186-188, 203, 204-205.

30. Electoral Vote of 1789, Maryland, NA; DenBoer, Brown, Hagermann, eds., *First Federal Elections*, 2:208, 220, 230, 231, 233, 234.

31. Forrest McDonald, *We The People* (Chicago, 1958), pp. 255-283.

32. George Washington to James Madison, Mount Vernon, 23 Sept. 1788, in *First Federal Elections*, edited by DenBoer, Brown, Hagermann, 2:254; Main, *Political Parties*, pp. 244-267.

33. Virginia, *Journal of the House of Delegates* [20 Oct.-30 Dec. 1788], pp. 14, 31-33; DenBoer, Brown., Hagermann, eds., *First Federal Elections*, 2:263, 268-269, 367-368, 384, 404-406; William Waller Hening, ed., *The Statutes at Large; Being A Collection of All the Laws of Virginia from the First Session of the Legislature in the Year 1619* vol. 12 (Richmond, 1823), c. 1, 17 Nov. 1788.

34. DenBoer, Brown, Hagermann, eds., *First Federal Elections*, 2:299-300, 305-306, 398-399, 400, 404; Electoral Vote of 1789, Virginia, NA.

35. DenBoer, Brown, Hagermann, eds., *First Federal Elections*, pp. 366-368, 384, 384-386, 387, 395, 401-402; Electoral Vote of 1789, Virginia, NA.

36. Delaware, *Votes and Proceedings of the House of Assembly*, 20 Oct. 1788, pp. 5-14; *Laws of the Delaware State Passed at the Session of the General Assembly, Commenced at Dover, on the 20th day of October, 1788* (Wilmington, 1788), pp. 1-6, 28 Oct. 1788.

37. Electoral Vote of 1789, Delaware, NA.

38. DenBoer, Brown, Hagermann, eds., *First Federal Elections*, 3:14-19, 29-31; Electoral Vote of 1789, New Jersey, NA.

39. McDonald, *We The People*, pp. 163-164; Main, *Political Parties*, pp. 174-211; Pennsylvania, *Debates of the General Assembly* [2 Sept.-4 Oct. 1788], pp.179-187.

40. Tench Coxe to James Madison, Philadelphia, 26 Sept. [1788], in *First*

Federal Elections, edited by Jensen and Becker, 1:289.

41. *The Statutes at Large of Pennsylvania from 1682 to 1801* vol. 13 (Harrisburg, 1908), c. 1373, 4 Oct. 1788; Pennsylvania, *Debates of the General Assembly* [2 Sept.-4 Oct. 1788], pp. 187-190.

42. Pennsylvania, *Debates of the General Assembly*, p. 190.

43. Jensen and Becker, eds., *First Federal Elections*, 1:303-370, 370-384.

44. Ibid., 1:374-375, 380-382, 390-400. For example, Westmoreland had 53 candidates receiving votes, only one of whom had as many as 100. See also James Dunwoodie to the Honorable Members of Council, 2 Feb. [1788], in 1:387-388.

45. Ibid., 1:380-381; Electoral Votes of 1789, Pennsylvania, NA.

46. Charles Thomson to George Read, New York, 21 Mar. 1789, George Read Papers, Historical Society of Delaware, Wilmington, Del.

47. Bickford and Bowling, *Birth of the Nation*, pp. 9-12; W. J. McDonald, *Action*, p. 3.

48. McDonald, *Action*, pp. 4-5.

4. NEW YORK ABSTAINS

1. Patricia U. Bonomi, *A Factious People* (New York, 1971); Countryman, *A People in Revolution*; Linda Grant DePauw, *The Eleventh Pillar* (Ithaca, N.Y., 1966); Main, *Political Parties*, pp. 120-155; McDonald, *We The People*, pp. 283-310; E. Wilder Spaulding, *New York in the Critical Period 1783-89* (New York, 1932), pp. 84-159; Young, *The Democratic Republicans*; DenBoer, Brown, Hagermann, eds., *First Federal Elections*, 3:191-564.

2. Main, *Parties*, pp. 149-150.

3. Ibid.

4. Spaulding, *Critical Period*, pp. 232-276; McDonald, *We The People*, pp. 287-310; DePauw, *Eleventh Pillar*, pp. 183-203; Richard B. Morris, "John Jay and the Adoption of the Federal Constitution in New York: A New Reading of Persons and Events," *New York History* 63 (April, 1982):133-164; Elliot, ed., *Debates*, 1:413; George Washington to John Jay, 3 Aug. 1788, in *The Correspondence and Public Papers of John Jay 1763-1826* (New York, 1890-1893), edited by Henry P. Johnston, 3:352; Ezra L'Hommedieu to John Smith, 20 July 1788, John Smith Papers, The New-York Historical Society, New York, N.Y. (hereinafter cited as NYHS); Robert Ernst, "The Long Island Delegates and the new York Ratifying Convention," *New York History* 70 (January, 1989):55-78.

5. Abraham B. Bancker to, 30 Aug. 1788, Bancker Family Correspondence, NYHS; H. G. Letter 12, [New York], 8 March 1789, in *The Papers of Alexander Hamilton* (New York, 1962), edited by Harold C. Syrett, 5:293-297.

6. Abraham B. Bancker to Evert Bancker, Albany, 20 Dec. 1788, Bancker

Family Papers, NYHS; Young, *The Democratic Republicans*, pp. 109-128.

7. John Jay to George Washington, 21 Sept. 1788, John Jay Papers, Columbia University, New York, N.Y. (hereinafter cited as CU); John Lamb to Mr. Oswald, n.p., n.d., and a second letter without target, place, or date, beginning with "The Federal Republicans in this State," John Lamb Papers, Box 5, nos. 46 and 47, NYHS; Henry Knox to George Washington, New York, 21 Dec. 1788, in *The Papers of George Washington, Presidential Series 1: September 1788-March 1789*, edited by W. W. Abbot and Dorothy Twohig (Charlottesville, Va., 1983), 1:195.

8. New York, *Senate Journal*, 12th session, 11 Dec. 1788, pp. 6-7; New York, *Assembly Journals*, 12th session, 11 Dec. 1788, pp. 6, 13, 18-20; Francis Newton Thorpe, ed., *The Federal and State Constitutions* (Washington, D.C., 1909), 5:2634-2635; Ernst, "The Long Island Delegates," pp.60-67; David Gelston to John Smith, York, 28 Dec. 1788, John Smith Papers.

9. New York, *Senate Journal*, 12th session, pp. 20-23.

10. New York *Assembly Journal*, 12th session, pp. 33-39.

11. *Daily Advertiser*, 13 Jan. 1789, and *The New York Journal and Weekly Register*, 5 Feb. 1789; DenBoer, Brown, Hagermann, eds., *First Federal Elections*, 3:303-311, 314-315, 318-319.

12. *Daily Advertiser*, 13 Jan. 1789; *The New York Journal and Weekly Register*, 5 Feb. 1789.

13. *Daily Advertiser*, 14 Jan. 1789; *The New York Journal and Weekly Register*, 12 Feb. 1789.

14. *Daily Advertiser*, 16 Jan. 1789; *The New York Journal and Weekly Register*, 26 Feb. 1789.

15. *Daily Advertiser*, 17 Jan. 1789; *The New York Journal and Weekly Register*, 26 Feb. 1789.

16. *Daily Advertiser*, 20 Jan. 1789, and *The New York Journal and Weekly Register*, 5, 12 Mar. 1789.

17. Henry Sewall to William Heath, New York, 6 Jan. 1789, and Tench Coxe to Benjamin Rush, 13 Jan. 1789, in *First Federal Elections*, edited by DenBoer, Brown, Hagermann, 3:311, 318; Abraham Bancker to Evert Bancker, n.d., received 10 Jan. 1789, Bancker Family Papers; New York, *Senate Journal*, 12th session, pp. 26-27; *Daily Advertiser*, 20, 21 Jan. 1789; New York, *Assembly Journal*, 12th session, p. 43.

18. Abraham Bancker to Evert Bancker, n.d., received Jan. 10, 1789, Bancker Family Papers.

19. *New York Journal and Weekly Register*, 15 Jan. 1789. See also John Lamb to John Smith, 17 Jan. 1789, John Smith Papers.

20. New York, *Senate Journal*, 12th session, pp. 40, 43-44; Cornelius C. Schoonmaker to Peter Van Gaasbeek, Albany, 3 Jan. 1789, Peter Van Gaasbeek Papers, Franklin D. Roosevelt Library, Hyde Park; New York, *Assembly Journal*, 12th session, pp. 63-64, 72-77.

21. DeWitt Clinton to John McKesson, New York, 18 Jan. 1789, George Clinton Gubernatorial and Personal Records (hereinafter cited as George Clinton Papers), New York State Archives, Albany, N.Y.; Melancton Smith notes, n.p., n.d., Melancton Smith Papers, Folder 37, New York State Library, Albany, New York (hereinafter cited as NYSL); New York, *Assembly Journal*, 12th session, pp. 72-73, 75-77, 95-99, 106; New York, *Senate Journal*, 12th session, pp. 39, 43-44, 50, 53-54, 56-57.

22. Alexander Hamilton to Samuel Jones, New York, 21 Jan. 1789, *Hamilton*, edited by Syrett, 5:244-246.

23. Ernst, "The Long Island Delegates," pp. 60-67; DeWitt Clinton to John McKesson, New York, Jan. 18, 1789, George Clinton Papers; New York *Assembly Journal*, 12th session, pp. 81-82; Melancton Smith to John Smith, New York, 10 Jan. 1789, John Smith Papers.

24. *Daily Advertiser*, 13 Feb. 1789; New York, *Assembly Journal*, 12th session, pp. 85-87.

25. *Daily Advertiser*, 13 Feb. 1789.

26. *Daily Advertiser*, 14 Feb. 1789.

27. New York, *Assembly Journal*, 12th session, pp. 85-88, 95-99; *Daily Advertiser*, 16 Feb. 1789; New York, *Senate Journal*, 12th session, p. 50.

28. *Daily Advertiser*, 17 Feb. 1789.

29. Ibid.

30. *Daily Advertiser*, 18 Feb. 1789.

31. New York, *Assembly Journal*, 12th session, pp. 100-103.

32. New York, *Senate Journal*, 12th session, pp. 51-53.

33. Madison, *Notes*, pp. 585-586; Farrand, *Records*, 2:500, 514, 515, 524-525.

34. Jeremiah Mason to John Woodworth, New Haven, 26 Jan. 1789, in *First Federal Elections*, edited by DenBoer, Brown, Hagermann, 3:345; John Smith to, n.p., n.d., and David Gelston to John Smith on 8 Jan. 1789, John Smith Papers; Hamilton to Theodore Sedgwick, New York, 29 Jan. 1789, in *Hamilton*, edited by Syrett, 5:250-251; John Lamb to John Smith, 7 Jan. 1789, John Lamb Papers.

35. Melancton Smith to John Smith, New York, 10 Jan. 1789, John Smith Papers.

36. Alexander Hamilton to James Wilson, New York, 25 Jan. 1789, in *Hamilton*, edited by Syrett, 5:247.

37. Horatio Gates to James Duane, 22 Feb. 1789, James Duane Papers, NYHS.

38. Election broadside, Jacob C. Ten Eyck et al, Albany, 19 Feb. 1789, Broadside Collection, NYPL; Charles Tillinghast, Melancton Smith, Mr. Connolly to various Committees, New York, 15 Apr. 1789, John Lamb Papers; Rufus King, Subject of a Conversation with Gov. Clinton, 12 June 1789, *Rufus King*, edited by King, 1:356; and Young, *Democratic Republicans*, pp. 3-6,

129-148.

39. Alexander Hamilton to Samuel Jones, New York, 21 Jan. 1789, in *Hamilton*, edited by Syrett, 5:244-246.

5. NEW RULES FOR THE GAME IN 1792

1. Bickford and Bowling, *Birth of the Nation*, and Margaret C. S. Chrisman, *The First Federal Congress 1789-1791* (Washington, D.C., 1989). Charlene Bangs Bickford and Helen E. Veit, eds., *Documentary History of the First Federal Congress of the United States of America* (Baltimore, Md., 1986), 4:659-663; McKnight, *Electoral System*, pp. 246-257.

2. New Hampshire, *Laws of New Hampshire, 1792-1801* vol. 6 (Concord, 1917), c. 16, 20 June 1792.

3. Rhode Island, *Acts of the Governor and General Assembly*, [Mar. 1787-Oct. 1794], Oct. 1792 session, p. 5; *Records of the State of Rhode Island* (Providence, 1865), 10:504-505.

4. *State Papers of Vermont* (Montpelier, 1970), 3:Part 5, 65-69, 82-88, 106-107, 182-183, 187-188, 199, 203; *State Papers of Vermont* (Montpelier, 1967), 15:43, 103.

5. North Carolina, *Laws of North Carolina at a General Assembly, Begun and Held at Newbern on the Fifteenth Day of November, in the Year of Our Lord One Thousand Seven Hundred and Ninety-Two* (Halifax, 1793), c. 15, 16, n.d.

6. Delaware, *Senate Journal* [1-3 Nov. 1792], pp.5-8; Peirce and Longley, *The People's President*, pp. 247-249.

7. *Laws of New York*, 15th session, c. 72, 12 Apr. 1792.

8. Article II, section 1, provides "Each State shall appoint, in such Manner as the Legislature thereof may direct" and says nothing about the role of governors and other bodies.

9. New York, *Senate Journal*, 15th session, 5 Jan. 1792, pp. 70-71, 78, and *Assembly Journal*, 15th session, 5 Jan. 1792, pp. 177-178, 204-206; *Laws of New York*, 15th session, c. 72, 12 Apr. 1792; *Daily Advertiser*, 5, 12, 14, 23 Jan. 1792.

10. Alexander Hamilton to George Washington, Philadelphia, 4 Apr. 1792 in *Hamilton*, edited by Syrett, 11:228-230 and editorial note on 226-228; Richard Henry Lee to Henry Lee, Richmond, 25 Mar. 1792, Myers Coll., NYPL; New York, *Senate Journal*, 16th session, 6 Nov. 1792, pp. 4-5, 6; *Laws of New York*, 16th session, c. 1, 19 Nov. 1792.

11. New York in 1825 tried a brief experiment where voters chose in congressional districts and these electors met and appointed two additional electors, but abandoned this method in favor of popular election on a general ticket in 1829. See *Laws of New York*, 48th session, c. 33, 15 Mar. 1825, and

Laws of New York, 52nd session, c. 139, 15 Apr. 1829.

12. Hofstadter, *The Idea of a Party System*, pp. 40-73; William N. Chambers, *Political Parties in a New Nation, The American Experience 1776-1809* (New York, 1963), pp. 17-52; Joseph Charles, *Origins of the American Party System*, Reprint (New York, 1961), pp. 3-53; Noble Cunningham, Jr., *The Jeffersonian Republicans, The Formation of Party Organization, 1789-1801* (Chapel Hill, N.C., 1957), p. 29.

13. James Madison to Edmund Pendleton, Philadelphia, 6 Dec. 1792, Hunt, *James Madison*, 6:121. See also Marcus Cunliffe, "The Elections of 1789 and 1792," in *American Presidential Elections*, edited by Arthur M. Schlesinger, Jr. (New York, 1971), 1:22-26.

14. Robert R. Livingston to Thomas Jefferson, New York, 20 Feb. 1791 in Robert R. Livingston Papers, NYHS; Dumas Malone, *Jefferson and the Rights of Man* (Boston, Mass., 1951), pp. 359-363.

15. Melancton Smith and Marinus Willett, New York, 30 Sept. 1792, a memorandum enclosed with the letter of James Monroe to James Madison, Fredericksburg, 9 Oct. 1792, and John Nicholson to James Madison, 3 Oct. 1792, *Papers of James Madison* (Charlottesville, Va., 1983), edited by Robert A. Rutland and Thomas A. Mason, 14:376-377, 378-380; Robert R. Livingston to Edward Livingston, Clermont, 1 Oct. 1792, Robert R. Livingston Papers.

16. John Beckley to James Madison, Philadelphia, 10 Sept. and 17 Oct. 1792, James Madison Papers, Rare Book and Manuscript Division, NYPL, Astor, Lenox and Tilden Foundations.

17. James Monroe to James Madison, Fredericksburg, 9 October 1792, *Madison*, edited by Rutland and Mason, 14:378.

18. Young, *Democratic Republicans*, pp. 324-341; Roseboom, *Presidential Elections*, p. 27; James Madison to Edmund Pendleton, Philadelphia, 6 Dec. 1792, *The Writings of James Madison* (New York, 1906), edited by Gaillard Hunt, 6:121; Alexander Hamilton to, Philadelphia, 21, 26 Sept. 1792, in *Hamilton*, edited by Syrett, 12:408, 480.

19. Spaulding, *George Clinton*, p. 208, quotes Wolcott. Spaulding's speculation that if Clinton had taken 14 votes from Adams's total, he would have been Vice President leaves open what it is that Clinton could have had to do to win those 14 and what consequences his actions would have had on the dynamics of the election. See also George Read to Gunning Bedford, Philadelphia, 30 Nov. 1792, George Read Papers, Historical Society of Delaware (hereinafter cited as HSD).

20. Electoral Vote of 1792, Connecticut, Massachusetts, New Hampshire, Rhode Island, and Vermont, NA. See also the agreement between Lot Hall and Paul Brigham, Windsor, 5 Dec. 1792, Paul Brigham Papers, University of Vermont, Burlington, Vt.

21. Electoral Votes of 1792, Maryland, Virginia, North Carolina, South Carolina, Georgia, and Kentucky, NA.

22. John Quincy Adams to John Adams, Boston, 8, 16 Dec. 1792, in *Writings of John Quincy Adams*, edited by Worthington C. Ford (New York, 1913), 1:120, 123.

23. *New York Journal*, 21 Nov. 1792.

24. Abraham Bancker to Evert Bancker, 25 Nov. 1792, Bancker Family Correspondence; John Beckley to James Madison, Philadelphia, 1 Aug. 1792, *Papers of James Madison*, edited by Rutland and Mason, 14:346, and 2 Sept. and 17 Oct. 1792, James Madison Papers, NYPL; Jabez D. Hammond, *History of Political Parties in the State of New York*, 3d ed. (Cooperstown, N.Y., 1845), 1:76-77; Jacob Morris to William Cooper, New York, 27 Jan. 1793, Jacob Morris Papers, New York State Historical Association, Cooperstown, N.Y. (hereinafter cited as NYSHA); Silas Talbot to Reverend Hitchcock, New York, 15 Dec. 1792, George Clinton Papers; Cunningham, *Jeffersonian Republicans*, pp. 45-49. See also Young, *Democratic Republicans*, p. 331; William Stuart to Griffith Evans, New York, 13 Dec. 1792, Griffith Evans Correspondence 1786-1848, Historical Society of Pennsylvania, Philadelphia (hereinafter cited as HSP); Alexander Hamilton to John Steele, 18 Oct. 1792, in *Hamilton*, edited by Syrett, 12:568-569.

25. Certificate of the New York electors, 1792, in James Duane Papers; the Electoral Votes of New York, 1792, NA.

26. Electoral Vote of 1792, New York, New Jersey, Delaware, and Pennsylvania, NA.

27. Cunliffe, "Elections of 1789 and 1792," p. 27.

28. W. J. McDonald, *Action*, pp. 5-6.

29. Cunningham, *Jeffersonian Republicans*, p. 35; Electoral Vote of 1792, Rhode Island, NA, noted that they voted for two persons, "one of whom for President and the other for Vice President." See Appendices A.1 for a summary of the electoral votes.

30. Robert R. Livingston to Edward Livingston, Clermont, 1 Oct. 1792, Robert R. Livingston Papers; Young, *Democratic Republicans*, p. 332; Best, *The Case Against Direct Election*, pp. 46-82.

31. John Quincy Adams to John Adams, Boston, 22 Dec. 1792, in *Writings*, edited by W. C. Ford, 1:131.

6. AN ELECTION WITHOUT WASHINGTON

1. Cunningham, *Jeffersonian Republicans*, pp. 50-88; Charles, *Origins of the American Party System*, pp. 91-140.

2. George Washington to John Jay, Philadelphia, 8 May 1796, in *John Jay*, edited by Johnston, 4:212.

3. George Washington to Alexander Hamilton, Philadelphia, 15 May 1796 in *Hamilton*, edited by Syrett, 20:177.

4. Robert Goodloe Harper to Alexander Hamilton, Raleigh, 4 Nov. 1796, in Ibid., 20:371; and John Beckley to William Irvine, 15 Sept. 1796, William Irvine Papers, HSP.

5. George Washington to Alexander Hamilton, Mount Vernon, 26 June 1796, and Alexander Hamilton to George Washington, New York, 5 July 1796, in *Hamilton*, edited by Syrett, 20:239, 247.

6. William Smith to Rufus King, Charleston, 23 July 1796, Rufus King Papers, NYHS. See also Page Smith, "The Election of 1796," in *American Presidential Elections*, edited by Schlesinger, 1:70-71; Roseboom, *American Presidential Elections*, p. 33; Robert R. Livingston to James Monroe, Clermont, 10 July 1795, Robert R. Livingston Papers.

7. Cunningham, *The Jeffersonian Republicans*, pp. 89-115; Smith, "Election of 1796," p. 70; John Beckley to DeWitt Clinton, Philadelphia, 11 Apr. 1796, DeWitt Clinton Papers, Rare Book and Manuscript Library, CU; John Beckley to James Monroe, Philadelphia, 1 June 1795, James Monroe Papers, Rare Books and Manuscript Division, NYPL, Astor, Lenox and Tilden Foundations; John Beckley to James Madison, Philadelphia, 20 June 1796, James Madison Papers, NYPL; Spaulding, *George Clinton*, p. 218; Robert R. Livingston to Edward Livingston, Clermont, 12 June 1796, Robert R. Livingston Papers; Young, *Democratic Republicans*, pp. 546-565.

8. John Beckley to James Monroe, Philadelphia, 17 Oct. 1796, James Monroe Papers, NYPL; *Greenleaf's New York Journal, & Patriotic Register*, 25 Oct. 1796; John Laurance to Rufus King, New York, 15 Oct. 1796, Rufus King Papers.

9. John Beckley to James Madison, Philadelphia, 15 Oct. 1796, James Madison Papers, NYPL.

10. Alexander Hamilton to, New York, 8 Nov. 1796, in *Hamilton*, edited by Syrett, 20:376-377; Forrest McDonald, *Alexander Hamilton* (New York, 1979), pp. 322-328, and 438 n. 45.

11. John Laurance to Rufus King, New York, 7 Nov. 1796, Rufus King Papers; Jonathan Dayton to Theodore Sedgwick, 12 Nov. 1796, *Hamilton*, edited by Syrett, 20:403-404.

12. Theodore Sedgwick to Jonathan Dayton, Stockbridge, 19 Nov. 1796, in *Hamilton*, edited by Syrett, 20:406.

13. George Cabot to Oliver Wolcott, Jr., Brookline, 30 Nov. 1796, Oliver Wolcott, Jr. Papers, Connecticut Historical Society, Hartford, Ct. (hereinafter cited as CHS).

14. Alexander Hamilton to, New York, 8 Nov. 1796, Theodore Sedgwick to Alexander Hamilton, Stockbridge, 19 Nov. 1796, and Stephen Higginson to Alexander Hamilton, Boston, 9 Dec. 1796, in *Hamilton*, edited by Syrett, 20:376-377, 402-407, 437-438.

15. Peirce and Longley, *People's President*, pp. 248-249, provides a summary table of how states chose electors; Electoral Vote of 1796, Massachusetts

and New Hampshire, NA; *Laws of New Hampshire* vol. 6 (Concord, 1917), c. 19, 16 June 1796.

16. Electoral Vote of 1796, Connecticut, NA.

17. Electoral Vote of 1796, Rhode Island, NA.

18. Electoral Vote of 1796, Vermont, NA.

19. Cunningham, *Jeffersonian Republicans*, pp. 94-97, 103-105; Electoral Vote of 1796, Maryland, NA.

20. Electoral Vote of 1796, Virginia, NA.

21. Electoral Vote of 1796, North Carolina, NA.

22. Electoral Vote of 1796, South Carolina, NA.

23. Electoral Votes of 1796, Georgia and Kentucky, NA. According to the *Newport Mercury*, 29 Nov. 1796 a question arose about Georgia because a legislative resolution rather than law prescribed the mode. The former did not require the assent of the governor, the latter did. According to Georgia newspapers, the state constitution did not authorize any legislative act which did not give the governor the opportunity to revise it.

24. Edward Rutledge to Henry Middleton Rutledge, 21 July 1796, Rutledge Papers in the Ferdinand J. Dreer Autograph Collection, HSP.

25. Electoral Vote of 1796, Tennessee, NA.

26. *Delaware Gazette*, 14, 17 Dec. 1796, complained about the legislative mode which kept Republicans from any proportional weight in presidential elections and wondered at the expectations "that 138 men, many of whom have hundreds of miles to travel, and many of whom are advanced in years, should all be able to attend on the *one* day set aside for the election, at this inclement season of the year."

27. Ibid.

28. Electoral Votes of 1796, Delaware, New Jersey, and Pennsylvania, NA. Some contemporaries pointed to Samuel Miles as the person who created the anomalous results by casting a vote for Jefferson and Pinckney. They assert that he was a faithless elector, but most scholars agree that party lines were still not that clear and that Miles had not publicly pledged to the Federalist ticket.

29. *Laws of New York, 1792-1797*, c. 32, 26 Mar. 1796.

30. Peter Van Gaasbeek to Ebenezer Foote, Kingston, 20 Mar. 1796, Ebenezer Foote Papers, NYSA.

31. *Greenleaf's New York Journal, & Patriotic Register*, Nov. 11, 1796. See also New York, *Senate Journal*, 20th session, 1 Nov. 1796, p. 4; Hammond, *History*, 1:101-103; New York, *Assembly Journal*, 20th session, 1 Nov. 1796, pp. 14-18; John Jay, Certificate for New York State Electors, 24 Nov. 1796, NYSL; Ebenezer Foote to Peter Van Gaasbeek, Newburgh, 7 Oct. 1796, and Peter Van Gaasbeek to Ebenezer Foote, Kingston, 24 [   ] 1796, Ebenezer Foote Papers, NYSL.

32. Robert Troup to Rufus King, New York, 16 Nov. 1796, Rufus King Papers.

33. DeWitt Clinton to Oliver Phelps, New York, 13 Nov. 1796, Phelps-Gorham Papers, NYSL.

34. George Clinton to Doctor Michael Leib, Greenwich, 19 Nov. 1796, George Clinton Papers.

35. *Greenleaf's New York Journal, & Patriotic Register*, 25 Oct. and 29 Nov. 1796.

36. *The Argus, or Greenleaf's New York Daily Advertiser*, 17 Dec. 1796. See also *Albany Register*, 12 Dec. 1796.

37. Lewis Morris to Lewis Morris, Jr., Morrisiana, 29 Dec. 1796, George Clinton Papers; Thomas L. Whitbeck to John Williams, Albany, 10 Dec. 1796, John Williams Papers, NYSL.

38. Alexander Hamilton to Rufus King, New York, 16 Dec. 1796, in *Hamilton*, edited by Syrett, 20:445; B[enjamin] Goodhue to Rufus King, Philadelphia, 15 Dec. 1796, Rufus King Papers; Aaron Burr to Oliver Phelps, New York, 16 Dec. 1796, Phelps-Gorham Papers; Lewis Morris to Lewis Morris, Jr., Morrisiana, 29 Dec. 1796, George Clinton Papers.

39. W. J. McDonald, *Action*, pp. 7-8.

40. See Appendices, A.2.

41. Noble E. Cunningham, ed., *Circular Letters of Congressmen to Their Constituents 1789-1829* (Chapel Hill, N.C., 1978), 1:61.

42. Robert Troup to Rufus King, New York, 20 Jan. 1797, Rufus King Papers; Nathaniel Smith to David Daggett, Philadelphia, 22 Dec. 1796, David Daggett Papers, Yale University, New Haven, Ct. (hereinafter cited as YU).

43. Alexander Hamilton to Rufus King, 15 Feb. 1797, Rufus King Papers.

44. Theodore Sedgwick to Rufus King, Stockbridge, 12 Mar. 1797, in *Rufus King*, edited by King, 2:156-157.

45. Stephen Higginson to Alexander Hamilton, Boston, 12 Jan. 1797, in *Hamilton*, edited by Syrett, 20:465.

46. Elkanah Watson to John Adams, Albany, 5 Mar. 1797, Elkanah Watson Papers, NYSL.

47. John Adams to Elkanah Watson, Philadelphia, 17 Mar. 1797, in Elkanah Watson Papers. See also Roseboom, *American Presidential Elections*, p. 35.

48. Cunningham, *Circular Letters*, 1:62.

7. PREPARATIONS FOR 1800

1. Miller, *Federalist Era*, pp. 210-250; Stephen Kurtz, *Presidency of John Adams* (Philadelphia, Pa., 1957), pp. 284-373; Cunningham, *Jeffersonian Republicans*, pp. 116-174.

2. Cunningham, *Jeffersonian Republicans*, pp. 144-146.

3. Virginia, *Journal of the House of Delegates* [2 Dec. 1799- 28 Jan. 1800], pp. 83-84, 91, 95; Miller, *Federalist Era*, p. 257.

4. Cunningham, *Jeffersonian Republicans*, pp. 146-147; John B. Watson to Timothy Pickering, Richmond, 19 Jan. 1800, Timothy Pickering Papers, Massachusetts Historical Society, Boston (hereinafter cited as MHS); *Newport Mercury*, 10 June 1800; *Acts and Laws of the Commonwealth of Massachusetts, 1800-1801*, c. 6, 6 June 1800, and c. 57, 15 Nov. 1800; Wilson Cary Nicholas to [Charles] Pinckney & [Jesse] Franklin, Warren, 12 July 1800, Wilson Cary Nicholas Papers, Library of Congress, Washington, D.C. (hereinafter cited as LC).

5.*American Citizen*, 14, 25 June 1800.

6. *The Providence Gazette*, 28 June 1800 for a Federalist reading.

7. New York, *Assembly Journal*, 22nd session, 2nd. meeting, 2 Jan. 1799, pp. 103-107.

8. Thomas Tillotson to Robert R. Livingston, 31 Jan. 1799, Robert R. Livingston Papers.

9. New York, *Assembly Journal*, 22nd session, 2nd meeting, pp. 103-107, and 23rd session, 28 Jan. 1800, pp. 89, 136; Francis Crawford to Ebenezer Foote, New Windsor, 1 Mar. 1799, Ebenezer Foote Papers, NYSL; Robert Troup to Rufus King, New York, 6 Nov. 1799, Rufus King Papers; Hammond, *History*, 1:127-128, 131-132; James Morton Smith, *Freedom's Fetters* (Ithaca, N.Y., 1956), pp. 390-398; Richard Harison to Timothy Pickering, 10 Apr. 1800, Timothy Pickering Papers.

10. *American Citizen*, 17 Mar. and 5 Apr. 1800.

11. Ibid.

12. Ibid.

13. Leonard Levy, *Freedom of Speech and Press in Early American History: Legacy of Suppression* (New York, 1963), pp. 249-309.

14. *American Citizen*, 17 Mar. and 5 Apr. 1800.

15. Ibid.

16. Ibid.

17. Ibid.

18. New York, *Assembly Journal*, 23d session, 28 Jan. 1800, p. 166. The *American Citizen*, 25 Mar. 1800 gives the vote as 54-49 against the measure; Henry Van Schaack to Theodore Sedgwick, Pittsfield, 16 Mar. 1800, Theodore Sedgwick Papers, MHS.

19. Harry Marlin Tinkcom, *The Republicans and Federalists in Pennsylvania 1790-1801* (Harrisburg, Pa., 1950), p. 227-241; Dumas Malone, *Jefferson and the Ordeal of Liberty* (Boston, Mass., 1962), pp.462-464; Chauncey Goodrich to John Treadwell, Philadelphia, 6 Jan. 1800, John Treadwell Papers, CHS; Thomas McKean to Thomas Jefferson, Lancaster, 7 Mar. 1800, Thomas Jefferson Papers, LC; and two items among the Drafts, Notes, Fragments, undated, unidentified, Box 3, Wilson Cary Nicholas Papers; John Marshall to [James Markham Marshall], Philadelphia, 4 Apr. 1800, in *The Papers of John Marshall* (Chapel Hill, N.C., 1984), edited by Charles T.

Cullen, 4:123-124.

20. *Senate Journal*, 6th Cong., 1st session, 2 Dec. 1799, pp. 23, 31, 33, 35, 40-43, 46, 49; *Senate Documents*, 6th Cong., 1st session, "Amendment proposed by Mr. Bingham" and "A Bill prescribing the mode of deciding disputed elections of President and Vice President of the United States, as agreed to be amended in Senate, 10 Mar. 1800."

21. *Senate Documents*, 6th Cong., 1st session, "A Bill prescribing the mode."

22. Ibid.

23. Ibid.

24. *Senate Documents*, 6th Cong., 1st session, Undated, Senator Nicholas' amendment; *Senate Journal*, 6th Cong., 1st session, pp. 57-59; Wilson Cary Nicholas, "I enclose you the copy of a bill that yesterday passed the Senate," in Wilson Cary Nicholas Papers, Drafts, Notes, Fragments, undated, unidentified, Box 3.

25. *Senate Journal*, 6th Cong., 1st session, p. 59; Cunningham, ed., *Letters of Congressmen*, 1:195, 200-201, 209.

26. *House Journal*, 6th Cong., 1st session, pp. 668-670, 675, 683; Cullen, ed., *John Marshall*, 4:36, 138-145.

27. *House Journal*, 6th Cong., 1st session, pp. 689-692.

28. Ibid., pp. 692-693.

29. *Senate Journal*, 6th Cong., 1st session, pp. 89-90; *Senate Documents*, 6th Cong., 1st session, *The Report of the Committee to Whom was Referred the Bill Sent from the Senate*, 25 Apr. 1800.

30. *House Journal*, 6th Cong., 1st session, pp. 707-709, 710; *Senate Journal*, 6th Cong., 1st session, p. 92. According to Cullen, ed. *Marshall*, 4:36, n. 8, the Senate's desire for a greater role in the selection of the executive met some success in the Twelfth Amendment, which assigned the contingency election for Vice President to the upper house.

8. THE ELECTION OF 1800

1. Thomas Jefferson to James Madison, Philadelphia, 4 Mar. 1800, James Madison Papers, LC.

2. Ibid.

3. Ibid.; Chauncey Goodrich to Jonathan Trumbull, Philadelphia, 8 May 1800, Jonathan Trumbull Papers, CHS.

4. "To the Electors of the County of Washington," Broadside, 17 Apr. [18]00, John Williams Papers; *American Citizen*, 19 Mar., 2, 4, 5, 9, 19 Apr. 1800; *Republican Watch Tower*, 12, 23 Apr. 1800; "Thoughts on the Subject of the ensuing election," Albany, 1 Apr. 1800, and "An Independent Elector, To the Electors of New York State," 4 Apr. 1800, Barber & Southwick, Broadside

Coll., NYPL.

5. G. W. Bancker to A. B. Bancker, Albany, 20 Apr. 1800 in Bancker Family Papers.

6. Robert Troup to Rufus King, New York, 9 Mar. 1800 in *Rufus King*, edited by King, 3:205, 208-209.

7. Cunningham, *Jeffersonian Republicans*, pp. 175-248; William Bingham to Rufus King, Philadelphia, 5 Mar. 1800 and Henry Van Schaack to Theodore Sedgwick, Pittsfield, 14 Feb. 1800, Theodore Sedgwick Papers; *Albany Register*, 10 June 1800.

8. James Nicholson to Albert Gallatin, 6 May 1800, Albert Gallatin Papers, microfilm edition, Scholarly Resources. See also Noble E. Cunningham, Jr., "The Election of 1800," in *American Presidential Elections*, edited by Schlesinger, Jr., 1:108; and *American Citizen*, 3 May 1800.

9. Robert Troup to Rufus King, New York, 29 Mar. 1800, Rufus King Papers; Peter A. Jay to the Editor of the *Daily Advertiser*, 26 Apr. 1800, John Jay Papers; George W. Bancker to Abraham B. Bancker, New York, 7 May 1800, Bancker Family Correspondence; Hammond, *History*, 1:134-135.

10. Alexander Hamilton to John Jay, New York, 7 May 1800 in *Hamilton*, edited by Syrett, 24:464-467.

11. Philip Schuyler to John Jay, New York, 7 May 1800 in *John Jay*, edited by Johnston, 4:273; Syrett, ed., *Hamilton*, 24:467, n. 4 point out that the Governor wrote at the bottom of the letter: "Proposing a measure for party purposes wh[ich] I think it w[oul]d not become me to adopt."

12. Miller, *Alexander Hamilton*, p. 514; Forrest McDonald, *Hamilton*, p. 446, n. 42, suggests this defense.

13. Henry Van Schaack to Theodore Sedgwick, Pittsfield, 9 Mar. 1800, Theodore Sedgwick Papers.

14. David H. Fischer, *Revolution of American Conservatism*, Reprint (New York, 1969), pp. 1-28.

15. [Matthew] L. Davis to Albert Gallatin, New York, 5 May 1800, Albert Gallatin Papers; Cunningham, "The Election of 1800," p. 110; Abraham Van Vechten to Ebenezer Foote, n.p., 27 May 1800, Ebenezer Foote Papers, NYSL.

16. Fisher Ames to Rufus King, Boston, 15 July 1800, in *Rufus King*, edited by King, 3:232.

17. George Cabot to Rufus King, n.p., 19 July 1800, in Ibid., III, 277; Robert Troup to Rufus King, 24 June and 14 Sept. 1800, Rufus King Papers; Aaron Burr to Robert R. Livingston, New York, 7, 24 Sept. 1800, Robert R. Livingston Papers.

18. Cunningham, "The Election of 1800," pp. 111-113.

19. Ibid., p. 111; William Pitt Beers to Ebenezer Foote, Albany, 24 May 1800, Ebenezer Foote Papers, NYSL; Timothy Pickering to Rufus King, Philadelphia, 7 May 1800, in *Rufus King*, edited by King, 3:232; Elizur Goodrich to David Daggett, Philadelphia, 12 May 1800, David Daggett Papers;

Kurtz, *Presidency of John Adams*, pp. 374-408.

20. Thomas Jefferson to Thomas Mann Randolph, Philadelphia, 7, 14 May 1800, Thomas Jefferson Papers, LC.

21. David Ogden to William Meredith, Newark, 19 Oct. 1800, in Meredith Papers, HSP.

22. Carl E. Prince, *New Jersey's Jeffersonian Republicans, The Genesis of an Early Party Machine 1789-1817* (Chapel Hill, N.C., 1964), pp. 41-68; *American Citizen*, 10 Oct. 1800; *Republican Watch Tower*, 18 Oct. 1800.

23. Charles Pinckney to Thomas Jefferson, 16 Oct. 1800, in *American Historical Review* 4 (1898):114-115, cited by Cunningham, *Jeffersonian Republicans*, p. 232.

24. Henry William DeSaussure to Timothy Pickering, Charleston, 12 Aug. 1800, Timothy Pickering Papers.

25. *Federal Gazette*, 3 Oct. 1800, cited in Cunningham, *Jeffersonian Republicans*, pp. 189-190.

26. *Federal Gazette*, 13 Aug. 1800, cited in Ibid.

27. Cunningham, *Jeffersonian Republicans*, pp. 192-193.

28. Ibid.

29. Pennsylvania, *Journal of the Senate*, 10th session, [3 Dec. 1799-17 Mar. 1800], pp. 68-69, 79-82; Pennsylvania, *Journal of the House of Representatives*, 10th session [3 Dec. 1799-17 Mar. 1800], p. 65.

30. Pennsylvania, *Journal of the Senate*, 10th session, pp. 69-70, 108.

31. Pennsylvania, *Journal of the House of Representatives*, 10th session, pp. 383-387; Tinckom, *Pennsylvania*, pp. 233-234.

32. Pennsylvania, *Journal of the Senate*, 10th session, pp. 266-267; Tinckom, *Pennsylvania*, p. 245.

33. John Nicholas to A. J. Dallas, Falmouth, 20 July 1800, and J. Dawson to A. J. Dallas, Fredericksburg, 28 Sept. 1800, in George Mifflin Dallas Collection, HSP; James Monroe to Thomas McKean, Richmond, 12 July 1800, McKean Papers, HSP.

34. Pennsylvania, *Journal of the Senate*, 11th session [5 Nov. 1800-27 Feb. 1801], pp. 11-12; Pennsylvania, *Journal of the House of Representatives*, 11th session, pp. 13-15; John Beckley to A. J. Dallas, Philadelphia, 7 Nov. 1800, George Mifflin Dallas Collection.

35. Pennsylvania, *Journal of the House of Representatives*, 11th session, pp. 49-54; *Gazette of the United States*, 5, 6 Nov. 1800; Tinckom, *Pennsylvania*, pp. 248-250; William Meredith to David Meredith, Philadelphia, 2 Dec. 1800, in Meredith Papers; Alexander J. Dallas to Thomas McKean, Philadelphia, 28 Nov. 1800, Thomas McKean Papers.

36. Robert Troup to Rufus King, 14 Sept. 1800, Rufus King Papers; Cunningham, "The Election of 1800," pp. 117-118; William North to his wife, Plainfield, 25 May 1800, William North Papers, NYSL; Hammond, *History*, 1:147; Kurtz, *Presidency of John Adams*, pp. 374-408; James Madison to

Thomas Jefferson, Williamsburg, 1 Nov. 1800, Thomas Jefferson Papers, LC.

37. Electoral Vote of 1800, New Jersey, NA; New Jersey, *Minutes of Joint Meetings of the General Assembly 1792-1804*, 30 Oct. 1800, Manuscript, New Jersey State Archives, Trenton, N.J.; *The Centinel of Freedom*, 4 Nov. 1800.

38. Cunningham, *Jeffersonian Republicans*, pp. 208-209; Abraham Bishop, *Connecticut Republicanism, An Oration on the Extent and Power of Political Delusion, Delivered in New Haven* (Philadelphia, Pa., 1800); William Bristol to David Daggett, n.p., 10 Sept. 1800, David Daggett Papers; *American Citizen*, 11 Oct. 1800; Electoral Vote of 1800, Connecticut, NA.

39. Electoral Vote of 1800, Delaware, NA; Delaware, *Journal of the House of Representatives* [3-5 Nov. 1800], pp. 4-15; Delaware, *Journal of the Senate* [3-5 Nov. 1800], pp. 3-10.

40. *American Citizen*, 22 Oct. 1800. See also *Republican Watch Tower*, 15, 25 Oct. 1800; Alexander L. McDonald to Peter A. Jay, New York, 18 Oct. 1800, John Jay Papers.

41. New York, *Assembly Journal*, 24th session, 1st meeting, 4 Nov. 1800, p. 5; Robert Troup to Rufus King, New York, 9 Aug. 1800, in *Rufus King*, edited by King, 3:289; New York, *Senate Journal*, 24th session, 1st meeting, pp. 9-10.

42. By his Excellency John Jay, Governor of the State of New-York, A PROCLAMATION, 7 Nov. 1800, Albany Institute Pamphlets no.803 in NYSL; John Jay to Pierre Van Cortlandt, Jr., 8 Nov. 1800, Sleepy Hollow Restorations for original, a copy of which is in the John Jay Papers; Robert Troup to Rufus King, New York, 9 Nov. 1800, in *Rufus King*, edited by King, 3:332; Ambrose Spencer to Robert R. Livingston, Hudson, 28 Nov. 1800, Robert R. Livingston to Ambrose Spencer, 30 Nov. 1800, and Robert R. Livingston to Edward Livingston, Clermont, 1 Dec. 1800 in Robert R. Livingston Papers. Electoral Votes 1800, New York, NA.

43. Lucius Wilmerding, Jr., *The Electoral College,* p. 183; Timothy Pickering to Rufus King, 7 Feb. 1801, in Rufus King Papers.

44. George W. Bancker, Albany, 10 Dec. 1800 in Bancker Family Papers. Massachusetts had already provided for filling vacancies: *Acts and Resolves 1796-97* (Boston, Mass., 1796), c. 9, 23 Nov. 1796, and *Acts and Laws of the Commonwealth of Massachusetts* (Boston, Mass., 1800), c. 57, 15 Nov. 1800.

45. Vermont, *Journal of the General Assembly*, 9 Oct. 1800, pp. 12-13, 110, 136-141, 187, 198, 199; William Niles to Nathaniel Niles, Pembroke, 4 Nov. 1800, in James Whitelaw Papers, Vermont Historical Society, Montpelier, Vt. (hereinafter cited as VtHi); Electoral Vote of 1800, Vermont, NA.

46. Cunningham, *Jeffersonian Republicans*, p. 189, n. 64; Risjord, *Chesapeake Politics*, p. 558; Electoral Vote of 1800, Maryland, NA.

47. *Acts and Laws of the Commonwealth of Massachusetts*, c. 6, 6 June 1800; *Gazette of the United States*, 21 Nov. 1800; Electoral Vote of 1800, Massachusetts, NA.

48. Electoral Vote of 1800, Georgia, NA; *Gazette of the United States*, 19 Nov. 1800; Georgia, *Journal of the House of Representatives* [3 Nov.-2 Dec. 1800], pp. 7-8, 14, 15, 19, 21, 26, 47; Georgia, *Journal of the Senate* [3 Nov.-2 Dec. 1800], pp. 12, 13, 19, 20, 25, 39, 46, 50.

49. *The United States Chronicle*, 6, 13, 28 Nov. and 11 Dec. 1800.

50. Electoral Vote of 1800, Rhode Island, NA.

51. *The Public Laws of the State of Rhode Island and Providence Plantations as Revised by a Committee, and Finally Enacted by the Honourable General Assembly at their Session in January, 1798* (Providence, 1798), "An Act relative to the Election of Senators and Representatives and of Electors," pp. 136-140, n.d.; *The Providence Gazette*, 1, 8, 15, 29 Nov. 1800; *Newport Mercury*, 2 Sept. and 4, 15, 18 Nov. 1800.

52. Risjord, *Chesapeake Politics*, pp. 556-563; *Virginia Argus*, 11 July 1800, reprinted as "Official Communications of the Republican Party in Virginia, 1800," in the Appendices to Cunningham, "The Election of 1800," pp. 144-147; Electoral Vote of 1800, Virginia, NA.

53. Electoral Vote of 1800, North Carolina, NA; *Gazette of the United States*, 12 Nov. 1800; Risjord, *Chesapeake Politics*, pp. 562-563.

54. New Hampshire, *Laws of New Hampshire*, vol. 6, c. 7, 14 June 1800; Electoral Vote of 1800, New Hampshire, NA.

55. *Gazette of the United States*, 29 Nov. 1800; Electoral Vote of 1800, Kentucky and Tennessee, NA.

56. Pennsylvania, *Journal of the Senate*, 11th session, 1st meeting, pp. 35-37, 66; Pennsylvania, *Journal of the House of Representatives*, 11th session, 1st meeting, pp. 90-93, 106; Tinckom, *Pennsylvania*, pp. 250-251; Nathan Penrose to A. J. Dallas, Tuesday, 6 o'clock P.M., in George Mifflin Dallas Papers; Jonathan Roberts to Jonathan Roberts, Sr., 3 Dec. 1800, in Jonathan Roberts Papers, HSP; Cunningham, *Jeffersonian Republicans*, p. 231.

57. Thomas McKean to Thomas Jefferson, Lancaster, 15 Dec. 1800, McKean Papers.

58. Thomas McKean to Thomas Jefferson, Lancaster, 10 Jan. 1801 with postscript dated Lancaster, 22 Jan. 1801, Thomas McKean Papers; Tinckom, *Pennsylvania*, pp. 245-247, 256-257.

59. Electoral Vote of 1800, Pennsylvania, NA.

60. Cunningham, "Election of 1800," pp. 127-128; Henry W. DeSaussure to John Treadwell, Columbia, 2 Dec. 1800, John Treadwell Papers; Electoral Vote of 1800, South Carolina, NA.

61. Abraham Van Vechten to Henry Glen, 26 Dec. 1800, Henry Glen Papers, Rare Book and Manuscript Division, NYPL, Astor, Lenox and Tilden Foundations. See also Robert Troup to Rufus King, New York, 4 Dec. 1800 in *Rufus King*, edited by King, 3:340; Benjamin Goodhue to Jeremiah Wadsworth, Salem, 21 Nov. 1800, Jeremiah Wadsworth Papers, CHS; Timothy Pickering to Rufus King, Easton, 27 Dec. 1800, Rufus King Papers; Elizur

Goodrich to David Daggett, Washington, 10 Dec. 1800, David Daggett Papers; and Henry Glen to John Jay, Washington, 20 Dec. 1800, John Jay Papers; Lewis Morris to William Meredith, Washington, 10 Dec. 1800, Meredith Papers.

62. Peter Freneau to Thomas Jefferson, Columbia, 2 Dec. 1800, Thomas Jefferson Papers, LC; Chauncey Goodrich to David Daggett, Washington, 12 Dec. 1800, David Daggett Papers: "Tis said here, on what authority I know not, that a single Vote in South Carolina is to be thrown from Mr. Burr to G. Clinton."

63. James Burrell to David Daggett, Providence, 15 Dec. 1800, and John Cotton Smith to David Daggett, Washington, 4, 18 Dec. 1800, David Daggett Papers. See Appendices, A.3.

9. THE CONTINGENCY ELECTION OF 1801

1. Cunningham, "Election of 1800," p. 131; James Madison to Thomas Jefferson, 21 Oct. and Orange, 20 Dec. 1800, James Madison Papers, LC; Raymond Walters, Jr., *Albert Gallatin, Jeffersonian Financier and Diplomat* (New York, 1957), p. 126; Robert A. Rutland, *James Madison, the Founding Father* (New York, 1987), pp. 165-167.

For Burr, see G. Jackson to James Madison, Washington, 5 Feb. 1801, James Madison Papers, LC; Chauncey Goodrich to David Daggett, Washington, 12 Dec. 1800, David Daggett Papers; Peter Freneau to Thomas Jefferson, Columbus, S.C., 2 Dec. 1800, Charles Pinckney to Thomas Jefferson, n.p., 8 Jan. 1801, and Thomas Jefferson to Aaron Burr, Washington, 15 Dec. 1800, Thomas Jefferson Papers, LC; *Annals*, 8th Cong., 1st session, p. 157; Joseph Lyman to Theodore Sedgwick, Hatfield, 26 Jan. 1801, Theodore Sedgwick Papers.

For notions of faithful and fair electors, see Elizur Goodrich to David Daggett, 8 Dec. 1800, David Daggett Papers; Uriah Tracy to Jeremiah Wadsworth, Washington, 7 Jan. 1801, Jonathan Trumbull Papers; Harrison Gray Otis to, Washington, 3 Dec. 1800, Harrison Gray Otis Papers, MHS; Theodore Sedgwick to Peter Van Schaack, Philadelphia, 9 May 1800, Theodore Sedgwick Papers.

2. Timothy Pickering to John Pickering, Boston, 31 Jan. 1801, Timothy Pickering Papers.

3. Roseboom, *Presidential Elections*, p. 45. Walters, *Gallatin*, p. 130, believes that Federalists, if unified, could have elected Burr on the first ballot, while Elizur Goodrich to David Daggett, Washington, 16 Jan. 1801, David Daggett Papers, thinks that Federalists could not prevent the choice of Jefferson. Strictly speaking, neither is correct.

4. *American Citizen*, 10 Jan. 1801.

5. *American Citizen*, 10 Feb. 1801.

6. Robert R. Livingston to Ambrose Spencer, Clermont, 16 Dec. 1800, Thomas Jefferson Papers, HSP; *Daily Advertiser*, 5 Jan. 1801; *Evening Post*, 17 Dec. 1803.

7. Daniel Hale to Ebenezer Foote, Albany, 3 Jan. 1801, Ebenezer Foote Papers, NYSL.

8. James McHenry to Rufus King, 2 Jan. 1801, Rufus King Papers. See also George W. Bancker to his father [A. B. Bancker], Albany, 31 Dec. 1800 and addendum 5 Jan. 1801, Bancker Family Correspondence; James Bill to Ebenezer Foote, Catskill, 12 Jan. 1801, Ebenezer Foote Papers, NYSL; Golds. Banyer to Henry Glen, Albany, 16 Feb. 1801, Henry Glen Papers, NYPL.

9. James Muse to Henry Glen, Philadelphia, 30 Jan. 1801, Henry Glen Papers, NYSHA.

10. Robert Troup to Rufus King, New York, 31 Dec. 1800, in *Rufus King*, edited by King, 3:358.

11. Elizur Goodrich to David Daggett, Washington, 25 Dec. 1800, David Daggett Papers.

12. Edward Livingston to Robert R. Livingston, Washington, 29 Jan. 1801, Robert R. Livingston Papers.

13. Thomas Jefferson to Tench Coxe, n.p., 31 Dec. 1800, and Hugh Henry Brackenridge to Thomas Jefferson, Pittsburgh, 19 Jan. 1801, Thomas Jefferson Papers, LC; Thomas McKean to Thomas Jefferson, Lancaster, 10 Jan. 1801, Thomas McKean Papers; Samuel Smith to Aaron Burr, Washington, 11 Jan. 1801 [original misdated 1800], Samuel Smith Papers, LC.

14. Thomas Jefferson to Andrew Ellicott, Washington, 18 Dec. 1800, Thomas Jefferson Papers, LC.

15. James Monroe to Thomas Jefferson, Richmond, 6, 27, Jan. 1801, James Monroe to Col. John Hoomes, Richmond, 14 Feb. 1801, and James Monroe to S. T. Mason and W. C. Nicholas, Richmond, 18 Feb. 1801 in *Writings of James Monroe*, Reprint (New York, 1969), edited by Stanislaus Murray Hamilton, 3:253-255, 257, 258-260, 260-261; Samuel Smith to Aaron Burr, Washington, 11 Jan. 1800, Samuel Smith Papers; James Madison to, 10 Jan. 1801, James Madison Papers, LC; Thomas McKean to Thomas Jefferson, Lancaster, 10 Jan. 1801 and Hugh H. Brackenridge to Thomas Jefferson, Pittsburgh, 19 Jan. 1801, Thomas Jefferson Papers, LC; James Hillhouse to Jeremiah Wadsworth, Washington, 3 Feb. 1801, Jonathan Trumbull Papers; Aaron Kitchell to E[benezer] Elmer, Washington, 11 Jan. 1801 and Joseph Hopper Nicholson to, Washington, 15 Jan. 1801 [original misdated 1800], Thomas Jefferson Papers, HSP; Timothy Pickering to Rufus King, Philadelphia, 5 Jan. 1801, in *Rufus King*, edited by King, 3:366; Robert Troup to Rufus King, New York, 12 Feb. 1801, Rufus King Papers; and Walters, *Gallatin*, p. 129.

16. Cunningham, "Election of 1800," p. 132.

17. *Daily Advertiser*, 16 Feb. 1801. Harrison Gray Otis to Sally Otis,

Washington, 9 Feb. [1801], Harrison Gray Otis Papers.

18. Harrison Gray Otis to Sally Otis, Wednesday [11 Feb. 1801], Harrison Gray Otis Papers, provides an account from one of the House tellers.

19. Ibid.

20. Theodore Sedgwick to Ashbel Strong, Washington, 19 Feb. 1801, Theodore Sedgwick Papers. See also Cunningham, "Election of 1800," p. 132; John Condit to Ebenezer Elmer, Washington, 15 Feb. 1800, and Uriah Tracy to, Washington, 16 Feb. 1801, Simon Gratz Collection, HSP.

21. Robert Troup to Rufus King, New York, 18 Feb. 1801, Rufus King Papers.

22. John Laurence to Rufus King, New York, 18 Feb. 1801 in *Rufus King*, edited by King, 3:393-394.

23. Harrison Gray Otis to Sally Otis, Washington, 9 Feb. [1801], Harrison Gray Otis Papers; Thomas Jefferson to Craven Peyton, Washington, 15 Jan. 1801, Thomas Jefferson Papers, Microfilm Edition, University of Virginia, Charlottesville, Va. (hereinafter cited as UVa); Wilson Cary Nicholas to James Madison, n.p., 1801, Wilson Cary Nicholas Papers; and Walters, *Gallatin*, pp. 130-131.

24. Samuel Smith to Aaron Burr, Washington, 11 Jan. 1801 [original misdated 1800], Samuel Smith Papers.

25. James Linn to Samuel Smith, Trenton, 10 Jan. 1803, Samuel Smith Papers; Kline, ed. *Aaron Burr*, I:489-490, n. 1 and n. 2; Theodorus Bailey to Thomas Tillotson, Washington City, 12 Feb. 1801, George Clinton Papers; and John F. Mercer to James Madison, Baltimore, 5 Jan. 1801 [original misdated 1800], James Madison Papers, LC.

26. John F. Mercer to James Madison, Baltimore, 5 Jan. 1801 [original misdated 1800], James Madison Papers, LC; two letters from G. Christie to Samuel Smith, Annapolis, both dated 19 Dec. 1802, Samuel Smith Papers; Theodore Sedgwick to Theodore Sedgwick Jr., Washington, 30 Jan. 1801, Theodore Sedgwick Papers; Uriah Tracy to Jeremiah Wadsworth, Washington, 7 Jan. 1801, Jonathan Trumbull Papers; John Cotton Smith to David Daggett, Washington, 13 Feb. 1801, David Daggett Papers.

27. Timothy Pickering to Dwight Foster, Washington, 4 Feb. 1801, Timothy Pickering Papers. See also *Daily Advertiser*, 5 Feb. 1801 for Centinel; 9 Feb. 1801 for A Federalist, taken from the *Philadelphia Gazette*; 11 Feb. 1801 for Crito; and 16 Feb. 1801 for Lucius, taken from the *Washington Federalist*; Peter Van Schaack to Theodore Sedgwick, Kinderhook, 9 Jan. 1801, and Theodore Sedgwick to Theodore Sedgwick, Jr., Washington, 11 Jan. 1801, Theodore Sedgwick Papers.

28. William Cooper to John Jay, Washington, 19 Dec. 1800, George Clinton Papers.

29. James Watson to Jeremiah Wadsworth, New York, 9 Feb. 1801, Jeremiah Wadsworth Papers.

30. Uriah Tracy to, Washington, 16 Feb. 1801, Simon Gratz Coll.

31. Cunningham, "Election of 1800," pp. 132-133; Harrison Gray Otis, undated memorandum [18? Feb. 1801], Harrison Gray Otis Papers; Samuel W. Dana to Oliver Wolcott, Jr., Washington, 11 Feb. 1801, Oliver Wolcott, Jr. Papers.

32. Uriah Tracy to, Washington, 16 Feb. 1801, Simon Gratz Coll.

33. Harrison Gray Otis to Sally Otis, Friday, 15 Feb. 1801, Harrison Gray Otis Papers.

34. Cunningham, "Election of 1800," pp. 132-133; James Watson to Jeremiah Wadsworth, New York, 9 Feb. 1801, Jeremiah Wadsworth Papers; Fisher Ames to Theodore Sedgwick, Dedham, 23, 26 Jan. 1801, and Henry Van Schaack to Theodore Sedgwick, Stockbridge, 9 Feb. 1801, and Theodore Sedgwick to Theodore Sedgwick, Jr., Washington, 16 Feb. 1801, Theodore Sedgwick Papers; Lewis Morris to William Meredith, Washington, 3 Feb. 1801, Meredith Papers; Thomas Mann Randolph, Jr., to Thomas Jefferson, 10 Jan. 1801, Thomas Jefferson Papers, UVa; John Vaughan to Thomas Jefferson, Wilmington, 10 Jan. 1801, Thomas Jefferson Papers, LC.

35. Cunningham, "Election of 1800," pp. 132-133; James A. Bayard to, Washington, 22 Feb. 1801, Thomas Jefferson Papers, HSP; Lewis Morris to William Meredith, Washington, 17 Feb. 1801, Meredith Papers.

36. Joseph Hopkinson to Henry Glen, Philadelphia, 22 Feb. 1801, Henry Glen Papers, NYSHA.

10. THE ELECTORAL COLLEGE IN 1801

1. Sayre and Parris, *Voting For President*, p. 42, point out that faithless electors have been a rarity in electoral college history.

2. Peirce and Longley, *The People's President*, pp. 248-249.

3. Homer Carey Hockett, *The Constitutional History of the United States 1776-1826* (New York, 1939), pp. 299-300, suggests that Congressman William Smith from South Carolina may have been the first to introduce a resolution to require electors to differentiate their votes for President and Vice President. Theodore Sedgwick to Rufus King, Stockbridge, 12 Mar. 1797, Rufus King Papers.

4. George Cabot to Rufus King, Brookline, 19 Mar. 1797, Rufus King Papers.

5. Ibid.

6. Thomas Jefferson to James Madison, 1 Jan. 1797, in *Writings of Thomas Jefferson* (New York, 1896), edited by Paul L. Ford, 7:99.

7. New York, *Senate Journal*, 22d session, 1st meeting, 9 Aug. 1798, p. 17, and 2nd meeting, 2 Jan. 1799, pp. 34-35, 39, 42-43; Hammond, *History*, 1:122; and Robert Troup to Rufus King, New York, 23 Jan. 1799, Rufus King

Papers; *Assembly Journal*, 22d session, 2d meeting, pp. 7, 12-13.

8. *Laws of New Hampshire*, 6:554-555; *Annals*, 5th Cong., 2d session, 13 Nov. 1797, p. 493, 3045; the Vermont resolutions can be found in many places, such as Massachusetts, *Acts and Laws, 1798-1799*, c. 154, 4 Mar. 1800; A Calm Observer in *The Monitor and Wilmington Repository*, 15 Nov. 1800.

9. Rhode Island, *Acts of the Governor and General Assembly*, June session 1800, "Report of the Committee Relative to Amendment of the Constitution," pp. 28-31; *The Providence Gazette*, 21 June 1800; and *The Newport Mercury*, 17 Dec. 1803.

10. [Maryland] *By the House of Delegates*, 9 Dec. 1800, broadside, Albany Institute Pamphlets, New York State Library; John Cotton Smith to David Daggett, Washington, 24 Nov. 1800, David Daggett Papers; *The Public Records of the State of Connecticut, 1800-1801* (Hartford, Conn., 1965), 10:221-223 and n. 37.

11. Wilson Cary Nicholas, "I transmit to you a resolution of the Genl. Assembly of North Carolina," Wilson Cary Nicholas Papers, Drafts, Notes, Fragments, undated, unidentified, Box 3.

12. *Annals*, 6th Cong., 2d session, pp. 942-946; *American State Papers: Documents, Legislative and Executive of the Congress of the United States* (Washington, D.C., 1834), 6th Congress, 2d session, no. 140, "Propositions to amend the Constitution."

13. John Dawson to James Madison, Washington, 18 Dec. 1800, James Madison Papers, LC.

14. Wilson Cary Nicholas to, with copies to [Charles] Pinckney and [Jesse] Franklin, Warren, 12 July 1800, Wilson Cary Nicholas Papers; and John Dawson to James Madison, New Brunswick, 28 Nov. 1799 and Hagerstown, 28 July 1800, James Madison Papers, LC.

15. Peirce and Longley, *The People's President*, Appendix B, "The Choice of Presidential Electors 1788-1836," pp. 309-311; Thomas Jefferson to James Monroe, Philadelphia, 16 Feb. 1800 and Thomas Jefferson to Thomas Mann Randolph, Philadelphia, 17 Feb. 1800, Thomas Jefferson Papers, LC.

16. Thomas Jefferson to James Monroe, Philadelphia, 12 Jan. 1800, Thomas Jefferson Papers, LC, and in *Writings of Thomas Jefferson*, edited by Ford, 7:401-402.

17. Dewey, "Madison's Views on Electoral Reform," pp. 140-145; Wilmerding, "Reform of the Electoral System," in *Political Science Quarterly* 64 (March, 1949):1-23, reprinted in Johnsen, ed., *Direct Election of the President*, pp. 45-63, believes Jefferson's reasoning "fallacious" but it makes evident that political calculation rather than ideological purity marked Jefferson's thinking.

18. *American Citizen*, 20 Nov. 1800.

19. *American Citizen*, 13, 15 Nov. 1800 for the excerpt from the *Aurora*; James Madison to [Thomas Jefferson], 15 Mar. 1800 and John Dawson to James Madison, Washington, 18 Dec. 1800, James Madison Papers, LC.

20. A True Republican, to the *Aurora*, in *American Citizen*, 3 Dec. 1800.
21. Ibid.
22. Ibid.

11. PARTISAN PRINCIPLES AND INTERESTS

1. Thomas Jefferson to Thomas Mann Randolph, Washington, 19 Feb. 1801, Thomas Jefferson Papers, LC; and Thomas Jefferson to John Wayles Eppes, Washington, 22 Feb. 1801, Thomas Jefferson Papers, UVa.
2. Leonard White, *The Jeffersonians, A Study in Administrative History* (New York, 1959), pp. 347-368; Thomas Jefferson to Levi Lincoln, 26 Aug. 1801, Levi Lincoln Papers, MHS; Nicholas Fish to Gouverneur Morris, New York, 14 Jan. 1802, Nicholas Fish Family Papers, Rare Book and Manuscript Library, CU; John Rutledge to Harrison Gray Otis, Newport, 15 Sept. 1801, Harrison Gray Otis Papers; Daniel Sheldon, Jr., to Oliver Wolcott, Jr., Washington, 3 July 1801, Oliver Wolcott, Jr. Papers.
3. Edward Livingston to Robert R. Livingston, New York, 17 Dec. 1801 and Gouverneur Morris to Robert R. Livingston, Washington, 20 Mar. 1802, Robert R. Livingston Papers.
4. Alexander J. Dallas to Robert R. Livingston, Philadelphia, 6 Apr. 1802, and Thomas Tillotson to Robert R. Livingston, New York, 13 May 1802, Robert R. Livingston Papers.
5. State of New York, *Messages From the Governors* (Albany, N.Y., 1909), edited by Charles Z. Lincoln, 2:471; New York, *Assembly Journal*, 24th session, 2d meeting, 27 Jan. 1801, p. 87; New York, *Senate Journal*, 24th session, 2d meeting, p. 60.
6. Jefferson to Gallatin, Monticello, 18 Sept. 1801, *Jefferson*, edited by Ford, 7:94.
7. Albert Gallatin to Thomas Jefferson, 14 Sept. 1801, in *Writings of Albert Gallatin* 3 vols. (Philadelphia, Pa., 1879), edited by Henry Adams, 1:49-52.
8. New York, *Messages From the Governors*, 2:513; New York, *Assembly Journal*, 25th session, pp. 34-35;New York, *Senate Journal*, 25th session, pp. 11-12, 12-13, 22; *Daily Advertiser*, 4 Feb. 1802.
9. *Annals*, 7th Cong., 1st session, 7 Dec. 1801, pp. 472, 509, 602-603, 629; the text of the Vermont resolution of 5 Nov. 1799 appears in a footnote on pp.542-544; William North to Benjamin Walker, 16 Jan. 1802, William North Papers.
10. Alexander Hamilton to Gouverneur Morris, New York, 4 Mar. 1802, in *Hamilton*, edited by Syrett, 25:558-560.
11. Alexander Hamilton to James A. Bayard, New York, 6, 12, [16-21] Apr. 1802, in Ibid., 25:587-589, 600-601, 605-610; Fischer, *American Conservatism*, pp. 110-128.

12. *Annals*, 7th Cong., 1st session, pp. 1285-1287.

13. Ibid., pp. 1287-1288.

14. Ibid., pp. 1289-1290; Wilson Cary Nicholas to James Madison, n.p., 1801, Wilson Cary Nicholas Papers.

15. *Annals*, 7th Cong., 1st session, pp. 1289-1290.

16. Ibid.   There are biographical sketches of most of these fourteen Congressmen in Fischer, *American Conservatism*, Appendix II, pp. 227-412.

17. *Annals*, 7th Cong., 1st session, pp. 259, 263-264.

18. *Annals*, 7th Cong., 1st session, pp. 303-304; memorandum in Drafts, Notes, fragments, undated, unidentified, Box 3, Wilson Cary Nicholas Papers.

19. Gouverneur Morris to the Speaker of the House of Assembly, Washington, 25 Dec. 1802, delivered on 26 Jan. 1803 in the House and reported in *Morning Chronicle*, 1 Feb. 1803, *Evening Post*, 1 Feb. 1803, and in many other newspapers.

20. A member of the committee of eleven at the Philadelphia Convention which proposed electing the executive magistrates by means of presidential electors, Morris gave an explanation in 1802 which cannot be confirmed by the official journal or Madison's records of the debates.

21. Thomas Jefferson to Levi Lincoln, Washington, 25 Oct. 1802, Levi Lincoln Papers.

22. *Morning Chronicle*, 25 Oct. 1802, reprints "A View of the Relative Strength of Parties in the United States, in the years 1800 and 1802," from the *National Intelligencer*, and the issues of 26, 27 Oct. contain additional useful data about the electoral college; Robert Troup to Rufus King, New York, 8 Jan. 1803, Rufus King Papers.

23. Thomas Jefferson to George Clinton, Washington, 17 May 1801 in *Writings of Thomas Jefferson*, edited by P. L. Ford, 3:53.

24. Samuel Osgood to James Madison, New York, 24 Apr. 1801, James Madison Papers, LC; Peter S. DuPonceau to Robert R. Livingston, Philadelphia, 2 Apr. 1802 and Thomas Tillotson to Robert R. Livingston, New York, 13 May 1802, Robert R. Livingston Papers; Cunningham, *Jeffersonian Republicans in Power* (Chapel Hill, N.C., 1963), pp. 203-204; Kline, ed., *Aaron Burr*, II, 653-655; Rutland, *Madison*, p. 168.

25. William Duane to Robert R. Livingston, Philadelphia, 15 Nov. 1802, Robert R. Livingston Papers; Spaulding, *George Clinton*, pp. 259-268; Egbert Benson to Oliver Wolcott, 9 Aug. 1802, Oliver Wolcott Papers; John Van Ness to Samuel Smith, New York, 2 Aug. 1802, Samuel Smith Papers; Justin Foote to Ebenezer Foote, Brooklyn, 2 Aug. 1802, Ebenezer Foote Papers, LC.

26. Egbert Benson to Oliver Wolcott, 9 Aug. 1802, Oliver Wolcott, Jr., Papers.

27. Kline, ed., *Aaron Burr*, 2:641-646, "Editorial Note: The Suppression of John Wood's *History,*" and pp. 724-728, "Editorial Note: The Pamphlet War," provide the definitive account of this episode. See also Cunningham,

Jeffersonian Republicans in Power, pp. 205-207; Peter R. Livingston to Robert R. Livingston, London, 15 Feb. 1802, William Wilson to Robert R. Livingston, Clermont, 6 July 1802, Ambrose Spencer to Robert R. Livingston, Hudson, 27 July 1802, Gouverneur Morris to Robert R. Livingston, Morrisiana, 21 Aug. and 10 Oct. 1802, Robert R. Livingston Papers; John P. Van Ness to William P. Van Ness, Washington, 9 June 1802, William Van Ness Papers, Rare Books and Manuscript Division, NYPL; George W. Bancker to Abraham B. Bancker, New York, 24 July 1802, Bancker Family Correspondence; Henry Van Schaack to Oliver Wolcott, Jr., Pittsfield, 23 Oct. 1802, Oliver Wolcott, Jr., Papers; Rufus King to Robert Troup, London, 19 July 1802, Robert Troup to Rufus King, New York, 24 Aug. 1802, and Robert Troup to Rufus King, New York, 12 Dec. 1802, Rufus King Papers; *Morning Chronicle* began publication in October, and represented the Burr-Republican interests as a counterweight to the DeWitt Clinton-Republican orientation of the *American Citizen.*

28. William Plumer to Oliver Peabody, Washington, 22 Dec. 1802 and to Nicholas Emery, Washington, 6 Jan. 1803, William Plumer Papers, LC; John Rutledge to Theodore Sedgwick, Washington, 11 Jan. 1802, Theodore Sedgwick Papers; *Annals*, 7th Cong., 2d session, 6 Dec. 1802, p. 449.

29. *Annals*, 7th Cong., 2d session, pp. 481-486.

30. Ibid., pp. 491-493; *Morning Chronicle*, 19 Feb. 1803.

31. John Quincy Adams to Rufus King, Boston, 8 Oct. 1802, in *Rufus King*, edited by King, 6:176.

32. James Hillhouse to [Jonathan Trumbull?], Washington, 14 Feb. 1803, Jonathan Trumbull Papers; John Taylor to Wilson Cary Nicholas, Caroline, 16 Sept. 1802, Wilson Cary Nicholas Papers. The *Republican Watch Tower*, 8 June 1803, made a comparison of the relative strengths of the two parties in the Seventh and Eighth Congresses; Marshall Smelser, *The Democratic Republic 1801-1815* (New York, 1968), p. 74, writes, "In the Seventh Congress the Republican-Federalist ratio was 69:36. After the election of 1802 it was 102:39. In the Senate the Republican advantage had been 18:13; now it was 25:9." The *Evening Post*, 1 Nov. 1803, identifies the party affiliation of members of both houses of Congress.

33. Richard E. Ellis, *The Jeffersonian Crisis: Courts and Politics in the Young Republic* (New York, 1971), pp. 36-52, 69-82; Justin Foote to Ebenezer Foote, New York, 29 Jan. 1802, Ebenezer Foote Papers, NYSL; George W. Bancker to Abraham B. Bancker, New York, 15 Mar. 1802, Bancker Family Correspondence, NYHS.

34. *Evening Post*, 13 June 1803.

35. Drew R. McCoy, *The Elusive Republic; Political Economy in Jeffersonian America* (New York, 1980), pp. 185-208; *Evening Post*, 21 June, 30 July, 1, 2 Aug. 1803.

36. Christopher Gore to Rufus King, London, 1 Nov. 1803, Rufus King Papers; William Plumer to Jeremiah Smith, Washington, 10 Feb. 1804, William

Plumer Papers.

37. Rufus King to, New York, 4 Nov. 1803, Rufus King Papers.

12. THE HOUSE INITIATES AN AMENDMENT

1. *The United States Chronicle*, 3 Nov. 1803; *Aurora*, 17 Oct. 1803 as quoted in *American Citizen*, 19 Oct. 1803.

2. *Annals*, 8th Cong., 1st session, 17 Oct. 1803, p. 375. See also *Morning Chronicle*, 14 Oct. 1803; *Republican Watch Tower*, 15 Oct. 1803; *Daily Advertiser*, 15 Oct. 1803 which reports a 97-38 advantage; William Plumer to Daniel Plumer, Washington, 15 Nov. 1803, William Plumer Papers, which estimates 103-39; Timothy Pickering to John Pickering, Washington, 17 Oct. 1803, Timothy Pickering Papers; *Daily Advertiser*, 22 Oct. 1803.

3. *Annals*, 8th Cong., 1st session, pp. 374-377; *Morning Chronicle*, 25 Oct. 1803; *Republican Watch Tower*, 29 Oct. 1803.

4. *Evening Post*, 26 Oct. 1803; *Daily Advertiser*, 27 Oct. 1803; *Annals*, 8th Cong., 1st session, p. 380. Joseph Bloomfield to Aaron Burr, Trenton, 14 Apr. and 2 Nov. 1803, in *Aaron Burr*, edited by Kline, 2:770-772, 793-794, explains that New Jersey had no one in attendance because a fight between Federalists and Republicans in the legislature prevented the passage of an election law for Representatives.

5. *Annals*, 8th Cong., 1st session, pp. 380-381.

6. Ibid., p. 383; *Evening Post*, 28 Oct. 1803; *Daily Advertiser*, 29 Oct. 1803.

7. *Annals*, 8th Cong., 1st session, pp. 490-495.

8. Ibid., pp. 420, 422.

9. Ibid., pp. 425-429.

10. Ibid., pp. 490-495, 496-497.

11. James Hillhouse to Jonathan Trumbull, Washington, 27 Oct. 1803, Jonathan Trumbull Papers.

12. *Annals*, 8th Cong., 1st session, pp. 516-535.

13. Ibid., pp. 535-543.

14. Ibid., p. 543.

15. *Evening Post*, 3 Nov. 1803; *Daily Advertiser*, 4 Nov. 1803; *Annals*, 8th Cong., 1st session, p. 544.

13. THE SENATE ADOPTS A DIFFERENT PLAN

1. DeWitt Clinton to Maria Clinton, Washington, 16 Oct. 1803, George Clinton Papers.

2. *Annals*, 8th Cong., 1st session, 17 Oct. 1803, pp. 16-17. See also

Morning Chronicle, 14 Oct. 1803, and *Republican Watch Tower*, 15 Oct. 1803; *Daily Advertiser*, 15 Oct. 1803, claims a 23-10 Republican advantage in the Senate; William Plumer to Daniel Plumer, Washington, 15 Nov. 1803, William Plumer Papers, sees a 25-9 margin.

3. Everett Somerville Brown, ed., *William Plumer's Memorandum of Proceedings in the United States Senate 1803-1807* (New York, 1923), pp. 15-17. Other sources for the debates are the *Annals;* Charles Francis Adams, ed., *Memoirs of John Quincy Adams, Comprising Portions of his Diary from 1795 to 1848*, Reprint (Freeport, N.Y., 1969); Timothy Pickering's letters to his son, John, Washington, 5 Dec. 1803, and to political figures in late 1803 and early 1804, Timothy Pickering Papers.

4. *Annals*, 8th Cong., 1st session, pp. 19-21; *William Plumer's Memorandum*, pp. 15-17; and Adams, ed., *Memoirs*, 1:265.

5. *William Plumer's Memorandum*, p. 17.

6. *Annals*, 8th Cong., 1st session, p. 22.

7. Ibid., pp. 22-23.

8. Ibid., p. 25. See also *William Plumer's Memorandum*, pp. 18-23.

9. Adams, ed., *Memoirs*, 1:265, 266; documents related to an incident in the United States Senate on 22 Oct. 1803 and letter of Wilson C. Nicholas to DeWitt Clinton, Washington, 27 Oct. 1803, DeWitt Clinton Papers; *William Plumer's Memorandum*, p. 26; John P. Van Ness to William P. Van Ness, Washington, 11 Nov. 1803, William P. Van Ness Papers; *Evening Post*, 10 Nov. 1803; *American Citizen*, 8 Nov. 1803; *The United States Chronicle*, 17 Nov. 1803.

10. William Eustis to, Washington, 12 Nov. 1803, William Eustis Papers, LC.

11. William Plumer to Daniel Plumer, Washington, 22 Nov. 1803, William Plumer Papers. See also *William Plumer's Memorandum*, pp. 32-33; *Annals*, 8th Cong., 1st session, p. 76; Timothy Pickering to John Pickering, Washington, 11 Nov. 1803, Timothy Pickering Papers; Rufus King to Christopher Gore, New York, 20 Nov. 1803, Rufus King Papers.

12. Jonathan Dayton to Aaron Burr, Washington, 17 Nov. 1803, in *Aaron Burr*, edited by Kline, 2:795.

13. *William Plumer's Memorandum*, p. 33.

14. *Annals*, 8th Cong., 1st session, pp. 81-84; *William Plumer's Memorandum*, pp. 35-36.

15. *Annals*, 8th Cong., 1st session, p. 84.

16. Ibid., p. 91.

17. Ibid., p. 87; Timothy Pickering to Governor Caleb Strong, Washington, 22 Nov. 1803, Timothy Pickering Papers.

18. *Annals*, 8th Cong., 1st session, pp. 97, 117-120.

19. Ibid., pp. 122-123.

20. Ibid., p. 98.

21. Ibid., pp. 99-101, 114-117.

22. Ibid., p. 106; Adams, ed., *Memoir*, 1:274, 275; *American Citizen*, 3, 19 Dec. 1803; Malcolm Bell, Jr., *Major Butler's Legacy, Five Generations of a Slaveholding Family* (Athens, Ga., 1987), pp. 95-96.

23. *Annals*, 8th Cong., 1st session, p. 124; *William Plumer's Memorandum*, pp. 40-43, 44-45.

24. Adams, ed., *Memoirs*, 1:274, 275; Thomas Dwight to John Williams, Washington, 16 Nov. 1803, Thomas Dwight Papers, MHS; James McHenry to Timothy Pickering, near Baltimore, 27 Oct. 1803, Timothy Pickering Papers; Alexander Stuart to John Breckinridge, Richmond, 25 Nov. 1803, Breckinridge Family Papers, LC; *American Citizen*, 3, 19 Dec. 1803.

25. *Annals*, 8th Cong., 1st session, p. 129.

26. Ibid., p. 129; Adams, *Memoirs*, 1:275.

27. *Annals*, 8th Cong., 1st session, p. 130.

28. Ibid.;*William Plumer's Memorandum*, p. 45.

29. *Annals*, 8th Cong., 1st session, pp. 130-132; Wilson Cary Nicholas to James Madison, n.p., 1801, Wilson Cary Nicholas Papers.

30. *Annals*, 8th Cong., 1st session, p. 136.

31. Ibid., pp. 136-137.

32. Ibid., pp. 137-139. Timothy Pickering to Benjamin Goodhue, Washington, 22 Dec. 1803, and Timothy Pickering to Stephen Higginson, n.p., 6, 7, 14 Jan. 1804, Timothy Pickering Papers.

33. William Plumer to Daniel Plumer, Washington, 5 Dec. 1803, William Plumer Papers.

34. *Annals*, 8th Cong., 1st session, pp. 159-180; Fischer, *American Conservatism*, pp. 23-24; Thomas McKean to Uriah Tracy, Lancaster, 14 Jan. 1804, and Thomas McKean to Timothy Pickering, Lancaster, 14 Jan. 1804 in Thomas McKean Papers.

35. *Annals*, 8th Cong., 1st session, p. 165.

36. Timothy Pickering to John Pickering, 8 Dec. 1803, Timothy Pickering Papers; *Morning Chronicle*, 22 Jan. 1804, Leonidas, "Who Shall Be Our Next Vice-President," no. 1, demonstrated that even without designation, the Republicans could gain the Presidency by having all of their electors vote for one candidate and then directing sixty of them to vote for the other. The Federalists did not have sufficient numbers of electors to make up the difference even if all of them voted for the second Republican. But Leonidas realized that Republicans might not always have such a commanding advantage among electors. Designation offered a better long-term solution.

37. *Annals*, 8th Cong., 1st session, pp. 175-180; *William Plumer's Memorandum*, pp. 50-53, 57-58; William Plumer, "Autobiography," p. 123, William Plumer Papers.

38. *Annals*, 8th Cong., 1st session, pp. 180-183.

39. Ibid., pp. 183-189; John Taylor to Wilson C. Nicholas, Caroline, 16

Sept. 1802, Wilson Cary Nicholas Papers.

40. *Annals*, 8th Cong., 1st session, p. 203. The election of 1824 demonstrated that designation did not close the door to contingency elections. It also pointed out how important it was that the Twelfth Amendment specified three highest instead of five.

41. Ibid., pp. 204-209; Timothy Pickering to John Pickering, 5 Dec. 1803, Timothy Pickering Papers; William Plumer, "Autobiography," pp. 123-124, William Plumer Papers; Wilson Cary Nicholas to DeWitt Clinton, Washington, 3 Dec. 1803, DeWitt Clinton Papers; *The United States Chronicle*, 29 Dec. 1803.

42. Wilson Cary Nicholas to DeWitt Clinton, Washington, 3 Dec. 1803, DeWitt Clinton Papers.

43. James Hillhouse to Jonathan Trumbull, Washington, 3 Dec. 1803, Jonathan Trumbull Papers; William Plumer to Thomas W. Thompson, n.p., n.d. and to Edward St. Loe Livermore, Washington, 24 Dec. 1803 in William Plumer Papers; and Plumer, *Memorandum*, p. 66.

14. THE HOUSE CONCURS

1. Timothy Pickering to John Pickering, Washington, 5 Dec. 1803, Timothy Pickering Papers; William Plumer to Daniel Plumer, Washington, 5 Dec. 1803, William Plumer Papers.

2. *Annals*, 8th Cong., 1st session, 17 Oct. 1803, p. 650.

3. Adams, ed., *Memoirs of John Quincy Adams*, 1:277.

4. *Annals*, 8th Cong., 1st session, pp. 663-665; 7 Dec. 1803; *Daily Advertiser*, 15 Dec. 1803.

5. *Annals*, 8th Cong., 1st session, pp. 665-666.

6. Ibid., pp. 667-675.

7. Ibid., p. 676.

8. Ibid., p. 677.

9. Simeon Baldwin, Speech of 7 Dec. 1803 in Baldwin Family Papers, YU, provides a full text, which in much abbreviated form appears in *Annals*, 8th Cong., 1st session, pp. 679-680.

10. Ibid.

11. Timothy Pickering to John Pickering, Washington, Dec. 8, 1803, and to David Cobb, Washington, Dec. 29, 1803 in Timothy Pickering Papers.

12. Ibid.

13. *Annals*, 8th Cong., 1st session, pp. 686-690; *American Citizen*, 13 Dec. 1803, "An Extract of a Letter to the Editor," Washington, 7 Dec. 1803.

14. *Annals*, 8th Cong., 1st session, pp. 686-691; Adams, ed., *Memoirs*, 1:277; Thomas Dwight to John Williams, Washington, 8 Dec. 1803, Thomas Dwight Papers.

15. *Annals*, 8th Cong., 1st session, pp. 700-705.

16. Ibid., p. 722.

17. Ibid., p. 762.

18. Ibid., pp. 707-711, 744-752, 753-758; Thomas Dwight to John Williams, Washington, 8 Dec. 1803, Thomas Dwight Papers.

19. *Annals*, 8th Cong., 1st session, pp. 765-771.

20. *Annals*, 8th Cong., 1st session, pp. 771-775.

21. *American Citizen*, 15 Dec. 1803, An Extract of a Letter from a Member of Congress to a Gentleman in this City, dated, Washington, 9 Dec. [1803], 6 o'clock P.M.; *Daily Advertiser*, 17 Dec. 1803.

22. Simeon Baldwin to Elizabeth Baldwin, Washington, 19 Dec. 1803, Baldwin Family Papers.

23. Benjamin Tallmadge to Jonathan Trumbull, Washington, 9 Dec. [original is misdated Nov.] 1803, Jonathan Trumbull Papers.

24. *Annals*, 8th Cong., 1st session, p. 777.

25. Adams, ed., *Memoirs*, 1:278; Samuel A. Otis to Aaron Burr, 11 Dec. 1803, in *Aaron Burr*, edited by Kline, 2:804-806; *Daily Advertiser*, 20 Dec. 1803; *Evening Post*, 23, 26 Dec. 1803.

15. RATIFICATION OF THE TWELFTH AMENDMENT

1. George Clinton to John Smith, Albany, 25 Dec. 1803, George Clinton Papers.

2. Thomas Jefferson to George Clinton, 31 Dec. 1803 and George Clinton to Thomas Jefferson, Albany, 20 Jan. 1804, Thomas Jefferson Papers, UVa.

3. Thomas Jefferson to Thomas McKean, Washington, 9 March 1801, Thomas McKean Papers; Jonathan Trumbull to Benjamin Tallmadge, 4 Jan. 1804, Jonathan Trumbull Papers.

4. Thomas Jefferson to Thomas McKean, Washington, 17 Jan. 1804, in Thomas McKean Papers.

5. Ibid.; Rutland, *Madison*, p. 168; Dewey, "Madison's Views on Electoral Reform," pp. 141-142; Thomas Jefferson to Martha Jefferson Randolph, Washington, 6 Nov. 1804, Thomas Jefferson Papers, UVa; William Plumer to Thomas W. Thompson, n.p., n.d., Box 7, William Plumer Papers.

6. James Hillhouse to Jeremiah Wadsworth, Washington, 23 Dec. 1803, Jonathan Trumbull Papers.

7. Uriah Tracy to Jeremiah Wadsworth, Washington, 27 Dec. 1803, Jonathan Trumbull Papers. The series of Timothy Pickering's letters include those to Governor Thomas McKean, Peter Gordon, and Andrew Ellicott, all dated Washington, Dec. 19, 1803, and many others, Timothy Pickering Papers. See also D. A. Sherman to Simeon Baldwin, New Haven, 31 Dec. 1803, Baldwin Family Papers; Uriah Tracy to Rufus King, Washington, 3 Jan. 1804, Rufus

King Papers; Uriah Tracy to Oliver Wolcott, Jr., Washington, 25 Dec. 1803, Oliver Wolcott, Jr. Papers; James Hillhouse to Jonathan Trumbull, 22 Dec. 1803, Jonathan Trumbull Papers. The pamphlet appears as Uriah Tracy, *Speech in the U.S. Senate, 2 Dec. 1803* (Washington, D.C., 1803).

8. James Hillhouse to Jonathan Trumbull, Washington, 27 Jan. 1804, Jonathan Trumbull Papers; North Carolina, *Journal of the House of Commons* [21 Nov.-22 Dec. 1803], pp. 55-59; North Carolina, *Journal of the Senate* [21 Nov.-22 Dec. 1803], pp. 51-52, 54-55; *Laws of North-Carolina At a General Assembly*, 1803, c. 3, n.d.; *Acts Passed at the First Session of the Twelfth General Assembly for the Commonwealth of Kentucky*, c. 74, 27 Dec. 1803; *Acts of the State of Ohio*, 1803, 2d session, "An act declaring the assent to an amendment," 30 Dec. 1803; Ohio, *Journal of the House of Representatives*, 1803, 2d session, pp. 51-52, 57, 58-60, 60-62; Ohio, *Journal of the Senate*, 1803, 2d session, pp. 54, 59, 63, 65; Virginia, *Statutes At Large*, edited by Samuel Shepherd (Richmond, Va., 1835-1836), 3:109-110.

9. Matthias Barton to Timothy Pickering, Lancaster, 27 Dec. 1803, and 9 Jan. 1804, Timothy Pickering Papers.

10. Maryland, *Votes and Proceedings of the Senate*, Nov. session, 1803, pp. 21, 22, 25; Maryland, *Votes and Proceedings of the House of Delegates*, Nov. session, 1803, pp. 60, 66;*Laws at a Session of the General Assembly of Maryland, Begun the 7th day of November, 1803*, c. 65, 7 Jan. 1804.

11. "Dissent of the Minority in the Senate and House of Representatives of the State of Delaware," Legislative Papers, Reports, 1804, Delaware State Archives.

12. Ibid.

13. Delaware, *Journal of the Senate* [8-27 Jan. 1804], pp. 7, 18-20, 21-22; Delaware, *Journal of the House of Representatives* [8-27 Jan. 1804], pp. 9-10, 11-13, 26-28; *Mirror of the Times, & General Advertiser*, 23 Jan. 1804; *The Federal Ark*, 24, 28, Jan. 1804; *Hudson Balance and Columbian Repository*, 7 Feb. 1804; *Republican Watch Tower*, 28 Jan. 1804; *The Newport Mercury*, 4 Feb. 1804; *The United States Chronicle*, 2 Feb. 1804; *The Providence Gazette*, 4 Feb. 1804.

14. Ibid.

15. Vermont, *Journals of the Adjourned Session of the Legislature*, 26 Jan. 1804, pp. 10-12, 16-18, 19-21, 22-24; *Acts and Laws Passed by the Legislature of the State of Vermont*, 1804, c. 2, 30 Jan. 1804; *The Newport Mercury*, 18 Feb. 1804.

16. George Cabot to Timothy Pickering, Boston, 10 Jan. 1804, Timothy Pickering Papers.

17. George Cabot to Enoch Titcomb, Boston, 3 Feb. 1804, Timothy Pickering Papers.

18. Colo. Lambr. Cadwallader, Trenton, 30 Dec. 1803, Timothy Pickering Papers.

19. *Laws of the State of New Jersey, 1703-1820* (Trenton, N.J., 1821), "An Act to ratify an amendment," 22 Feb. 1804.

20. *The Public Statutes at Large of the United States of America, 1789-1845* vol. 2 (Boston, 1845), c. 50, 26 Mar. 1804.

21. New York, *Assembly Journal*, 27th session, 31 Jan. 1804, p. 6. See also Hammond, *History*, I, 195; New York, *Senate Journal*, 26th session, 25 Jan. 1803, pp. 26-28, 35; *Evening Post* and *Morning Chronicle*, 22 Feb. 1803; *Daily Advertiser* and *Morning Chronicle*, 23 Feb. 1803; *Daily Advertiser*, 2 Mar. 1803.

22. New York, *Assembly Journal*, 26th session, 25 Jan. 1803, pp. 74, 142, 169, 225; *Daily Advertiser*, 9 Mar. 1803; *Morning Chronicle*, 14 Mar. 1803; John Williams to David Thomas, Washington County, 9 Apr. 1804, John Williams Papers.

23. *Republican Watch Tower*, 7 Mar. 1804; New York, *Assembly Journal*, 27th session, 31 Jan. 1804, pp. 48, 52-53, 148; New York, *Senate Journal*, 27th session, p. 14; House, *Twelfth Amendment*, pp. 59-61; *American Citizen*, 14 Feb. 1803; *Morning Chronicle*, 15 Feb. 1804.

24. Benjamin Bourne to Timothy Pickering, Bristol, 16 Jan. 1804, Timothy Pickering Papers; *The Newport Mercury*, 7, 14, 21, 22 Jan. and 10, 17 Mar. 1800; *The United States Chronicle*, 29 Mar. 1804; *The Providence Gazette*, 14 Jan. 1804; William Plumer to Jeremiah Smith, Washington, 15 Mar. 1804, William Plumer Papers; *Acts Passed by the General Assembly of the State of Rhode-Island and Providence Plantations, Holden at Providence, on the last Monday of February, A.D. 1804*, "An act to ratify," 1 Mar. 1804.

25. *An Act and Resolutions of the General Assembly of the State of South Carolina Passed in May, 1804* (Columbia, S.C., 1804), Report and Resolutions, pp. 5-6; Henry William DeSaussure to Timothy Pickering, Charleston, 26 Feb. 1804, Timothy Pickering Papers; *Journals of the Senate and House of Representatives of the State of Georgia at an Extra Session of the General Assembly thereof, held in May, MDCCCIV*, pp. 4-5, 5, 6, 7, 9; *Acts of the General Assembly of the State of Georgia, Passed at the Session of May and November, 1804* (Louisville, Ga., 1805), "An Act to declare the approbation and assent of this State, to the amendment," 19 May 1804.

26. Jonathan Trumbull to Benjamin Tallmadge, Lebanon, 28 Dec. 1803, Jonathan Trumbull Papers; Governor Trumbull's address and the vote of the lower house appear in the *Hartford Courant*, May 16 and June 6, 1804, respectively.

27. Fischer, *American Conservatism*, p. 229.

28. New Hampshire, *Journal of the House of Representatives*, 6 June 1804, pp. 42-43, 46-47.

29. See also New Hampshire, *Journal of the House of Representatives*, 23 Nov. 1803, pp. 122-124; New Hampshire, *Journal of the House of Representatives*, 6 June 1804, pp. 5, 23, 38; New Hampshire, *Journal of the Senate*, 6

June 1804, pp. 17-19, 25.

30. New Hampshire, *Journal of the House*, 6 June 1804, pp. 61-64; New Hampshire, *Journal of the Senate*, 6 June 1804, p. 28.

31. House, *Twelfth Amendment*, pp. 59-61;*Acts Passed at the Second Session of the Fifth General Assembly of the State of Tennessee* (Knoxville, Tenn., 1804), c. 2, 27 July 1804; Tennessee, *Journal of the Senate*, 5th General Assembly, 2d session, 1804, pp. 24, 25; George W. Campbell to Samuel H. Smith, Knoxville, 27 July 1804, George W. Campbell Papers, LC.

16. THE ELECTION OF 1804

1. Rufus King to [Christopher Gore], New York, 4 Jan. 1804, Rufus King Papers.

2. Timothy Pickering to Rufus Putnam, Washington, 6 Dec. 1803, and to Theophilus Parsons, Washington, 30 Dec. 1803, Timothy Pickering Papers; Thomas Rodney told his son, Caesar A. Rodney, Congressman from Delaware, Washington [District] Mississippi Territory, 28 Dec. 1803, Rodney Family Papers, LC.

3. Cunningham, *Jeffersonian Republicans in Power*, pp. 211-212; Manning Dauer, "Election of 1804," in *American Presidential Elections 1789-1968*, edited by Schlesinger, Jr., 1:161; Spaulding, *George Clinton*, pp. 275-276. See also Thomas Jefferson, "Memorandum of a Conversation with Burr," 26 Jan. 1804, in *Aaron Burr*, edited by Kline, 2:819-824; *American Citizen*, 14 Feb. 1804; William Plumer to Jeremiah Smith, Washington, 10, 24 Feb. 1804, William Plumer Papers, LC; T[homas] D[wight] to Theodore Sedgwick, Washington, 27 Feb. 1804, Theodore Sedgwick Papers; C. A. Rodney to George Read, Washington, 27 Feb. 1804, Rodney Collection, Historical Society of Delaware, Wilmington, Del.; Allan B. Magruder to John Breckinridge, Lexington, 23 June 1804 and John Breckinridge to Mr. Huston, Editor of the *Palladium*, 5 July 1804, Breckinridge Family Papers; *American Citizen*, 10, 17 Aug. 1804, which answer charges of a Virginia-New York alliance in [Kentucky]*Guardian of Freedom*, 30 June 1804; Linda Kerber, *Federalists In Dissent* (Ithaca, N.Y., 1970), pp. 23-66.

4. George Clinton to Pierre Van Cortlandt, Jr., Albany, 10 Mar. 1804, Pierre Van Cortlandt, Jr., Papers, NYPL.

5. Martin Chittenden to Dr. Joseph D. Farnsworth, 1 Mar. 1804, Farnsworth Collection, VtHi.

6. Dauer, "Election of 1804," p. 162. See also *Republican Watch Tower*, 30 July 1803; T[homas] D[wight] to Theodore Sedgwick, Washington, 27 Feb. 1804, Theodore Sedgwick Papers.

7. Peirce and Longley, *The People's President*, Appendix B, p. 248.

8. W. C. Ford, ed., *The Writings of John Quincy Adams*, 3:62-68; Massa-

chusetts, *Acts and Resolves 1804-1805* (Boston, Mass., 1804), c. 21, 15 June 1804.

9. Anonymous,*A Defense of the Legislature of Massachusetts or the Rights of New England Vindicated* (Boston, Mass., 1804), p. 16.

10. Ibid.; Barnabas Bidwell, *An Address to the People of Massachusetts* (Boston, Mass., 1804), pp. 3-18.

11. Paul Goodman, *The Democratic-Republicans of Massachusetts,* pp. 154-181; Electoral Vote of 1804, Massachusetts, NA.

12. New Hampshire, *Journal of the House,* 6 June 1804, pp. 26-27, 52, 64; New Hampshire, *Journal of the Senate,* 6 June 1804, pp. 8, 17-18, 30;*Laws of the State of New Hampshire,* June 1804, "An Act directing the mode of balloting and appointing Electors," 21 June 1804; Electoral Vote of 1804, New Hampshire, NA.

13. *Acts and Laws of the State of Connecticut in America 1799-1806* (Hartford, Conn., 1805), p. 529; Electoral Vote of 1804, Connecticut, NA.

14. Electoral Vote of 1804, Rhode Island, NA.

15. Vermont, *Journals of the General Assembly,* 11 Oct. 1804, pp. 25-26.

16. Ibid., p. 278; Electoral Vote of 1804, Vermont, NA.

17. *Hudson Balance and Columbian Repository,* 6 Nov. 1804; *American Citizen,* 29 May and 18 June 1804.

18. *Albany Register,* 9 Nov. 1804.

19. *Laws of New York,* 28th session, c. 2, 12 Nov. 1804.

20. *Hudson Balance and Columbian Repository,* 11 Dec. 1804.

21. *American Citizen,* 11 Dec. 1804; Electoral Vote 1804, New York, NA.

22. Joseph Bloomfield to Dr. E. Elmer, Trenton, 5 Mar. 1804, Miscellaneous C Manuscripts, NYHS; *Acts of the Twenty-Eighth General Assembly of the State of New Jersey* (Trenton, N.J., 1804), c. 116, 25 Feb. 1804; *The True American,* 26 Nov. 1804; Electoral Votes of 1804, New Jersey, NA.

23. *The Statutes at Large of Pennsylvania from 1802 to 1805,* vol. 17 (Harrisburg, Pa., 1915), c. 2231, 2 Feb. 1802.

24. Thomas McKean to Thomas Jefferson, Lancaster, 7 Feb. 1803, and 10 Feb. 1805, Thomas McKean Papers, HSP; Electoral Vote of 1804, Pennsylvania, Legislative Division, NA; *National Intelligencer,* 10 Dec. 1804.

25. Electoral Vote of 1804, Delaware, NA.

26. Electoral Votes of 1804, Maryland, NA.

27. *A Digest of the Laws of Maryland* (Washington, D.C., 1804), 2:48-49.

28. *Acts at a General Assembly of the Commonwealth of Virginia Begun the Fifth Day of December One thousand Eight Hundred and Three* (Richmond, Va., 1804), c. 112, 21 Jan. 1804; Electoral Vote of 1804, Virginia, NA.

29. *Laws of North-Carolina at a General Assembly begun the 21st day of November, One Thousand Eight Hundred and Three* (Raleigh, N.C., 1803), c. 5, n.d.; Electoral Vote of 1804, North Carolina, NA.

30. *Acts and Resolutions of the General Assembly of the State of South-*

Carolina Passed in December, 1803 (Columbia, S.C., 1804), Resolution of the House of Representatives, 14 Dec. 1803; Electoral Vote of 1804, South Carolina, NA.

31. Electoral Vote of 1804, Georgia, NA.

32. *Acts Passed at the First Session of the Twelfth General Assembly for the Commonwealth of Kentucky* (Frankfort, Ky., 1804), c. 71, 24 Dec. 1803; Electoral Vote of 1804, Kentucky, NA.

33. Electoral Vote of 1804, Tennessee, NA.

34. Ohio, *Journal of the Senate*, 1803, 2d session, p. 11; *Acts of the State of Ohio*, 2d session of the General Assembly, 1803, c. 15, 20 June 1804; Electoral Vote of 1804, Ohio, NA.

35. *Albany Register*, 26 Feb. 1805, reprints this account from the *National Intelligencer*, 15 Feb. 1805.

EPILOGUE

1. John Quincy Adams to Rufus King, Boston, 8 Oct. 1802, in *Rufus King*, edited by King, 4:176; *Republican Watch Tower*, 8, 15 June 1803; *Evening Post*, 1 Nov. 1803; Smelser, *Democratic Republic*, p. 74.

2. Jefferson to Gallatin, Monticello, 18 Sept. 1801, *Writings of Thomas Jefferson*, edited by P. L. Ford, 7:94; Thomas Jefferson to Thomas McKean, Washington, 17 Jan. 1804, Thomas McKean Papers.

3. Kline, ed., *Aaron Burr* 2:795; McCormick, *Presidential Game*, pp. 76-116.

4. Peirce and Longley, *The People's President*, p. 131, indicates over 500; Slonim, "The Electoral College," p. 35, puts the figure at "close to seven hundred proposals" since 1789.

Select Bibliography

This bibliography includes all manuscript and most printed sources cited. It does not list well-known public records, such as the journals and session laws of various state legislatures, all of which are fully identified in the notes.

MANUSCRIPTS

Columbia University. Rare Book and Manuscript Library. New York, N.Y.
  DeWitt Clinton Papers.
  Nicholas Fish Family Papers.
  John Jay Papers.

Connecticut Historical Society. Hartford, Conn.
  John Treadwell Papers.
  Jonathan Trumbull Papers.
  Jeremiah Wadsworth Papers.
  Oliver Wolcott Papers.

Delaware State Archives. Dover, Del.
  Legislative Papers, Reports, 1804.

Franklin D. Roosevelt Library. Hyde Park, N.Y.
  Peter Van Gaasbeek Papers.

Historical Society of Delaware. Wilmington, Del.
  George Read Papers.
  Richard S. Rodney Collection.

Historical Society of Pennsylvania. Philadelphia, Pa.
        George Mifflin Dallas Collection.
        Ferdinand J. Dreer Autograph Collection.
        Griffith Evans Correspondence.
        Simon Gratz Collection.
        William Irvine Papers.
        Thomas Jefferson Papers.
        Thomas McKean Papers.
        Meredith Papers.
        Jonathan Roberts Papers.

Library of Congress. Washington, D.C.
        Breckinridge Family Papers.
        George W. Campbell Papers.
        William Eustis Papers.
        Ebenezer Foote Papers.
        Thomas Jefferson Papers.
        James Madison Papers.
        Wilson Cary Nicholas Papers.
        William Plumer Papers.
        Rodney Family Papers.
        Samuel Smith Papers.

Massachusetts Historical Society. Boston, Mass.
        Thomas Dwight Papers.
        Levi Lincoln Papers.
        Harrison Gray Otis Papers.
        Timothy Pickering Papers.
        Theodore Sedgwick Papers.

National Archives. Washington, D.C.
        Electoral Votes. 1788-1804.

New Jersey State Archives. Trenton, N.J.
        Minutes of Joint Meetings of the General Assembly
        1792-1804.

The New-York Historical Society. New York, N.Y.
        Bancker Family Correspondence.
        James Duane Papers.
        Rufus King Papers.
        John Lamb Papers.
        Robert R. Livingston Papers.
        John McKesson Papers.

Miscellaneous C Manuscripts.
John Smith Papers.

New York Public Library. Rare Books and Manuscript Division. New York, N.Y. Astor, Lenox and Tilden Foundations (for those collections marked by an asterisk).
Henry Glen Papers.*
James Madison Papers.*
James Monroe Papers.
Myers Collection.
Philip Schuyler Papers.
Pierre Van Cortlandt Papers.*
William P. Van Ness Papers.

New York State Archives. Albany, N. Y.
George Clinton Gubernatorial and Personal
Records, Series A0142

New York State Library. Albany, N.Y.
Ebenezer Foote Papers.
William North Papers.
Phelps-Gorham Papers.
Henry Rutgers Papers.
Melancton Smith Papers.
Elkanah Watson Papers.
John Williams Papers.

New York State Historical Association. Cooperstown, N.Y.
Henry Glen Papers.
Jacob Morris Papers.

Scholarly Resources, Wilmington, Del.
Albert Gallatin Papers.

University of Vermont Library. Burlington, Vt.
Paul Brigham Papers.

University of Virginia Library. Manuscripts Division, Special
Collections Department. Charlottesville, Va.
Thomas Jefferson Papers.

Vermont Historical Society. Montpelier, Vt.
Farnsworth Collection.
John White, Jr., Papers.

James Whitelaw Papers.

Yale University Library. Manuscripts and Archives. New Haven, Conn.
    Baldwin Family Papers.
    David Daggett Papers.

PRINTED PRIMARY MATERIALS

Abbot, W. W., and Twohig, Dorothy. Eds. *The Papers of George Washington*. Presidential Series 1: September 1788-March 1789. Charlottesville, Va., 1987.

Adams, Charles Francis. Ed. *Memoirs of John Quincy Adams, comprising portions of his Diary from 1795 to 1848*. Reprint. Freeport, N.Y., 1969.

---. Ed. *The Works of John Adams*. 10 vols. Boston, Mass., 1850-1856.

Adams, Henry. Ed. *Writings of Albert Gallatin*. 3 vols. Philadelphia, Pa., 1879.

Andrews, James DeWitt. Ed. *The Works of James Wilson, Being the Public Discourses upon Jurisprudence and the Political Sciences*. 2 vols. Chicago, 1896.

Annals of the Congress of the United States, 1789-1824. 42 vols. Washington, D.C., 1834-1856.

Bickford, Charlene Bangs and Veit, Helen E. Eds. *Documentary History of the First Federal Congress of the United States of America, 4 March 1789-3 March 1791*. Vol.4, *Legislative Histories: Amendments to the Constitution through Foreign Officers Bill*. Baltimore, Md., 1986.

Borden, Morton. Ed. *The Antifederalist Papers*. East Lansing, Mich., 1965.

Brown, Everett Somerville. Ed. *William Plumer's Memorandum of Proceedings in the United States Senate 1803-1807*. New York, 1923.

Cullen, Charles T. Ed. *The Papers of John Marshall*. Vol.4, *Correspondence and Papers, January 1799-October 1800*. Chapel Hill, N.C., 1984.

Cunningham, Noble E. Ed. *Circular Letters of Congressmen to Their Constituents 1789-1829*. 3 vols. Chapel Hill, N.C., 1978.

DenBoer, Gordon. Ed. *The Documentary History of the First Federal Elections*. Vol.2, *Elections in Connecticut, Delaware, Maryland, Virginia, and Georgia*. Madison, Wisc., 1984.

DenBoer, Gordon; Brown, Lucy Trumbull; and Hagermann, Charles D. Eds. *The Documentary History of the First Federal Elections 1788-1790*. Vol.3, *Elections in New Jersey and New York*. Madison, Wisc., 1986.

Edward Mead Earle. Ed. *The Federalist*. New York, 1937.

Eliot, Jonathan. Ed. *The Debates in the Several State Conventions on the Adoption of the Federal Constitution as Recommended by the General*

Convention at Philadelphia in 1787. Philadelphia, Pa., 1836.

Farrand, Max. Ed. *Records of the Federal Convention*. 3 vols. New Haven, Conn., 1911.

Ford, Paul Leicester. Ed. *Pamphlets on the Constitution of the United States, Published During Its Discussion by the People 1787-1788*. Brooklyn, N.Y., 1888.

---. Ed. *Writings of Thomas Jefferson*. 10 vols. New York, 1892-1899.

Ford, Worthington Chauncey. Ed. *Writings of John Quincy Adams*. 7 vols. New York, 1913-1917.

Hamilton, Stanislaus M. Ed. *The Writings of James Monroe*. 7 vols. Reprint. New York, 1969.

Historical Statistics of the United States to 1957. Washington, D.C., 1960.

Hunt, Gaillard. Ed. *The Writings of James Madison*. 9 vols. New York, 1900-1910.

Jensen, Merrill. Ed, *The Documentary History of the Ratification of the Constitution by the States*. 3 vols. Madison, Wisc., 1978.

Jensen, Merrill, and Becker, Robert A. Eds. *The Documentary History of the First Federal Elections*. Vol.1, *Elections in South Carolina, Pennsylvania, Massachusetts, and New Hampshire*. Madison, Wisc., 1976.

Johnston, Henry P. Ed. *The Correspondence and Public Papers of John Jay 1763-1826*. 4 vols. New York, 1890-1893.

Kenyon, Cecelia. Ed. *The Antifederalists*. Indianapolis, Ind., 1966.

King, Charles. Ed. *The Life and Correspondence of Rufus King*. 6 vols. New York, 1894-1900.

Kline, Mary Jo. Ed. *Political Correspondence and Public Papers of Aaron Burr*. 2 vols. Princeton, N.J., 1983.

Lee, Richard H. *Letters From The Federal Farmer to the Republican*. Edited by Walter Hartwell Bennett. University, Ala., 1977.

Madison, James. *Notes of Debates in the Federal Convention of 1787 Reported by James Madison*. Edited by Adrienne Koch. Athens, Ohio, 1966.

Rutland, Robert A., and Mason, Thomas A. Eds. *The Papers of James Madison*. Vol.14, *6 April 1791-16 March 1793*. Charlottesville, Va., 1983.

Syrett, Harold C. Ed. *The Papers of Alexander Hamilton*. 27 vols. New York, 1961-1987.

Thorpe, Francis Newton. Ed. *The Federal and State Constitutions, Colonial Charters, and Other Organic Laws of the State, Territories, and Colonies Now or Heretofore Forming the United States of America*. 7 vols. Washington, D.C., 1909.

NEWSPAPERS

[Albany, N.Y.]	*Albany Register.*
[Dover, Del.]	*True American.*
[Hartford, Conn.]	*Connecticut Courant.*
[Hudson, N.Y.]	*Hudson Balance and Columbian Repository.*
[New Haven, Conn.]	*Connecticut Journal.*
[New Haven, Conn.]	*New Haven Gazette.*
[New York]	*American Citizen.*
[New York]	*Daily Advertiser.*
[New York]	*Evening Post.*
[New York]	*Morning Chronicle.*
[New York]	*New York Journal and Weekly Register.*
[New York]	*Republican Watch Tower.*
[Newark, N.J.]	*Centinel of Freedom.*
[Newport, R.I.]	*The Newport Mercury.*
[Philadelphia]	*Gazette of the United States.*
[Portsmouth]	*New Hampshire Gazette.*
[Poughkeepsie, N.Y.]	*Poughkeepsie Journal.*
[Providence, R.I.]	*The Providence Gazette.*
[Providence, R.I.]	*The United States Chronicle.*
[Trenton, N.J.]	*True American.*
[Washington, D.C.]	*The National Intelligencer.*
[Wilmington, Del.]	*Mirror of the Times & General Advertiser.*
[Wilmington, Del.]	*The Monitor and Wilmington Depository.*

SECONDARY SOURCES

Ames, Herman V. "The Proposed Amendments to the Constitution of the United States During the First Century of its History." *Annual Report of the American Historical Association for 1896.* Washington, D.C., 1897.

Appleby, Joyce. *Capitalism and a New Social Order.* New York, 1984.

Bailyn, Bernard. *Origins of American Politics.* New York, 1967.

Banner, James M. *To the Hartford Convention: The Federalists and the Origins of Party Politics in Massachusetts, 1789-1815.* New York, 1970.

Banning, Lance. Ed. *After the Constitution.* Belmont, Calif., 1989.

Best, Judith. *The Case Against Direct Election of the President: A Defense of the Electoral College.* Ithaca, N.Y., 1971.

Bickel, Alexander M. *Reform and Continuity: The Electoral College, the Convention, and the Party System.* New York, 1971.

Bickford, Charlene Bangs, and Bowling, Kenneth R. *Birth of the Nation: The*

First Federal Congress 1789-1791. New York, 1989.

Bonomi, Patricia U. *A Factious People*. New York, 1971.

Borden, Morton. *Parties and Politics in the Early Republic, 1789-1815*. New York, 1967.

Buel, Richard, Jr. *Securing the Revolution: Ideology in American Politics, 1789-1815*. Ithaca, N.Y., 1972.

Chambers, William N. *Political Parties in a New Nation*. New York, 1963.

Charles, Joseph. *The Origins of the American Party System*. Reprint. New York, 1961.

Chrisman, Margaret C. S. *The First Federal Congress 1789-1791*. Washington, D.C., 1989.

Congressional Quarterly. *Presidential Elections Since 1789*. Washington, D.C., 1987.

Corwin, Edward S. *The President, Office and Powers*. New York, 1948.

Countryman, Edward. *A People in Revolution: The American Revolution and Political Society in New York 1760-1790*. Baltimore, Md., 1981.

Cunningham, Noble E. *The Jeffersonian Republicans: the formation of party organizations 1789-1801*. Chapel Hill, N.C., 1957.

---. *The Jeffersonian Republicans in Power: Party Operations 1801-1809*. Chapel Hill, N.C., 1963.

Dangerfield, George. *Chancellor Robert R. Livingston*. New York, 1960.

DePauw, Linda Grant. *The Eleventh Pillar*. Ithaca, N.Y., 1966.

Dewey, Donald O. "Madison's Views on Electoral Reform." *The Western Political Quarterly* 15 (March, 1962): 140-145.

Diamond, Martin. *The Electoral College and the American Idea of Democracy*. Washington, D.C., 1977.

Dougherty, J. Hampden. *The Electoral System of the United States*. New York, 1906.

Ellis, Richard E. *The Jeffersonian Crisis: Courts and Politics in the Young Republic*. New York, 1971.

Ernst, Robert. "The Long Island Delegates and the New York Ratifying Convention." *New York History* 70 (January, 1989): 55-78.

Feerick, John D. "The Electoral College--Its Defects and Dangers." *New York State Bar Journal* 40 (August, 1968): 317-330.

Fischer, David Hackett. *The Revolution of American Conservatism*. Reprint. New York, 1969.

Fox, Dixon Ryan. *The Decline of Aristocracy in the Politics of New York*. New York, 1918.

Goodman, Paul. *The Democratic-Republicans of Massachusetts*. Cambridge, Mass., 1964.

Hammond, Jabez D. *The History of Political Parties in the State of New York*. 3d ed. 2 vols. Cooperstown, N.Y., 1845.

Hockett, Homer Carey. *The Constitutional History of the United States 1776-*

1826. New York, 1939.

Hofstadter, Richard B. *The Idea of a Party System*. Berkeley, Calif., 1969.

Holcombe, John Walker. *The Electoral College*. Washington, D.C., 1913.

House, Lolabel. *A Study of the Twelfth Amendment of the Constitution of the United States*. Philadelphia, Pa., 1901.

Jackson, Joseph. *Survey of the Electoral College in the Political System of the United States*. Washington, D.C., 1945.

Johnsen, Julia E. Comp. *Direct Election of the President*. New York, 1949.

Kallenbach, Joseph E. *The American Chief Executive: The Presidency and the Governorship*. New York, 1966.

---. "Our Electoral College Gerrymander." *Midwest Journal of Political Science* 4 (May, 1960): 162-191.

Kammen, Michael. *People of Paradox, An Enquiry Concerning the Origins of American Civilization*. Reprint. New York, 1973.

Kerber, Linda. *Federalists in Dissent*. Ithaca, N.Y., 1970.

Kurtz, Stephen. *The Presidency of John Adams*. Philadelphia, Pa., 1957.

Levy, Leonard. *Freedom of Speech and Press in Early American History: Legacy of Suppression*. New York, 1963.

Lomask, Milton. *Aaron Burr, The Years from Princeton to Vice President 1756-1805*. New York, 1979.

Longley, Lawrence D., and Braun, Alan G. *The Politics of Electoral College Reform*. New Haven, Conn., 1972.

Main, Jackson Turner. *Political Parties Before the Constitution*. Reprint. New York, 1974.

Malone, Dumas. *Jefferson and the Ordeal of Liberty*. Boston, Mass., 1962.

---. *Jefferson and the Rights of Man*. Boston, Mass., 1951.

Matthews, Donald R. Ed. *Perspectives on Presidential Selection*. Washington, D.C., 1973.

McCormick, Richard P. *The Presidential Game*. New York, 1982.

McCoy, Drew R. *The Elusive Republic: Political Economy in Jeffersonian America*. New York, 1980.

McDonald, Forrest. *Alexander Hamilton*. New York, 1979.

---. *We The People*. Chicago, 1958.

McDonald, W. J. *The Action of the Senate and House of Representatives 1789-1873*. Washington, D.C., 1876.

McKnight, David A. *The Electoral System of the United States*. Philadelphia, Pa., 1878.

Miller, John C. *Alexander Hamilton and the Growth of the New Nation*. New York, 1964.

---. *The Federalist Era 1789-1801*. New York, 1960.

Morris, Richard B. "John Jay and the Adoption of the Federal Constitution in New York: A New Reading of Persons and Events." *New York History* 63 (April, 1982): 133-164.

Murrin, John M.   "The Great Inversion, or Court versus Country: A Comparison of the Revolution Settlements in England 1688-1721 and America 1776-1816." In *Three British Revolutions: 1641, 1688, 1776.* Edited by J. G. A. Pocock. Princeton, N.J., 1980.

O'Neill, Charles A. *The American Electoral System.* New York, 1887.

Peirce, Neal R., and Longley, Lawrence D. *The People's President: The Electoral College in American History and the Direct-vote Alternative.* New Haven, Conn., 1981.

Peterson, Svend. *A Statistical History of the American Presidential Elections.* New York, 1963.

Pocock, J. G. A. *The Machiavellian Moment, Florentine Political Thought and the Atlantic Republican Tradition.* Princeton, N.J., 1975.

Prince, Carl E. *New Jersey's Jeffersonian Republicans, The Genesis of an Early Party Machine 1789-1817.* Chapel Hill, N.C., 1964.

Risjord, Norman K. *Chesapeake Politics 1781-1800.* New York, 1978.

Roche, John P.   "The Electoral College: A Note on American Political Mythology." *Dissent* 8 (Spring, 1961): 197-199.

Roseboom, Eugene. *A History of Presidential Elections.* New York, 1959.

Rossiter, Clinton. *1787: The Grand Convention.* New York, 1987.

Rutland, Robert. *James Madison, The Founding Father.* New York, 1987.

Sayre, Wallace S., and Parris, Judith H. *Voting for President: The Electoral College and the American Political System.* Washington, D.C., 1970.

Schlesinger, Arthur M., Jr. Ed. *American Presidential Elections.* Vol.1. New York, 1971.

Shalhope, Robert. *The Roots of Democracy: American Thought and Culture 1760-1800.* Boston, Mass., 1990.

Sindler, Allan P.   "Presidential Election Methods and Urban-Ethnic Interests." *Law and Contemporary Problems* 27 (Spring, 1962): 213-233.

Slonim, Shlomo. "The Electoral College at Philadelphia: The Evolution of an Ad Hoc Congress for the Selection of a President." *Journal of American History* 73 (June, 1986): 35-58.

Smelser, Marshall. *The Democratic Republic 1801-1815.* New York, 1968.

Smith, James Morton. *Freedom's Fetters.* Ithaca, N.Y., 1956.

Spaulding, E. Wilder.   *His Excellency George Clinton, Critic of the Constitution.* New York, 1938.

---. *New York in the Critical Period 1783-1789.* New York, 1932.

Stanwood, Edwin. *A History of the Presidency from 1788 to 1897.* Boston, Mass., 1912.

Susman, Thomas M. "State of Inhabitancy of Presidential and Vice Presidential Candidates and the Electoral College Vote." *Texas Law Review* 47 (May, 1969): 779-792.

Sydnor, Charles S. *Gentlemen Freeholders, Political Practices in Washington's Virginia.* Chapel Hill, N.C., 1952.

Thach, Charles C., Jr. *The Creation of the Presidency 1775-1789, A Study in Constitutional History*. Baltimore, Md., 1969.

Tinkcom, Harry Marlin. *The Republicans and Federalists in Pennsylvania 1790-1801*. Harrisburg, Pa., 1950.

Walters, Raymond, Jr. *Albert Gallatin, Jeffersonian Financier and Diplomat*. New York, 1957.

Wheeler, I. H. *A Letter in Regard to the Electoral Votes; The Mode of Counting from 1789 to 1873, with Precedents, Debates, Arguments, and Interesting Facts Collated From Official Records*. Washington, D.C., 1876.

White, Leonard. *The Jeffersonians: A Study in Administrative History*. New York, 1959.

Wilmerding, Lucius Jr. *The Electoral College*. New Brunswick, N.J., 1958.

Wood, Gordon S. *The Creation of the American Republic 1776-1787*. Chapel Hill, N.C., 1969.

Young, Alfred F. *The Democratic Republicans of New York*. Chapel Hill, N.C., 1967.

Young, James Sterling. *The Washington Community 1800-1828*. New York, 1966.

Index

About the Author

TADAHISA KURODA received his B.A. in history from Yale College and his M.A. and Ph.D. from Columbia University. He has taught at Mount Vernon College in Washington, D.C. and is presently Professor of History and Associate Dean of the Faculty at Skidmore College in Saratoga Springs, New York.